# THE PROFESSION OF ENGLISH LETTERS

*STUDIES IN SOCIAL HISTORY*

*edited by*

*HAROLD PERKIN*

*Lecturer in Social History, University of Manchester*

| | |
|---|---|
| THE OUTLAWS OF MEDIEVAL LEGEND | Maurice Keen |
| RELIGIOUS TOLERATION IN ENGLAND, 1787–1833 | Ursula Henriques |
| LEARNING AND LIVING, 1790–1960: A Study in the History of the English Adult Education Movement | J. F. C. Harrison |
| HEAVENS BELOW: Utopian Experiments in England, 1560–1960 | W. H. G. Armytage |
| FROM CHARITY TO SOCIAL WORK in England and the United States | Kathleen Woodroofe |
| ENGLISH LANDED SOCIETY in the Eighteenth Century | G. E. Mingay |
| ENGLISH LANDED SOCIETY in the Nineteenth Century | F. M. L. Thompson |
| A SOCIAL HISTORY OF THE FRENCH REVOLUTION | Norman Hampson |
| CHURCHES AND THE WORKING CLASSES IN VICTORIAN ENGLAND | K. S. Inglis |
| A SOCIAL HISTORY OF ENGLISH MUSIC | E. D. Mackerness |
| THE PROFESSION OF ENGLISH LETTERS | J. W. Saunders |

# THE PROFESSION OF ENGLISH LETTERS

by

J. W. Saunders

*Lecturer in English Literature*
*University of Leeds*

LONDON: Routledge and Kegan Paul

TORONTO: University of Toronto Press

*First published 1964*
*in Great Britain by*
*Routledge and Kegan Paul Limited*
*and in Canada by*
*University of Toronto Press*

*Printed in Great Britain by*
*W. & J. Mackay & Co. Ltd., Chatham*

# Contents

# Acknowledgements

THE author acknowledges in these few inadequate words his deep gratitude to the support of all those who have helped him up a most daunting and uncharted mountain: Mr. F. W. Bateson, who in early years at Oxford encouraged first enquiries; Professor Sidney Raybould, who made possible a context of scholarship amid the hurlyburly of extra-mural life; and Mr. Harold Perkin, general editor of this series, who has the remarkable gift of knowing the right road for all his specialists; the editors of *Essays in Criticism* and *A Journal of English Literary History*, who published, more than ten years ago now, first essays into the subject; and, above all, those friends, who would prefer not to be named, who pushed hard when the route was darkest and most steep.

J.W.S.

*27 March 1964*

# I

## Letters—Human and not so Human

*Human life without some form of poetry is not human life at all but animal existence.*

RANDALL JARRELL[1]

THE producers of literature now work within one of the major industries of the world. According to UNESCO statistics, the annual global production of books (that is, documents of fifty pages or more) runs to 5,000,000,000 copies in 3,000 different languages. There are in addition 30,000 newspapers, including 8,000 dailies, with a total circulation of more than 250,000,000, and 22,000 periodicals with a circulation of about 200,000,000.[2] In short, an inconceivable amount of printed paper circulates every day. And the industry is still in its infancy. Only ninety-two copies of daily newspapers circulate per thousand of the world's population; fewer than forty languages can be properly called literate, and three-quarters of the world's total is produced by only ten countries. There is a long way to go, then, before saturation point: underprivileged nations have still to attain parity with their more highly civilized neighbours, in this as in other respects. All this growth is inevitable, granted the printing press and universal literacy, but frightening nevertheless. After all, only 600 years ago a polyglot could

[1] *Poetry and the Age* (1955).
[2] *Vide*, R. G. Parker, *Books for All* (1956).

have read through the world's entire annual output within comfortable working hours.

In the United Kingdom we have learned to accept almost without a thought the miracle of production and distribution which, almost every breakfast of the year, provides us with national newspapers selling 4,000,000 copies and more. We are beginning to take for granted the records broken, almost every year now, by the national book trade: in 1960 the total of new books and new editions was 23,783, compared with 17,137 in 1937, the best of the pre-war years.[1] We are also a nation of public library ticket holders, and borrow between us every year something like 400,000,000 books. The national libraries, which have an obligation under the Copyright Acts, are hardly able to find space to store one copy of everything: at Oxford, for instance, the extension to the Bodleian Library, planned in 1928 to provide storage space for a hundred years, will not suffice for even fifty. And yet this is the age, we were told, when books would be superseded by television.

It is high time we paused and thought. What is it all *for*? Why does the literature industry thus survive, and thrive? What, after all, *is* literature? It is a loose term given to every variety from the 'sales literature' of commercial firms to the 'literature bookstalls' of political parties. Most literary terms become debased in time and only a purist would want to pin down language, a living thing, as if it were a dead specimen. But it is desirable that the word be examined to see if any explanation is to be found, echoing among its connotations, of the enormous power of the literature industry.

Literature is difficult to see as a whole because, although it is sold as such, it is not primarily a commodity at all. It will not stand still to be defined like steel or oil or other materials, which we describe by referring to their qualities and properties. When one has described a book in accurate bibliographical terms, naming its title, author, publisher, place and date of publication, its size, number of pages, kind of binding, and so on, one has not even begun to describe it as literature. Further,

[1] The year's figures are usually published in *The Bookseller* in the first January number.

a book cannot easily be defined in terms of its function, because there is no clear link between the many individual functions served by particular books and the general term, literature, which ought to cover them all. Nor is a facile definition possible in terms of public need. Books and wool may both be said to be produced to earn money, but whereas wool serves a clear purpose, originating in the need of people for warm clothing, the function of books, which also earn money for the producers, is complicated by the way single needs in human beings tend to merge with others, blur and become something different from expectation.

It might seem that there were certain common tastes, fixed and predictable, which literature might be said to satisfy: the circulation figures of journals like the *Daily Mirror*, the *Daily Express*, the *News of the World*, *Woman*, and so on, indicate that such a formula might exist. Up to a point, this is true. The difficulty is that the sales of these journals would rapidly slump if their editors rested content with a fixed formula. No matter how much a man reads he expects every reading experience to provide something new, something he has not met before. He wants to read what he likes, certainly, but if the writer does nothing more than give him what he likes, he is quite ungratefully dissatisfied. Indeed, very often he cannot tell what he likes until he has been offered the something new which he finds he likes. Human nature at large exhibits this dualism, this demand for the known and need for the unknown, but the arts, and literature in particular, live by it. The names adopted by the best-selling form of non-fiction, the *news*paper, and by the best-selling form of fiction, the *novel*, testify to the demand for the new. In no other trade, not even women's dressmaking, are the merchants driven, at evey dateline, to seek new angles and new gimmicks, revaluations and new looks, before they can sell even that which is known to be popular. *Mutatis mutandis*, the same truth applies to all levels of literature. Here then, if anywhere, in the search for newness, one must begin a definition of literature.

Indeed, if the audiences of literature were not committed so fundamentally to the necessity of seeking the new, literature could never be a convenient means to an end for propagandists, for instance, who act on the assumption, like salesmen, that there is always room for converting people to new tastes and new ways of thought. Since audiences always remain unpredictable, it is always possible for literature to be exploited by the salesman and the propagandist, the preacher and the politician, the dream-pedlar and the exhibitionist, and many others, who work within literature for a non-literary end. There are many kinds of 'newness': the word needs narrowing down.

In Roget the synonyms of literature are given as letters, polite literature, *belles-lettres*, the muses, humanities, the republic of letters, and *literae humaniores*. Most of these terms imply a comparison, between the human and the not-so-human, between things which are less, and things which are more, human, civilized and beautiful. *Polite literature* implies writing that is civilized, cultured and good-mannered, and the silent distinction is only superficially describable in terms of social class, in terms of 'highbrow' and 'lowbrow', or 'U' and 'Non-U', or similar words. Fundamentally the word distinguishes between polite people advanced in the things which make men human beings, and the barbarians. Cicero argued that it was the man who was educated in the arts of expression who was also the man polished in humanity, and later thinkers have tended to agree with him, even when they make the point unflatteringly, like Daniel Defoe: 'As the rational soul distinguishes us from brutes, so education carries on the distinction, and makes some less brutish than others'.[1] A *republic of letters* may be said to be a community of books, or writers, dedicated in an admirable spirit of Ciceronian egalitarianism to the common weal, the cause of the polite arts. The phrase has the connotation that humanity can be nurtured by literature in as many different ways as there are individuals qualified to nourish. The *humanities*, or *literae humaniores*, were originally those studies, of Greek and Latin authors, which were held for long centuries to be more human than others, and therefore the subjects providing the best preparation for civilized living and the best foundation of education. More specifically, the term *belles-lettres* implies a distinction between books which call for taste and imagination and books which are merely useful, between literature which serves the spirit of man and literature which serves his material

[1] *Essay upon Projects* (1698), 'Of Academies'.

needs. Even more precisely, the allusion to the Muses recalls the nine imaginative arts which, in the opinion of the Greeks, were more spiritual than others, and therefore defended by separate goddesses: these were the arts of epic poetry, love poetry, sacred poetry, lyric poetry, tragedy, comedy, dancing and song, history and astronomy.

When we say a thing several times over, using different words each time, we usually clarify what we mean. A clear hard core of meaning emerges from these comparisons, a picture of literature as an art intimately connected with the things of the imagination and the spirit which makes men human. And a moment's reflection will suffice to add that, of course, it is our curiosity in these very things which lies behind our expectation of the new in literature. Animals and barbarians are only curious about things under their noses. Human beings, and in particular civilized human beings, are insatiably curious to the limits of their imagination. We are all curious about ourselves and our neighbours, how we tick, who we are, what we do here. The fact is as well known to the news editor, looking for 'human interest' stories, as it was to the ancient philosophers who first established a profession of letters. We join clubs, we gossip over the garden wall, we cheerfully hypothesize all the time about other people's behaviour. But there is a limit to the satisfaction of our curiosity in daily conversation and observation. Most of us are well aware that we are poor observers, that we do not know people half as well as we should like. There are some individuals much wiser than we are, because perhaps they are more sensitive or more subtle or more profound. And so we turn to these few in the search for enlightenment. It is this need which makes us listen to the bards, the story-tellers, the table-talkers, the writers. When reality fails us or falls short, we turn to art and to fiction, to the pattern-makers who give us insight by developing our imagination.

Henry James had this in mind when he remarked to H. G. Wells: 'It is art that *makes* life, makes interest, makes importance . . . and I know of no substitute whatever for the force and beauty of its process.' Art is in no sense a repository of knowledge, like an encyclopaedia or a dictionary: it provides no precise answers. It is possible to agree with Bertrand Russell's mischievous suggestion that 'a poet is an unimportant person whose views are of no consequence', and yet in another sense to argue that poets are among the most important people in the world. Outside his special province the poet is no more important than any other private citizen, but if he is a poet, a literary artist, an artist, he is also a specialist in certain explorations of the imagination which lie beyond the reach of other forms of knowledge. For precise information about human nature we call in the doctor and the psychiatrist, the sociologist and perhaps the theologian. But precise certainties do not exist in the realm of the imagination with which poetry, and other literature, and other art, is primarily and intimately concerned. The artist is less concerned with what *is* true than with what *might* be true. It is a fact that human society has not as yet developed sufficiently far to obviate the need for art: most of what we want to know about human nature lies outside the terrain explored by precise scientists. And one agrees with F. L. Lucas: 'For persons of intelligence and vitality, life can be lived with far fewer certainties than is commonly supposed.' But if the security of certainties is not available, human beings have to come to terms with the open questions to which there are no sure answers, and it is this service which James suggests the artists, and not least the literary artists, provide.

It follows that within the vast mass of the literature industry, the total output of which is concerned with enlightening mankind about itself and its environment, there is a section or part more valuable than the rest because it is more deeply concerned with the exploration of the imagination, the provision of new thoughts, ideas and hypotheses with which literature at its highest and best is involved. It is this part which we seem to have in mind when we talk about the 'profession of letters.' The literary historian who seeks to record the history of the profession is compelled to distinguish between the many kinds of literary activity which have led, in time, to the modern literature industry. Now, it is relatively easy for him to ignore the mass of an impossible quantity by eliminating, on grounds of aesthetic quality, the great majority of writings, writers and literary forms. The difficulty is that most of the usual aesthetic eliminations are decidedly unfair to the devoted craftsmen who work in the humbler levels. It simply is not true that, for instance, all daily journalism is undeserving of mention. Literature occurs where men are enlightened by writing. The enlightenment is everything; nothing else really matters. The best examples of enlightenment occur when literature calls into play the whole man and above all his imagination. And it is surprising in how many odd places literature happens; and conversely, surprising how often it does not happen in places where we have every right to expect it.

When little George is compelled by his mother to write a proper thank-you letter to his aunt for a birthday present, George, the literate child, pens a carefully correct letter; not a comma out of place, not a word misspelled, not a construction obscure. But because George has done all this but nothing more, the letter is apt to be cold, dry, unimaginative, unexciting, and completely worthless as literature. On the other hand, young Henry, technically the illiterate one, happens to like his aunt better; he pens in his grubby hand several sheets of untidy paper, full of blots and howlers of every variety, but somehow the words convey something warm and exciting, something his aunt will treasure. Literature is full of examples of Georges and Henrys, sometimes in the same person. Sir Walter Scott's *Ivanhoe* is a superb yarn, a first-class example of technical skill, written by a man who knows his trade inside out. On the other hand, his *Heart of Midlothian* rambles, falls into disparate parts, is far too long, contains a good deal of shabby characterization, and was quite shamelessly padded out, a third longer than it need have been, in order to earn in one long novel the money offered by the publisher for two. All the same, there is no doubt which is the better book, which is truly literature. In one, Scott, like George, seems unable to write meaningfully: the book runs away from life and enlightenment. In the other, for all the grubbiness, Scott, like Henry, has commented profoundly upon life, and the faults are relatively insignificant.

Another difficulty about discriminating between one book and another is that in the words we are always aware of the writer himself, of his uniqueness as a person, and of the life he sees about him, and these presences stand in the way of an objective opinion about an artefact, unconnected now that it is complete with its creator. If the writer is a little man, little in humanity, and if his insight into other men is limited, his book will be a mean book, no matter how good his technique or gift of the gab.

If he is a big man, big in humanity, and his insight into other men is profound, his book is apt to be an important book, sometimes in spite of itself. After all, the pleasures of literature are the pleasures of the varied human scene at its best: conversation with, observation of, an infinite variety of excellent human beings whose potential is more readily available to us in books than anywhere else. And the great authors lie on our bookshelves, superbly different from each other, and superbly indifferent to the attempts of critics to make them conform with each other. Above a certain level, at any rate, *de gustibus non disputemus*. Some critics, more austere than others, argue that it is precisely disputation about tastes, and the transcending of individual judgments by absolute principles, that makes up the distinctive function of literary criticism. The difficulty is that most of us put a higher price on a relatively insignificant document by a great writer, whatever its intrinsic worth, than on an important document by a lesser writer. In the last analysis, literature is valuable because it gives insight into human nature, and insight unlike literary structure is not readily definable in absolute terms.

What a man has to say, and the kind of person he is to say it, predetermines in many important respects how he says it. And yet 'what a man has to say' needs qualification. One thinks of slight poems, which add very little, if anything, to the store of human knowledge and yet have high value as literature. One also thinks of grave encyclopaedic works which vastly contribute to human knowledge, and yet have little or no value as literature. It is worth repeating that literature is not a storehouse of factual knowledge. A railway timetable stores away multitudes of facts, but is not literature. A letter from his wife puts a man in possession of all kinds of domestic knowledge which he needs to have, but has no literary value unless it does something else. And the something else has nothing to do with literariness in the sense of technical skill. Each year historians, economists, psychologists, philosophers, and all kinds of other professors of knowledge, contribute to the human store invaluable books which help explain the human situation, but none of these is necessarily an addition to literature. There seems to be a specifically literary enquiry, an imaginative enquiry into the things that make men human, which needs to take place in addition to the historical enquiry, or the economic enquiry, or whatever it happens to be. For this reason works of fiction, like poems, novels and plays, where the imagination has full play, are normally conceded an automatic right to the title of literature, while works of non-fiction, in a sense, have to earn their passage. It is not the factual content, then, but the view of those facts, the perspective and its attached values, which is the heart of the literary worth of a book. The facts of Herodotus or Gibbon or Macaulay may well be declared false by a modern historian equipped with better knowledge; but the modern historian has to be something other than a good historian to stand by their side as a man of letters. In literature, unlike history, it is not *what is true* that matters, but *what a man believes to be true*, and there is ample room for divergent and indeed contradictory perspectives.

All subjects, then, are proper to literature, and no subject is in itself more proper than another. There are no subject frontiers for the imagination. The literary historian attempts to categorize works in their kinds, but good literature, when it comes along, has a habit of standing out of its category. One feels sympathy for literary editors, like the editor of the *Times Literary Supplement*, which each week categorizes the books reviewed under the various headings of agriculture, architecture, education, history, industry, philosophy, psychology, religion, and so on, with a separate section reserved for 'literature and literary criticism'. In fact, since there are separate sections for the various literary arts, fiction, poetry, drama, biography and so on, literature dwindles until it includes only literary criticism! And one wonders in what category the editor of the day would have placed great works like Burke's *Reflections on the French Revolution*, Ruskin's *Unto this Last*, Newman's *Apologia*, Browne's *Religio Medici* or Bunyan's *Pilgrim's Progress*? I am suggesting, in other words, that the field of English Letters extends vastly over all the acres, from the *Authorized Translation* on one hand to comic papers on the other, and that all this field is cultivated by men and women who have an opportunity, however slender, of joining the profession of letters. Fortunately, most of the important writers confine themselves, in the main, to the major imaginative forms, the poem and the play, the biography and the novel, the essay and the story. But we should keep in mind the salutary warning that literature can occur anywhere.

Like the school examiner, confronted with questions to which there is no unique answer, the reader evaluating literary work can only 'mark by impression'. We have to recognise wisdom and insight by the impression it makes upon us; there is no absolute scale of values, no cosmic measuring stick, which we can use. The heights and depths of human imagination are infinite and inexhaustible, capable of being continually scaled and mined, without loss or diminution, for all time. Our individual impressions will largely be determined by the state of our own growth. It is an experience to come across a new book for the first time, no matter how cheap and shoddy wiser men may find it. If for instance, one has never read one of the glossy modern thrillers, in which the heroes are always taking three fingers of rye and the blonde heroines are voluptuous in bar after bar, the book adds something to experience, not much perhaps, but something. The experience diminishes to zero with further reading. But for a little while the author concerned has made a small contribution to literature. There is always a first time for a child to be introduced to Pooh Bear and Mr. Toad, not to mention Billy Bunter and Dan Dare.

In much the same way, society at large will evolve continually changing evaluations of even the great writers; like individuals, societies will develop changing tastes in literature, dependent upon the state of their growth. If the nineteenth century could ignore Donne and Dryden, while the twentieth century rediscovers them, it would be foolish to claim a general insensitivity in our forebears and better standards of taste in ourselves. Society then and now had different interests and needs. Clearly, revaluation will go on for ever. There is no special reason to believe that the best standards of modern criticism would have been better for previous generations than those they fashioned themselves. We do what Dryden did, what Sidney, what Coleridge: we rewrite the history of the past in our own image. Literary historians, if they are to be honest, must stand aside, as far as they can without losing their own, necessary, contemporaneousness, from the narrowing effects of this natural process, and must aim to be latitudinarians, broadly tolerant of all the many aspects of literature. Within the profession of letters there are many kinds of wisdom and insight, and one ought to be wakeful to them all.

One last point in this introductory chapter. The origin and development of the literary profession will not become very clear unless it is seen that the ultimate end of literature, this particular exploration of the human situation through imaginative means, is served seldom directly, and almost always obliquely. Relatively little literature is written for the sake of literature. Most writers approach their work with all kinds of other motives which, though secondary, greatly influence the development of the profession. Bishop Fuller listed five different motives for his *History of the Worthies of England*: 'to gain some glory to God', 'to preserve the memories of the dead', 'to present examples to the living', 'to entertain the reader with delight', and lastly, '(which I am not ashamed publicly to profess) to procure some honest profit to myself'.[1] Fuller reminds us of some of the main strands in the evolution of the profession, of the entertainers who sought to earn a living by delighting customers, of the devout men who saw in literature a means of praising God and sought no other reward, of the patriots who assumed that literature was an essential part of a nation's well-being, and who sought a social status, with rewards of cash or kind, commensurate with their social usefulness, and of the teachers who exploited the didactic qualities of literature as a means to an end, while maintaining their primary interests and earning their chief rewards in some other occupation. It is the interplay between these secondary motives and others like them, and the primary, imaginative justification of all literature, which will determine the course of the story I shall tell in the following pages.

It is a tumultuous scene. The stage is crowded with bards and balladists, divines and dons, courtiers and clowns; with amateurs, professionals, amateur professionals, professional amateurs, and all kinds of rank intermediate; with writers whom society has turned into pensioners and prisoners, squires and spies, laureates and lepers, richmen and rogues. In the wings stand patrons who love literature and patrons who love themselves, Maecenases and mass audiences, fan clubs and coteries, and all the machinery, of manuscripts, periodicals, anthologies,

[1] Ed. Nuttall (1840), p. 1.

private editions, subscription editions, pulpits, stages, radio microphones and all else, by which the writers of different times have established their profession and its lines of communication. It is a tumultuous scene in which tolerance of infinite variety is both a necessity and a virtue.

# II

## In the Beginning

*Thow medlest the with makynges· and mygest go sey thi sauter*
*And bidde for hem that giveth the bred· for there ar bokes ynowe.*

(LANGLAND, *Piers Plowman*, XII, B. 16)

THE story of the profession of English letters begins in the middle of the fourteenth century, because it is then that the English language can be said to begin. The 'Old English' of King Alfred's time had been exposed to successive invasions from abroad, which had deepened the differences, already existing, between the 'English' spoken in different parts of the country, with the result that there were at least four forms of the language, Northumbrian, Midland, Southern and Kentish. These dialects, besides competing with each other, were challenged as the language of the realm by Anglo-Norman, the speech of the ruling dynasties, and Latin, the international language of the Church and the universities. At the beginning of the fourteenth century educated Englishmen of necessity had to be trilingual, and most written literature was not in English at all. But as merchants and other middle-class men, the professional managers of the manorial estates, the stewards, reeves and bailiffs, and the yeoman-landowners became increasingly more important and powerful in the social scale, their language, English, began to supersede Latin and French in legal and political affairs. By

1356 English was allowed in the London Sheriff's Courts, and by 1362 in all law courts. In 1363 Parliament was opened for the first time in English by Edward III, who was the first king to know the language well (Richard II was the first to have it as his mother tongue). These were the first steps by which the dialect of London and the south-eastern Midlands became, in a long process which took 200 years to complete, the national language, the 'Queen's English' of Elizabeth's time.

But despite the new nationalism of the age, and the renascent sense of nationhood and community, symbolized by the English victories in the Hundred Years War at Crecy and Poitiers, fourteenth-century Englishmen were completely unaware that later historians would regard them as standing at the beginning of things and would have been mystified if one of their writers, Geoffrey Chaucer, had been called the Father of English Letters. As far as they were concerned, the world was a very old world, which could not conceivably last very much longer; there was nothing really new under the sun; the pattern of all things, including literature, had been determined by masters who had died centuries before; and, since originality was impossible, there was no alternative but to join the dance of life, each man in the proper station appointed him by long eras of convention and tradition. The English Profession of Letters begins, then, by inheriting from the past established patterns of conduct and performance which had been shared by generations of Christian writers throughout Europe. It would be best, first, to determine precisely what the sources of these patterns were. There were three main sources: the church, and the literature of devotion and instruction specifically attributable to its work; the secular community, and the literature of entertainment which it fostered; and classical culture and literature, although it was not until the so-called Augustan age of the early eighteenth century that neo-classicism was in any sense predominant. The Court, which might have been expected to provide a fourth distinctive source, while continuing throughout history to be a powerful patron of letters, did not intervene decisively in the development of letters. Indeed, the medieval kings were much too busily engaged in politics and in the internecine struggles culminating in the long war with France and in the civil wars of York and Lancaster, to establish a courtly culture which was more than a reflection of the culture of the Church and an extension of feudal civilization.

Let us begin, then, with the Church. Before the invention of the printing press, at a time when all books were manuscripts, the great majority of writers and readers—defining writers as those who composed books recorded in manuscript, and readers, for the time being, as those capable of reading manuscripts for themselves—were churchmen. Among the writers of the period between 1350 and 1500 may be listed Osbern Bokenham, the Augustinian friar of Stoke Clare; John Capgrave, the monk of Lynn; Walter Hilton, the Augustinian canon; Julian of Norwich, the recluse; William Langland, a clerk in minor orders; John Lydgate, the priest of Bury St. Edmunds; Reginald Pecock, Bishop of St. Asaph and Chichester; Ranulf Higden, the monk of Chester; John Trevisa, Vicar of Berkely; John Wyclif, Rector of Lutterworth, and other priests. Apart from a few great noblemen and lawyers, the book-owners who possessed libraries of their own tended to be the better-endowed clergy, the bishops, the cathedral clergy, members of the collegiate churches and the university teachers (who were all clerics). The larger libraries belonged to the secular cathedrals of York, London, Exeter, Lichfield, Hereford, Lincoln, Salisbury, Chichester and Wells, or, here and there, to the better-endowed collegiate churches. Such libraries as the universities possessed owed their origin to churchmen: at Oxford, for instance, a hundred years before the royal patronage of Duke Humphrey of Gloucester, an extra-college library had been founded by Bishop Thomas Cobham, and all the early librarians were chaplains to the university. When one considers how large a proportion of the total population, and an even larger proportion of the literate population, were in orders of some kind, secular or regular, the predominance of the Church is not surprising.

The majority of the books in the medieval libraries were in Latin, and most of the others in French. English came slowly into its own, as far as the Church was concerned. The Church required books in English only to fulfil its pastoral function as a teacher: books to instruct not only laymen who might have no Latin, but also many of the lower clergy, secular and regular, and of the nuns, who might have very little. There was a need, then, for catechisms, missals and other liturgical books, and for compendia of dogma and ethics, books of psalms and sermons, saints' lives, translations of and commentaries upon parts of the Bible, and other didactic works. This emphasis upon the pious and the didactic dominated the book market for centuries to come. It was taken over by the printers: typically the largest quantities of stock recorded in the will of Thomas Bassandyne, the Edinburgh printer, in 1579, consisted of 20,640 'Single Catechissis', 1,440 'Psalms of preis', and 1,400 'Doubill catechissis', and as late as 1658 William London's *Catalogue of the most vendible Books in England* required as much space for books of Divinity as for all other kinds of books put together. The medieval book, apart from the service books, which seems to have been as popular as any other was Richard Rolle of Hampole's *Pricke of Conscience*, a long poem dealing with the life of Man and its uncertainty; this book has survived to the present day in 114 different manuscripts, fifty more than the *Canterbury Tales*, ninety-three more than Lydgate's *Troy Book*.

Here, then, in the Church is the first large strand to be woven into the story of the profession of letters. These Church writers were amateurs in every sense. They earned nothing from their literary labours, which were considered duties comparable with any other kind of monastic or pastoral work. And literature was not an end in itself but a means to an end. Writing was an occasional duty undertaken by the few who had an avocation for it, as others had an avocation for masonry or carpentry. Even those like John Lydgate, who devoted all his time to writing and teaching, and who composed over 250 literary works, of which the three longest run, immensely, to 36,000 lines, 30,000 lines, and 20,000 lines respectively, shared the same kind of attitude to writing as a colleague whose sole literary labour of a lifetime might have been to prepare for local use a single volume of catechisms. Indeed, it is likely that the Lydgates were encouraged to develop their literary gifts for no better reason than that men with a flair for writing relieved others within the monastic or diocesan community from the necessity of contributing to the fulfilment of this kind of chore.

The train of events which brought a literary work into being may be summarized as follows. The writer would be commanded, urged or requested to turn his attention to such-and-such a subject by a person under whom he owed some 'obedience'. This person might be the archbishop or bishop or other Church dignitary, secular or regular, in whose see, chapter, monastery or college the writer had a recognized public position; or he might be the nobleman in whose household the writer served, primarily, as a private chaplain, tutor, secretary or other assistant. Or, in the rare instances where the writer had a national reputation for his literary abilities, the command might come from the highest dignitaries of the state: Lydgate undertook his *Troy Book* at the request of Henry V, and his *Fall of Princess* at the request of Duke Humphrey of Gloucester. In the course of his studies, the writer would commit his work to 'foul papers'. that is to say, to autograph manuscripts on which the work was first roughed out and then polished. The completed manuscript would then pass to a professional scrivener, or firm of scriveners, who would prepare the requisite copies: a fair copy, suitably 'illuminated', inscribed on vellum or parchment, durably bound, for the use of the patron, if any such special reader were involved, and one or two others, less expensively produced, for domestic use in the community for which the work was intended. In time it might well happen that requests for further copies reached the writer from individuals within the community, or from the relatives of persons who already had a copy, or from elsewhere, and the writer, using his original foul papers, would prepare for the scriveners additional editions (which, incidentally, might differ in major respects, as the result of revisions and rewriting, from the copy first published). But since there was no law of copyright, and since the work once in circulation belonged to the community rather than to the author, transcriptions might well be made of which he could not conceivably have knowledge, and then transcriptions of transcriptions, and so on *ad infinitum*, during the life of the work.

As an instance, a considerable spacing throughout the period of manuscript circulation is evident in the five extant copies of Gavin Douglas's early sixteenth-century translation of the *Aeneid*. The earliest text, known as the Gale MS., inscribed 'the first correck coppy nixt efter the Translatioun', was written out for an intimate friend by 'master Matho Geddes, Scribe or Writar to the Translatar', and, since it bears marginal glosses in Douglas's hand, must be dated prior to 1522, the year of the author's death. Then follow transcriptions for unconnected enthusiasts: the Elphynstoun MS., inscribed 'W. Hay, 1527'; the Ruthven MS., believed to date between 1530 and 1540; the Lambeth MS., transcribed on 2 February 1546, and the Bath MS., dated in a colophon 1547. The work was finally edited for print by Urry in 1553. Scribes commonly charged a penny or twopence a leaf, for plain work, with 'rubrishing' extra. Prices varied: there is on record a note that a certain Thomas Burgh had Bokenham's *Legends of the Saints*, all ten thousand lines, transcribed in Cambridge in 1447 at a cost of thirty shillings, that is, thirty lines or so for a penny. But it is clear that the cost of transcription would not deter anyone keen to have a copy.

The scriveners were indeed the 'booksellers' of the day. Their market was predominantly 'bespoke', with very little speculative bookmaking. The first books manufactured for general retail trade in England came from abroad, Breviaries and Books of Hours, written in Flanders; the Low Countries, and in particular the cities of Bruges, Antwerp and Brussels, were the first European centres of mercantile bookmaking. And in England a certain amount of retail trading in manuscripts took place at the great fairs, under the sponsorship of grocers and mercers, at the universities, where the name *stationarii* was first heard, and along Paternoster Row in London. But there were relatively few items of scrivener's merchandise about which there was any guarantee of a general sale, and manuscripts were usually 'made to measure' a particular customer rather than sold 'ready-made'.

The author had no control over his work once it had passed beyond the bounds of his own community. Indeed, very often the only name on a manuscript would be the name of the scribe, the author lost in anonymity. For this reason we know the names of relatively few medieval writers. There was inherent in the nature of things a tradition of anonymity. Because the writers felt themselves to be unworthy successors of the great masters, not to be compared with Cicero and Virgil among the classics or Augustine and Boethius among the scholastics, they preferred to remain impersonal in their works. And when they found themselves intruding, they felt bound to apologize for themselves, even to treat themselves with contempt. When Langland appears personally in his story of *Piers Plowman*, it is as a 'lunatik', a 'lene thing', who ought to be doing something more useful than scribbling. Although John Gower, the author of the *Confessio Amantis*, was a cultivated man able to write in Latin and French as well as in excellent English, he refers to himself as a 'burel clerk', unacquainted with the sciences of eloquence and rhetoric. Geoffrey Chaucer appears in the *Canterbury Tales* as a shy and retiring man, a butt for the Host:

> Thou lookest as thou woldest fynde an hare,
> For evere upon the ground I se thee stare.

Maybe Langland and Chaucer play with the convention of humility to achieve humorous effects, and maybe Gower is prouder of his own literary skills than he says, but nevertheless the convention was strongly based upon hard facts. It was a fact that the rhetoricians had turned writing into a highly skilled trade in which amateurs, that is to say all those who were not professionally engaged in teaching and studying rhetoric, felt naturally hesitant and diffident. It was also a fact that the English language, in comparison with Latin and French, was *gauche* and *parvenu*; as John Skelton suggests, in the *Boke of Phyllyp Sparowe:*

> Our natural tongue is rude
> And hard to be ennuede
> With pollyshed tearmes lustye
> Oure language is so rustye
> So cankered and so ful
> Of frowardes and so dul
> That if I wold apply
> To write ornatly
> I wot not where to finde
> Termes to serue my mynde.

The writers were bound to find their own works, as a result, rude, simple, blunt, base and barbarous.

Moreover, the circumstances under which books were produced were such as would encourage anonymity. Books belonged to the small first audience of the writer's own community; within his own circle his authorship was well known, so that there was no need for him to place his name to the manuscript.

When transcribed manuscripts travelled outwards, away from the intimate circle to groups unknown to the writer and beyond his control, there was no point in adding the author's name. The outer groups were interested in the work not the writer, and very few authors were national names in the modern sense. In any case, there was a very real difficulty about names; before the universal adoption of surnames, so many monks and other clerics working within the same community had the same Christian name, so that there was no means of distinguishing for the outsider one from the other. And intellectual pride, individual genius, literary immortality, and all such conceptions had to await the competitive environment and the resurgent nationalism of the Renaissance before they effected fundamental change in the attitudes of writers to their work. It is probable that something like four-fifths of all medieval literature circulated in anonymous manuscripts, and all these writers will remain for ever unknown to us. E. P. Goldschmidt summarizes the attitude of Church writers thus: 'They valued extant old books more highly than any recent elucubrations and they put the work of the scribe and the copyist above that of the authors. The real task of the scholars in their view was not the vain excogitation of novelties but a discovery of great old books, their multiplication and the placing of copies where they would be accessible to future generations of readers.'[1]

But the Church provides only one of the main origins of the profession of letters. Merging with the culture of the Church, not distinct from it but mutually interdependent, and yet deriving in part at least from different roots, is the literature of the secular feudal communities. There are many manuscripts extant of works which seem to have been primarily intended as entertainment, with instruction as a secondary purpose if indeed instruction can be said to be present at all. There are the romances, Arthurian and non-Arthurian, tales of courtly love and chivalry; the ballads sung in the manorial halls and on the village greens; the tales of Chaucer and Gower and a few others. Then there are books which are instructive but not in a religious sense: books about health, diet, cookery, natural science, gardening, hunting, fishing, astrology, alchemy, dream lore and travel. Some of these books were in wide circulation. There are

[1] *Medieval Texts and their first appearance in print* (1943), p. 112.

thirty manuscripts extant of the vernacular version of Mandeville's *Travels*, forty-six of Lydgate's *Dietary*, and more than nineteen fifteenth-century manuscripts of *The Master of Game*, a translation of Gaston de Foix's *Livre de Chasse*. And outside the ranks of these manuscripts which have survived, we are aware of the vast, lost literature of medieval England, songs and tales and romances which are no longer extant because they were never committed to manuscript at all, or if they were their manuscripts have perished.

All this literature fundamentally derives from an oral tradition. Every European nation from pagan times has had its minstrels and travelling bards, its *ioculatores* and troubadours, *jougleurs* and *trouvères*, scops and gleemen. They have been explained historically as one of the products of the collapse of the Roman Empire, when professional entertainers and '*scenici infames*' were cast out of their metropolitan homes by the united disapproval of the barbarian conquerors and the leaders of the early Christian Church, who alike regarded fiction as decadent and immoral. This explanation may help to describe the particular efflorescence of troubadour literature from the fifth century onwards, but the minstrels existed long before there was a Roman empire at all. All communities taking the first steps towards civilization seem to have found the need for bards, whose function as in the modern Welsh Eisteddfodau was closely connected with religion. These bards, like Homer, were employed to preserve in metrical form, the form best calculated to assist memorization and thus transmission from one generation to the next, the religious legends and early history, half historical, half mythical, of the community, The bards, then, were the authors of each new nation's holy books, the repositories of the highest truths in which men believed, and they were revered for their priesthood. But as civilization became more sophisticated their primeval and epic function was fragmented and taken over by religious dignitaries, dramatists, chronologers and scholars. In fourteenth-century England there was little left of the bard; but there was still a welcome place by the open hearth for the travelling minstrel, with his romances of long ago and his traditional ballads, and there was still a place in each community for a resident story-teller, who enlivened the winter evenings with recitations and readings from memory or manuscript. Through these intermediaries, literature reached a wide audience among all classes, literate and illiterate.

In Church literature the audience explored the truth about Man, the truth unargued as such in Christian communities; sometimes this truth was a matter of dogma, to be learned in the manner of catechisms by numbers; sometimes, on the other hand, it was a mystical truth, to be caught only in oblique glimpses and through arduous journeys of the imagination. Langland's *Piers Plowman* has something of both aspects: on the one hand, the writer strives to simplify his meaning into catechistical categories—the three piles of the tree of charity, the trinity of dowel, dobet and dobest, the four virtues, the five wits, the seven deadly sins, the ten commandments, the ten orders of angels, and so on; on the other hand, his poem has six or more concurrent meanings, the literal, the social, the moral, the anagogical, the historical and the personal, and in all this complexity there are no fixed points to direct the imagination out of obscurity. In secular literature, the audience explored a different kind of truth, the unverifiable truth of imaginative fiction; sometimes this truth could be related as fact, strange facts about geography as in Mandeville or strange facts about physiology, as in the medical handbooks; sometimes it was concealed in outright fiction and was digested by the audience as a by-product of makebelieve. There is no antithesis, then, between Church writers and secular writers; each might be factual or imaginative, according to his inclinations and abilities. The Churchman might range in his imagination into anti-clerical and even heretical attitudes; the secular writer might frame his fiction within a structure of religious ideas which were devoutly orthodox. Chaucer's *Parson's Tale* is not out of place on the Canterbury pilgrimage, and the Mak plays are an essential part, for all their knockabout farce, of the Wakefield Cycle. This coexistence, of the devout and the profane, of the *fabliaux* and the hagiologies, of the moralities and the interludes, of the sermons and the romances, was an indispensable essential in the evolution of literature.

The literary profession needed both sources. The Churchmen connected literature with pleasures less transient than those of leisure entertainment, with the profounder truths of human nature. The minstrels connected literature with joyful recreation and with the open questions of human nature which dogma naturally tends to close and seal.

All literature remained essentially local. The literary centres were the centres in which literature was read aloud: the manorial halls of the countryside and the guildhalls of the town, the Churches and the market places, the village greens and the taverns, the earthen theatres in the round and the cobbled streets of theatrical pageants. There was no national public for the writers, but rather, scattered throughout England, many local publics, which were often connected, through the lord of the manor and the parish priest, with the feudal Court in London or with the diocesan cities, but seldom with each other. Literature was thus decentralized through a number of scattered and isolated literary neighbourhoods, and as such was much more closely a communal art, rooted to the community which gave it life, than at any time in later literary history. This fragmentation was itself a reflection of the strongly regional nature of medieval England. From the times of the Saxon division of the country into the four nations of Northumbria, Mercia, Wessex and Kent, England had never been unified, in any real sense of the word. And the tradition of regional differences and autonomies was to linger on, erupting in all kinds of local rebellions in the sixteenth century, and was still to be an effective force as late as the Civil Wars of the seventeenth century.

The writers, divine and secular, tended to be those members of the middle class, upper and lower, who had the flair for composition and recitation. More often than not they were quite obscure people of insignificant rank. The extraordinary thing about medieval literature is that so little of it was written by the aristocrats of State and Church, who might have been expected to exercise leadership in literate activities. Of the Church writers already named, only one was a bishop, and the greatest of them, Langland, seems to have had little higher social status than a labourer. Among the secular writers working before 1500, only Charles of Orleans, nephew of Charles VI of France, can claim royal blood; it would seem that this prince's English poems, written while he was a prisoner in this country, were the only royal works of the period; the Hals and Hotspurs, apparently, were not literary men. Scotland was little better than England: there is only King James I (1394–1437), the *grant auteur* of *The Kingis Quair*. England has a few literary noblemen and knights: Antony Wydeville, Earl Rivers, the translator; Sir John Fortescue (1394–1474), at one time Chief Justice of the King's Bench and author of the *Governance of England*; Sir Thomas Malory, of whom we know very little, and Sir John Mandeville, if he existed at all, of whom we know nothing. In both countries, at least until the sixteenth century, writing was the province of lesser men, priests and monks, Civil Servants and schoolteachers.

Geoffrey Chaucer, socially, was more highly placed than most. At least he started life as a courtier, and became Clerk of the King's Works, owing much to the patronage of princes of the royal house; but he was the son of a vintner, he was appointed a commissioner surveying the walls, ditches, bridges and sewers along the Thames, and he never attained knightly status. We should call him a senior Civil Servant rather than a courtier in his own right. John Gower was a wealthy merchant with the rank of esquire and with courtly connexions, who nevertheless occupied a lower place in public life than Chaucer. Thomas Occleve was a clerk in the Privy Seal Office, Robert Henryson a grammar-school master in Dunfermline, Margery Kempe the daughter of a former mayor of Lynn and the wife of a burgess, and so on downwards through the social scale to the Blind Harrys and the even obscurer minstrels whose names are not recorded at all. The drama of the period, too, is in middle-class hands. According to F. M. Salter, the author of the Chester Mystery Cycle was not, as tradition has it, Ranulf Higden, but another monk, the abbot of St. Werburgh's, Henry Francis.[1] According to J. S. Purvis, an author of the York Cycle was John de Greystock, the secretary to the Archbishop of the day.[2] These are the only two medieval plays about the authorship of which we might hazard a guess. All the other dramatists are completely obscured in anonymity, as they could hardly have been if they had had any social status worthy of note.

Social initiative, of course, of all kinds, devolved upon the middle classes in times when the hereditary nobility and other leaders were from generation to generation endlessly busy in

[1] *Mediaeval Drama in Chester* (Toronto, 1955), p. 48.

[2] In a public lecture in York in 1951: the evidence is in the nature of things highly tentative.

the turmoils of war. A few years ago a Member of Parliament explained to me why, despite his interest in poetry, he never wrote any:

> There isn't the time
> To bother with rhyme
> In a parliament neatly divided.
> I don't mind devoting
> Some moments to noting
> The poems by others provided. . . .

Something like the same attitude must have been common among those who were the leaders of medieval society: they left literature, as they left music and architecture and estate management and many other specialized problems, to those whose social duty it was to be expert with them. A very different attitude prevailed in later centuries. Until the Renaissance, then, the most dynamic forces behind the development of English Literature were middle class in origin, English rather than Anglo-French, of the gilds and the yeomanry rather than of the Court and the aristocracy. This fact was to have potent influence upon the development of a literary profession at the crucial time when printing presses came into use.

Certainly, the first steps toward developing a national public which could support a national profession came from a thrusting, vital middle class. It is clear, for instance, that literacy became increasingly the possession of the whole middle class and that the ability to read a manuscript for oneself, instead of relying upon oral means of communication, encouraged an increasing multiplication of manuscripts, and later of printed books, in the very kinds of literature which middle-class readers preferred.

The output of the first printers faithfully reflected the tastes expressed in manuscripts. Although William Caxton, for instance, concentrated for the most part on works of piety and devotion, nearly a third of his publications were books of entertainment, including eight romances and thirteen volumes of poetry; he also published prose translations, like his version of the Flemish beast-epic, *Reynart the Foxe*, and handbooks of information, like his *Doctrinal of Health*. It used to be argued that Caxton fashioned rather than followed popular taste, but a comparison of his titles with those of contemporary manuscripts suggests that he was primarily the servant, though an enlightened one, of his public of book-buyers.

Figures about literacy are difficult to estimate. But Sir Thomas More left on record his belief, in 1533, that in England 'farre more than fowre partes of all the whole divided into tenne coulde never read englishe yet'.[1] His argument, at the point of this estimate, is critical of the need for an English translation of the Bible, one of the demands of the newly literate classes which was in the highest degree and in many directions potential of revolution, and therefore it is to be presumed that if he had honestly been able to cast his percentage of illiteracy higher, he would have done so. When he calculates 'farre more than fowre partes of . . . tenne', avoiding directly saying half, or more than half, or six-tenths, we conclude that his guess is that something like 45 per cent of the population, and not much more, were illiterate. By subtraction, we find that he believed that more than half of the population could read, quite an extraordinarily high proportion. After all, in 1845 it was estimated then that 33 per cent of the total male, and 49 per cent of the total female, population were illiterate, and it would seem that if he was right in the 300 years after More there had been no permanent increase in literacy of any significant degree. More's figures seem to be supported by the Act of Parliament under Henry VIII in 1543, 'for the advancement of true religion and for the abolishment of the contrary', which forbade the reading of an English Bible by women, artificers, prentices, journeymen, serving-men of the rank of yeomen or under, husbandmen and labourers—clearly an astonishing statute to promulgate if there had not been widespread literacy among these lower orders of society.

Certainly, there is plenty of evidence that great numbers of people could read. Extant household accounts of the period reveal that the women and the servants were able to keep written records; manuscript posters in public places were displayed; labels were used on women's toilet boxes, and letters of the alphabet on children's porringers. And there is the evidence of wills. These are notoriously inadequate as record of book-ownership. In 7,568 wills of the fourteenth and fifteenth centuries examined by M. Deanesly, only 338 mentioned books at all, and most of these were Latin rather than English, and works of

[1] *Works* (1557), p. 850.

piety and devotion rather than books of secular entertainment.[1] This is rather disappointing, and the more so when the eagle eyes of inventory-takers go to great trouble to find books, even looking in one instance among the malt, wheat and sacks in the kiln, and when the testators remember other items of property as insignificant as 'one piece of whitt fyshe. vi d.' But one suspects that, as a general rule, only books of special monetary, prestige or sentimental value were named in wills, and that for the most part books were included, without specification, among the household paper in the family chest, or in the miscellaneous item recorded as the 'residewe' or as 'al other my householde stuffe'. Certainly, I have found no mention of books in the wills of prominent Elizabethans who certainly possessed them, men like Sir Thomas Walsingham, Sir Francis Drake, Sir Thomas Gresham, Sir Thomas White, and the Earl of Southampton. But if medieval wills are inadequate in this respect, they do provide, in the signatures of witnesses, evidence about the incidence of ability to sign a name. It is not uncommon to find 60 or 70 per cent of the witnesses literate, at least in this elementary way, and to discover that tailors and mariners, merchants and smiths, ropers and cooks were often literate, while gentlemen sometimes signed their name with a mark. The evidence is uneven, but certainly some major advance in literacy took place between 1350 and 1500, if only as the result of the increase in the provision of grammar schools in this period, chiefly under the patronage of gilds and leading aldermen of the towns. There was a great variety of schools, some for choristers and some which took in girls as 'petties', some attached to cathedrals and some to collegiate houses, some to gilds and hospitals and chantries, and some with independent governing bodies, the forebears of some of the great public schools of the future, and it is likely that all this educational activity had its effect.

And hence so many of the literary phenomena of the age, like the multiplication of manuscripts in English. G. C. Coulton estimated that for every one page of English written in the thirteenth century there were two or three in the fourteenth and ten in the fifteenth century. There was a multiplication also, clearly for people of modest means, of utilitarian manuscripts,

[1] 'Vernacular Books in England in the Fourteenth and Fifteenth Centuries', *Modern Language Review* (October 1920).

written in quires, unbound, without illuminations or embellishments, consisting sometimes only of single poems, like Lydgate's *Temple of Glas*, or short devotional treatises, like *The Abbey of the Holy Ghost*. Hence also the development of drama almost exclusively as a middle-class art: the great Mystery Cycles were sponsored by the trade gilds of the towns, in York, Chester, Wakefield, Coventry, London, Cambridge, Beverley, Canterbury, Newcastle, Norwich, Winchester, Worcester, Edinburgh, Kendal, Reading, Witney, Lincoln, Preston, and dozens of other places; the Miracles or Saints Plays were sponsored by the religious or charitable gilds, middle-class organizations again operating chiefly in the towns; and the few professional companies of actors which went on tour with plays like *The Castell of Perseverance* were dependent upon communal patronage to fill their 'rounds', which, to judge from the dimensions of the round at St. Just in Cornwall, had accommodation for as many as 4,000 spectators. Hence, too, that perceptible widening of the appeal of writers like Chaucer who began their literary careers as Court poets, catering for the tastes of a few patrons accustomed to the styles and modes of Anglo-French literature, but who gradually increase their Englishness until in later years they can write of millers and of reeves as happily as of knights and monks.

In all this story, so far, there has been little mention of patronage. The emphasis has been upon the collective support given to writers by the whole communities in which they worked, religious or secular. While it is true, as Samuel Moore suggests, that 'it is not much of an exaggeration to say that every English writer before 1475 (or perhaps 1500) had a patron',[1] the patronage of the day was in a different category from the Classical conception, exemplified by the relationship between say, Maecenas and Horace and Virgil, which was not revived in England until the sixteenth century. The third great source of the English profession of letters, classical example, was not indeed effective until Tudor times. Neither drama nor poetry is much influenced by classical models, nor the kinds of literature available to the writer, nor the functions of writers within society. Something is heard from medieval writers of the classical notion that a writer confers immortality upon his patron, perpetuating his

[1] 'General Aspects of Literary Patronage in the Middle Ages', *The Library* (October 1913), p. 374.

fame for future generations, but there is nothing of the assurance and certainty of later Renaissance writers. Basically, medieval writers did not think themselves good enough to confer fame upon themselves, let alone their patrons. Notice John Gower's hesitation in embarking upon this theme at the beginning of his *Confessio Amantis*:

> Forthi good is that we also
> In oure tyme among ous hiere
> Do wryte of newe some matiere,
> Ensampled of these olde wyse
> So that it myhte in such a wyse
> When we ben ded and elleswhere,
> Beleve to the worlds ere
> In tyme comende after this. . . .
>
> For hier in erthe amonges ous,
> If noman write hou that it stode,
> The pris of hem that weren goode
> Scholde, as who seith, a gret partie
> Be lost. . . .

It little became the writers of an old world, which had seen its best days and was fast hasting to its divinely appointed end, to make any grandiose claims about the future.

Nevertheless, influential patrons existed, men who were not writers themselves, but who suggested or commanded themes and who had the capacity to reward in cash or kind. Gower had Richard II; Chaucer had John of Gaunt and other royal princes, Occleve and Lydgate, Henry V; George Ashby, Margaret of Anjou; John Trevisa, Sir Thomas Berkeley, and so on. Other famous fifteenth-century patrons included James Butler, the fourth Earl of Ormonde, Cardinal Beaufort, Walter Lord Hungerford, and other noblemen, the Warwicks and Salisburys and Suffolks, as well as rich London merchants. There are plenty of dedications, epistles excusatory, epistles mendicant, and notes about works written by request, although the volume of this kind of prefatory matter is on nothing like the scale it assumed in the sixteenth century. The great difference between medieval and Renaissance writers was a difference of social security. In the sixteenth century, as we shall see, the writer more often than not deserted the home community into which he was born and went to London to seek his fortune; it was an economic necessity for him to interest a patron in his writing and thus earn a place in society; if he failed, he either starved or went home. But the medieval writer belonged very firmly to a local community which he would only rarely have any desire to leave; within this community he was completely dependent upon its head, religious or secular, whether he were a writer or not. What he sought from his patron was the permission to serve him in the special capacity of writer. He would not expect special rewards, except for occasional gratuities; he would not expect social promotion on account of his literary skills; he was happy if he would be allowed to earn his bread and board by specializing in writing chores rather than in other kinds of activity. There was nothing abject or servile, therefore, in his approach to the great men, and they, too, were correspondingly modest and helpful.

Here, then, in fifteenth-century England, were the rudiments necessary to the formation of a profession of letters. First, the Church found a practical need for literature in the vernacular, and gave to such writings a status of dignity and profundity, and to its writers an accepted place in the Christian community. Second, arising from the oral recitations and readings within local communities, a wide variety of literary subjects became available to writers and, with increasing literacy, a wide variety of audiences who could read manuscripts for themselves. Third, in Church and State, and assisted by patrons, individuals were seeking the means whereby they might devote much of their working time to the writing of books. Literature was still an avocation rather than a vocation; no man depended upon it for his living; no man claimed that it was worthy of lifelong devotion and dedication. But in Lydgate's voluminosity, 130,000 lines from one man's lifetime, and in the wide circulation of imaginative fictions like the *Canterbury Tales*, *Piers Plowman* and *Confessio Amantis*, and in the vast interest taken by all classes in the local communities in the plays and ballads of the period and in the widening circulation of manuscripts of all kinds and subjects, the elements were gathered together for transmutation in later years.

# III

## The Renaissance Amateurs

*As long as art remains a parasite*
*On any class of persons it's alright;*
*The only thing it must be is attendant,*
*The only thing it mustn't, independent.*

W. H. AUDEN

THE very word *profession* is singularly rich in connotations and overtones, and it would be unfair and unwise to define it too precisely. Originating as a term for an act or professing, an open declaration or avowal, it came to imply a dedication to a particular vocation or calling, and then the vocation itself and the collective body of people engaged in it. Traditionally the three great professions are those of divinity, law, and medicine; but the word has been applied to many other vocations, to all forms of employment, in fact, which are not mechanical and which require some degree of learning, in particular to callings of a learned, scientific or artistic kind. In modern times the number of professional letters designate, which one can add to one's name, including those awarded by learned bodies with a professional rather than a purely academic relevance, and excluding university degrees and medical degrees (except those referring to the membership of colleges), has risen to the extraordinary total of 167.[1] From the beginning the word has increasingly

[1] R. Lewis and A. Maude, *Professional People* (1952), p. 275.

gathered some sense of the reward given for services rendered: doctors and lawyers are traditionally fee-taking advisers, and other professionals have become salaried servants of the community. Today, when we refer to 'professional artists' or professional footballers', we isolate this sense of reward and give it exclusive importance. In defence of the scale of rewards, and in defence therefore of the means to a livelihood shared by the collective body engaged in a vocation, many professional organizations are in effect 'closed shops', with powers of exclusion and admittance which are used to limit the size of membership.

The historian of the profession of letters may catch points of comparison with other professions, similarities here, distinctions there, but is bound to map out his unique terrain in the lines of its own nature. The literary profession has very rarely attempted to establish any kind of collective body with an entity and powers of its own. Academies of writers have existed in different places at different times, but with the possible exception of seventeenth-century Italy these have not been all-inclusive, and therefore exclusive. Professional unions, like the National Union of Journalists, have nothing to do with the essential pursuits of literature to which the profession of letters may be said to be dedicated. Nor have the rewards of the profession very much direct value in seeking a definition; as has already been suggested, rewards in cash or in kind may be so indirect as to be relatively negligible compared with the sense of dedication offered by the writer himself. The true literary professional makes his life, rather than his livelihood, in the writing of books. But when all this is said, there remains a sense of a learned calling, with some kind of corporate togetherness shared by those who follow it, dedicated to high ends, and dependent upon the establishment of a social status which makes it possible, whatever the particular system of rewards, for many men to devote their lives towards it.

At the beginning of the sixteenth century it might have seemed extremely likely that England would soon have its literary profession. Looking back upon those times, conditions appear to have been ripe and ready. Wider literacy, the development of the printing press and of the market for printed books, the ending of 200 years of international and civil war, increasing prosperity and luxury, and above all, the revived interest in *belles-lettres*, which was a consequence of the Renaissance—all this might well have betokened the immediate establishment of a profession of letters. But in the event things were not so simple. The kind of society fashioned under the Tudors advanced a literary profession in some respects, but in others held it back for another century and a half. Literature suddenly came to enjoy a national importance and esteem it had never been vouchsafed in the Middle Ages, but simultaneously obstacles of a particularly harassing and immovable kind were placed in the way of those who sought to devote their lives to literature. The truth is that the great Renaissance courtiers were apt to regard literature, like all the other arts, as an avocation rather than a vocation, best pursued therefore by amateurs.

The new high status of literature seems to date from the time in the 1520's when Continental and particularly Italian ideas about *belles-lettres* began to be absorbed and accepted here. The agency of change was the Court. Henry VII had been content to employ as his 'poet laureate' a Frenchman, Bernard André of Toulouse. Such an appointment was unacceptable to Henry VIII, not only because of the rising nationalism of those years, but also because it offended one of the cardinal laws of Renaissance culture. According to Castiglione's *Il Cortegiano*, the most influential of the many contemporary handbooks of courtesy, circulating widely throughout Europe after its publication in 1527, the ideal courtier had to be, in the words of Hoby's Elizabethan translation, 'more than indifferently well seene at the leaste in those studies, which they call Humanitie', and skilled 'in writing both rime and prose, and especially in this our vulgar tunge.'[1] If the prince himself were to represent the 'floure of Courtlines' (Henry VIII, of course, was determined to have a Court second to none in Europe), he had to have men about him who were experienced in the writing, reading and criticism of English literature.

From this time the monarchs themselves set an example. According to Erasmus, Henry had always loved poetry, and he composed both music and verse. Queen Anne Boleyn, like her brother George, was a poet. Others of his queens cultivated literary interests and became leading patrons. Later, James VI of Scotland wrote *Ane Schort Treatise* on the *Reulis and cautelis*

[1] Ed. J. E. Ashbee, pp. 73, 302, 383.

*to be observit and eschewit in Scottis Poesie* (1584), assuming the leadership, that is to say, of a poetic school, and he continued to write verse after his accession to the throne of England. As for Elizabeth, her courtiers thought her the greatest poet who had ever lived, 'be it in Ode, Elegie, Epigram, or other kinde of poeme Heroick or Lyricke wherein it shall please her Maiestie to employ her penne, euen by as much oddes as her owne excellent estate and degree exceedeth all the rest of her most humble vassalls'.[1] John Vandernoodt, a visiting merchant of Brabant, found her, so he says, a second Sappho, 'perfecte in all good exercises of the wit, namely, the artes and liberall sciences'—his list includes languages, eloquence, music, dancing, painting, imagery and poetry.[2] Nor is this flattery entirely extravagant; we know that she danced energetically, that she played the lute and virginals, that she wrote 'anthems or things in metre', and at least one poem, 'Importune me no more', which is still included in modern anthologies, and that she had six languages and translated, into prose or verse, Xenophon, Tacitus, Sallust, Boethius, Plutarch, Cicero, Horace, Euripides and Isocrates—no mean achievement, although it is only fair to add that a modern editress thought the 'Boethius indifferent, Plutarch bad, and Horace worse, being in many places entirely unintelligible'.[3] It was evidently important that the monarchs should at least try to be good writers. Even Lady Jane Grey, Foxe reports, when denied pen and ink in the Tower, managed to scratch out a poem with a pin!

More important still, the Tudor princes gathered about them the men who could write. The Renaissance was uniquely the period when literature and statesmanship were accomplishments which normally went together. There were very few writers who could not have been said to be, in a very real sense, courtiers first and writers second. If for the sake of convenience we define the 'Renaissance' as the period between, say, 1520 and 1650, it can fairly be said that half the writers of the age earned their living wholly at Court, that most of the others were de-

[1] George Puttenham, *Arte of English Poesie* (1589). G. Gregory Smith, ed., *Elizabethan Critical Essays* (1904), II. 66.

[2] *A Theatre wherein be represented . . . the miseries & calamities that follow the voluptuous Worldlings, &c.* (1569).

[3] C. Pemberton, *Queen Elizabeth's Englishings* (Early English Text Society, 1899), p. xi.

pendent for a major part of their income, in various ways, upon courtly patronage, and that nearly all the great important writers were either courtiers in their own right or satellites utterly dependent upon the courtly system. Most writers were of humble origin, but by the time of their death four-fifths would have been described by Thomas Wilson, the Elizabethan commentator, as *nobiles*, that is to say, as members of the top fifth of the social scale.

The great names provide an impressive roll call. The following courtiers have all some reputation as writers (some of them were among the greatest writers of the day): Sir William Alexander, Earl of Stirling, Secretary for Scotland; Sir Francis Bacon, Viscount St. Albans, Lord Chancellor; Sir William Berkeley, Governor of Virginia; Sir Francis Bryan, Lord Marshal of Ireland; Lucius Cary, Viscount Falkland, Secretary of State; William Cecil, Lord Burghley, Chief Secretary of State; Sir John Cheke, Secretary of State; Sir John Davies, Lord Chief Justice; Robert Devereux, Earl of Essex, Earl Marshal; Sir Edward Dyer, Chancellor of the Garter; Sir Richard Fanshawe, Privy Councillor; James Graham, Marquis of Montrose, Lieutenant-General; Fulke Greville, Lord Brooke, Chancellor of the Exchequer; Edward Herbert, Lord Herbert of Cherbury, Ambassador to France; Mary Herbert, Countess of Pembroke; Henry Howard, Earl of Surrey, Lieutenant-General; Sir Thomas More, Lord Chancellor; Sir Albertus Morton, Secretary of State; Henry Parker, Lord Morley, Privy Councillor; Matthew Parker, Archbishop of Canterbury; Sir Walter Raleigh, Privy Councillor; Thomas Sackville, Earl of Dorset, Lord Treasurer; Edward Seymour, Duke of Somerset, Protector of the Realm; Sir Philip Sidney, Joint Master of Ordnance; Thomas, Lord Vaux, Privy Councillor; Edward de Vere, Earl of Oxford, Lord Great Chamberlain; Sir Henry Wotton, Ambassador; Sir Thomas Wyatt, Privy Councillor.

And then the lesser courtiers (again including some of the greatest writers of the age): Sir Robert Aytoun, Secretary to Queen Henrietta Maria; Sir Lodowick Bryskett, Clerk to the Munster Council; Richard Carew, Deputy Lieutenant of Cornwall; Sir Thomas Chaloner, Clerk to the Privy Council; George Chapman, Sewer to Prince Henry; Abraham Cowley, Secretary to Queen Henrietta Maria; Samuel Daniel, Gentleman of the

Chamber; John Donne, Dean of St. Paul's; Giles Fletcher, Ambassador to Moscow; Abraham Fraunce, Queen's Solicitor; Sir John Harington, High Sheriff of Somerset; John Heywood, Sewer of the Chamber; James Howell, Historiographer Royal; Ben Jonson, the King's Poet; John Leland, Regius Antiquarius; John Lyly, Clerk Controller at the Revels Office; Anthony Munday, Queen's Messenger of the Bedchamber; Thomas Norton, Leader of the Commons; John Skelton, Regius Orator; Edmund Spenser, Sheriff of Cork; Thomas Sternhold, Groom of the Robes; Joshua Sylvester, Groom of the Chamber; Cyril Tourneur, Secretary to Sir Edward Cecil; Edmund Waller, Commissioner for Trade.

And so on through all the rings of the Court outwards from the person of the Monarch. At every degree literary men are to be found. Among the members of Parliament of the period are to be found literary names: Sir Francis Bacon, Richard Carew, Sir John Cheke, Sir John Davies, John Donne, Sir Richard Fanshawe, Giles Fletcher (the Elder), George Gascoigne, Sidney Godolphin, Sir Arthur Gorges, John Lyly, Andrew Marvell, Thomas Norton, Sir Edwin Sandys, Thomas Sternhold, Sir John Suckling, and Edmund Waller, and many, many others. Statesmanship and literature went hand in hand.

Literature, it would seem, had a personal and private function for the courtier; it was necessary to his life. And this private function was so important that it retarded, in a serious way, the development of the public functions of literature. To put the point another way, the most surprising thing about the literary history of the period is that although the printing presses lay available to fulfil all kinds of educative function, religious, political and social, the writers of the day were much more interested, in the main, in the kind of literature which circulated in manuscript or by word of mouth and which was not intended for publication beyond the confines of the Court. For the courtier and the writers dependent upon him, letters were primarily an instrument of courtly converse and entertainment. At Court, literature was a formal essential of ceremonial; it was the agent of flattery, love-making, condolence and congratulation, the means whereby courtiers exchanged comments with each other about virtually every happening in their lives; it was the means whereby the new nationalism asserted itself against the rival courts of Europe; and, above all, it was the instrument whereby the language was 'purified' and made more graceful, a 'Queen's English' worthy of the realm.

Lyrical poetry and poetic plays were the commonest forms of literature. Plays and poems were written for and recited at the great state occasions, the visits, progresses and processions of the princes. Where we moderns use prose addresses of welcome, eked out with bunting, the Elizabethans used verse, sometimes inscribing it on hoardings which were torchlit by night. Among the writers of this ceremonial verse were the great Earl of Essex, Sir Francis Bacon, Sir Philip Sidney, Sir Edward Dyer and Fulke Greville, as well as poets of a lower social standing, like John Skelton, Edmund Spenser and Sir John Davies. Less spectacularly, but more intimately, poetry was employed in masques, parlour games and exercises of wit. It was the means whereby the courtier discussed experience and pondered, in death-bed or death-cell verses, the approach of death. Sir Henry Wotton said that Essex used to *think* in verse—to 'evaporate his thoughts in a sonnet' was his common way. More recently, it has been said of Raleigh that his verses were 'a part of that strange charm with which he won the Queen's favour, a spiritual adornment, a manifestation of riches and beauty, like his pale satins and the pearl eardrops he wore in his ears'.[1]

Raleigh's poems are indeed the types of his age, although, as is inevitable with manuscript poetry, only thirty-four survive which can be attributed with any certainty to him. There are poems to the Queen; one he had slipped into 'my lady Laitons pocket'; one that was intended to be his own epitaph, another an elegy for Sidney; others are alleged to have been written the night before his death; and there are literary exercises, trials of wits with his friends, like his reply to Marlowe's *Come live with me and be my love*, his poem *The Lie*, to which other poets wrote replies, or the acrostic of three poems in one, *In the grace of wit*, as well as commendatory verses for Spenser, Gorges and Gascoigne.

All this poetic activity transformed the attitude of Englishmen towards their own language. Even in the seventeenth century there were writers who were dissatisfied with English; Waller, for instance, held that

[1] A. Latham, *The Poems of Sir Walter Raleigh* (1929), p. 12.

Poets that lasting marble seek,
Must carve in Latin, or in Greek;
We write in sand. . . .
(*Of English Verse*)

But this medieval modesty about the language had become almost extinct by Waller's time. The transformation took place during the reign of Elizabeth. Richard Foster Jones places the turning-point at 'not earlier than 1575 nor later than 1580',[1] as sudden as that, and attributes the revolution of opinion, in large measure, to the influence of the Court poets who wrote Tottel's *Songes and Sonettes* and similar works. In 1560 Barnabe Googe patriotically insisted that if Chaucer, Homer, Virgil and Ovid were alive,

All these myght well be sure
Theyr matches here to fynde.
So much doth England florishe now
With men of Muses kynde.
(*The Zodyake of Life*)

Before long, Nashe was proudly proclaiming that 'the Poets of our time . . . haue cleansed our language from barbarisme, and made the vulgar sort, here in London . . . to aspire to a richer puritie of speach than is communicated with the Comminalty of any Nation under heauen'.[2] By the end of the century everyone is saying the same thing—scholars like Mulcaster and Holinshed, journalists like Webbe and Meres, courtly satellites like Chapman and Daniel, courtiers like Sidney and Puttenham.

Looking back to this first golden age of letters, the contemporary pride in English seems natural enough, but in many ways it was illogical. Elizabethan English was far from being a settled language: vocabulary was unstable, grammar imperfect, spelling chaotic, and there was no uniform law regarding, for instance, the importing of foreign words, the coining of neologisms and the revival of archaisms. Indeed, it is not difficult to find a writer about language contradicting himself on details: latinizations were bad because they were foreign to the Anglo-Saxon genius of the language, but were good because they enriched the supply of necessary words; monosyllabic words were good because historically they were the best English, but were bad

[1] *The Triumph of the English Language* (1953), p. 211.
[2] *Pierce Penilesse* (1592), in A. B. Grosart, ed., *Complete Works*, II. 61.

because in the mass they lacked elegance; and so on. Humanism and patriotism were often opposed forces, creating tensions which were unresolved because most Elizabethans wanted to have the best of both worlds.

What pleased and excited everybody was something in essence quite illogical, one of those compromises, quite arbitrary, full of inherent contradictions, with which English history has been particularly associated. The courtiers took the law into their own hands, defying wherever necessary the scholars, the Humanists, and the Continental examples, and made up the rules as they went along, establishing a Queen's English as the language of the realm; George Puttenham describes it as the 'usuall speach of the Court, and that of London and the shires lying about London within lx. myles, and not much aboue'.[1] So great was the authority of the Court that nobody questioned its decisions. The courtier thus had the advantage of being able to decide linguistic questions, as others, strictly on their merits. If a word, a device, seemed right in its context, if it *worked*, the courtier gave it his *imprimatur*. Sidney makes the point about oratory, but in a context which makes it equally applicable to literature:

> Undoubtedly (at least to my opinion undoubtedly) I have found in divers smal learned Courtiers, a more sound stile, then in some professors of learning, of which I can gesse no other cause, but that the Courtier following that which by practise he findeth fittest to nature, therein (though he know it not) doth according to art, thogh not by art: where the other using art to show art and not hide art (as in these casses he shuld do) flieth from nature, & indeed abuseth art.[2]

Others aped the courtier. In the words of John Hoskyns, an Oxford don, sergeant-at-law and M.P., writing about 1599:

> . . . we study according to the predominancy of courtly inclinations: whilst mathematics were in requests, all our similitudes came from lines, circles and angles; whilst moral philosophy is now a while spoken of, it is rudeness not to be sententious. And for my part I'll make one. I have used and outworn six several styles since I was first Fellow of New College, and am yet able to bear the fashion of the writing company.[3]

[1] G. Gregory Smith, *op. cit.* II. 150.
[2] *Defence of Poesie*, A. Feuillerat, ed., *Works of Sidney* (1923), III. 43.
[3] *Directions for Speech and Style*, ed. H. H. Hudson (1935), p. 39.

Sidney, damning the professors, is particularly critical of literariness, affections of diction, excessive alliteration, and a mechanical use of the figures of speech of the rhetoricians, faults that can be summed up in the one word *unnaturalness*. But if the courtier were asked how he knew what was unnatural and what was not, he rested his case upon his own instincts and judgments, deriving from long experience of what was done at Court. As George Turberville neatly sums up,

> The courtier knows what best becomes,
> in every kind of case:
> His nature is, what so he doth
> to decke with gallant grace,
> The greatest clarkes in ither artes,
> can hardly do the leeke:
> For learning sundry times is there
> where iudgement is to seeke.
> (*Tragical Tales*, 1587)

It follows that the man with the gift of golden speech, the man with a contribution to make to the glorification of the language, was readily acceptable at Court. The right man would find the way clear for all kinds of social and political promotion. Looking back, it may seem odd to us that good writing served as a kind of entrance examination to politics, but perhaps there have been systems far worse. After all, good writing meant more than the ability to flatter a patron and brighten social intercourse. It implied, as I have indicated, a linguistic skill of national importance. Good writing also advertises intelligence and wit. A capacity to deal with the different situations imposed upon the poet by his material might indicate a valuable adaptability and versatility. The manipulation of metre and language displayed the vital social requisites of gracefulness and graciousness; no boor nor barbarian could survive the test. Literature also reveals a man's originality, imagination, resourcefulness, loyalty, perhaps even courage.

At any rate, the road to the Court at London proved immensely attractive to the writers of the period. Tudor statesmen prided themselves on their *carrière ouverte aux talents*, a system which enabled the bright, ambitious boy with literary gifts to find his way, through scholarships and patronage, to a good school and university, and afterwards perhaps to a place in the Inns of Court, ultimately to a position in the body politic worthy of his gifts. The registers of Oxford University reveal that among students admitted to the colleges between 1567 and 1622 only eighty-four were the sons of noblemen, 590 the sons of knights, 902 the sons of esquires, 985 the sons of clergy and 3,615 the sons of gentlemen, while 6,635 were the sons of 'plebeians'. Rather more than half the students, in modern terms, were lower middle class or working class in origin. These figures compare well with the position today, although we tend too easily to think of the modern system of scholarships and State grants as uniquely egalitarian in educational opportunity. During the seventeenth century a new trend took effect; the old prejudice that letters did not become a nobleman was steadily worn away, and education began to spread more widely, not down, but up the social scale. But it was not until the eighteenth century that the universities came to be regarded as finishing school solely for young gentry; in the Renaissance they were still wide open to all comers. Theoretically, they prepared young men for careers in the Church and in certain of the traditional professions, such as law, but in practice, although three-quarters of the writers of the period went to a university, and a quarter on to the Inns of Court, very few took up the professions of the Church and of the law. There were much more attractive alternative possibilities.

The nucleus of courtly society might be likened to a solar system. The monarch, like the sun, at the centre, was surrounded first by a circle of great noblemen, the leaders of the factions which, as Sir Robert Naunton said of Elizabeth, she 'both made, upheld, and weakened, as her own great judgement advised'. These 'inner planets'—Wolsey, More, Burghley, Leicester, Buckingham, Falkland, and their kind—had their own satellites: lesser courtiers, inferior kinsmen, secretaries, chaplains, physicians, lawyers, tutors, and so on. Beyond these revolved the 'outer planets', the lesser noblemen whose orbits might yet bring them occasionally within the monarch's confidence, and each with his own satellites. Salaries were small; the real rewards of courtly service came from the fees and gratuities of suitors and litigants, the emoluments attached to all kinds of sinecure offices, the profits from the leasing of royal lands, and the yield from charters, licences and monopolies granted by letters patent. As Sir John Neale suggests, the noblemen was 'poised upon a great credit structure';[1] at any time the source of his wealth might be denied him, by order of the monarch, and the result might well be ruin not only for the principal himself but for all those attendant upon his largesse (Essex, for instance, was £10,000 in debt at his fall). But while the risks were enormous, the rewards of courtly service were vast, too, and this was the magnet that attracted Shakespeare from Stratford and Marlowe from Canterbury.

After all, without courtly patronage a clergyman might have to remain in a country living worth little more than the wage of a labourer, a lawyer would remain a 'pettifogger' rather than one of the elect who earned £10,000 a year or more, and the mere Master of a Cambridge college would earn less than a player in one of the liveried, acting companies. At Court there were a hundred profitable ways of reaching the top of a profession, or of using a profession to set up in business as a *rentier* or *entrepreneur*. The aim of every ambitious young man was to attract the attention of a nobleman, the greater the better, and thus to enter profitably into orbit as a satellite. Great fleas and little fleas indeed, but there are worse organizations of society than the parasitical.

The writer came into the system perhaps as a secretary (Spenser), a house poet (Daniel), a liveried player (Shakespeare), a political agent (Marlowe), a chaplain (Herrick), an antiquarian (Jonson), a tutor (Skelton), a lawyer (Fraunce), and so on. He might find himself sequestered from the political hurlyburly, like Shakespeare at the Globe, or like Daniel in receipt of lifelong patronage, free to devote himself towards a purely literary profession. Or he might find himself involved, like Spenser and Marlowe, in dangerous active service, unable perhaps to concentrate upon literature at all. He took his chances, and his writing remained his trump card. Sir John Davies's appointment as Attorney-General for Ireland has been attributed to King James's liking for *Nosce Teipsum*. Samuel Daniel in 1604 earned as a result of his *Panegyricke Congratulatory* the post of licenser of the Queen's Revels. More flamboyantly, William

[1] 'The Elizabethan Political Scene', *Proceedings of the British Academy*, XXXIV (1948), p. 116.

Grey, a writer of the mid-sixteenth century with a flair for ballads, earned the status of esquire, a seat in Parliament, the post of Chamberlain and Receiver in the Court of General Surveyors, and gifts of land and property in the town of Reading, which made him the owner of two of the three inns in the town, 197 houses, four corn mills and two fulling mills. Edmund Spenser, Michael Drayton, John Heywood, Barnabe Googe, Abraham Fraunce and many, many others owed everything to the literature that advertised their talents.

The effect of the concentration of literary talent at Court was the establishment of a highly elaborate literary system, but one which was confined almost exclusively within the bounds of courtly society, and one which was dedicated to an amateur conception of letters. Writers might well have received rewards, in cash or in kind, commensurate with the rewards of other, more professional times; but literature itself was not the immediate *raison d'être* of the system. And the public impact of the writings produced was essentially limited. The primary audience, compared with that of the time of Chaucer, had shrunk from a neighbourhood to a courtly set. Sir Thomas Wyatt wrote, primarily, for the Earl of Surrey, Sir Francis Bryan, Lord Vaux, Viscount Rochford and other close friends, and for some of the Court ladies. Sir Philip Sidney wrote for his sister Mary, his mistress Stella, and other Court ladies, and for close friends like Dyer and Greville and such attendant gentlemen as were privileged to join his 'Areopagus'. At a social level rather lower, John Donne wrote for friends who were associated with him at the university, at Lincoln's Inn, and in politics: men like Sir Henry Wotton, Sir John Davies, Sir Henry Goodyere, John Hoskyns, Sir Richard Baker and so on. Ben Jonson wrote for the 'Sons of Ben', originally a group of political associates, including Sir Robert Cotton, Inigo Jones, Hugh Holland and others, meeting at the Mermaid as the 'Right Worshipfull Fraternitie of Sirenaical Gentlemen'. And so on outwards through all the groups of gentry attendant upon and imitating the manners of the Court. It usually failed to strike the Court writer that his writings should be preserved for any audience outside the circle of friends; they were committed to manuscript, but not to print, and as a result so many poems, plays, masques and dissertations have been utterly lost to posterity. As B. H.

Newdigate pointed out, Drayton's 'gatherings of shepherds and shepherdesses who met for song and dance on Cotswold, on the banks of the Trent and Avon, or on the Elizian plains, were not just fictions of Drayton's muse, or echoes from Theocritus or Mantuan'.[1] These groups provided the real home of literature during this period.

The group system had its advantages. In essence, the group prepared its members, through mutual competition and co-operation, for the service of the monarch. Greville would write one poem in direct competition with Dyer—*Grace for Zenith*, for instance, matching *A Fancy*. Sidney would write another in reply to, say, Greville's *Shepherd's Conceit of Prometheus*. When Spenser joined them, he knew he had the best poets of the day to compete against. In this sense, the group served as a 'finishing school', where members polished each other's art which, like the taste for clothes, or the ear for a compliment, or the aptitude for dancing or fencing or riding, was very much a matter of doing the right things in the right way, in a game where every man tried to dazzle and outvie his competitors. More seriously, a group restricted, ideally at least, to those who were equals or near-equals in social status—no poet was likely to get a frank and helpful opinion from a man who was markedly his social inferior, and mere idle flattery sharpened no wits—co-operated in the formulation of critical principles, a sense of values, indispensable to Court life and to the individual writers. Isolated in his own judgment a writer could make a fool of himself, in speech as in behaviour, like Malvolio. There is a good story about Gabriel Harvey, the don and friend of Spenser, at Audley End in 1578, when he trusted his own judgment with disastrous results. Quite sure he knew the ropes, he dressed himself in exaggerated Italian clothes, paid his betters utterly absurd compliments, and pushed about in the throng with the battle-cry 'Give me entrance and lett me alone. Give me footing, and I will find elbow room.' Of course, this *gaffe* marked the end of Harvey's courtly career. Similarly with writing: fired with self-centred ambition, it was very easy for a man to overwrite (or underwrite, if he were timid) and lose the game. The merest step off a delicate balance, and the writer ran the risk of charges of indecorum and braggadocio that might damn his whole career.

[1] *Michael Drayton and his Circle* (1941), p. 40.

When John Southern, an ambitious satellite, wrote into a love poem these lines

> I doo not meane
> To sing you now: but *Dian*, when you haue bene
> More gretious unto mee: I wyll sing you better. . . .
> (*Pandora*, 1584)

he may have merely put into words a common bribe, but the ungracious proposition hardly recommended him for courtly service. Indeed, he has gone down in history, in Ritson's words, as an 'arrogant and absurd coxcomb'.

The disadvantage of the circle of friends as a source of literature is that convivial company often reduces the art to 'rymes', 'ridles', and 'dapper ditties'. All sorts of parlour games were played, particularly in verse. Renaissance poets loved inventing anagrams and cryptograms, where the lines were in code or contained a hidden meaning. They wrote acrostics and those more complicated variants, acrostiteliosticha, where the first *and* last letters of the lines make up words. They contrived poems where all the lines ended in the same letter. They exploited metrical devices like the Petrarchan sestina (used by Spenser in the *Shepheardes Calender*), in which the rhyme scheme rings, like the peal of bells, ABCDEF, FABCDE, EFABCD, and so on, all down the page. They amused themselves, as Dylan Thomas has in our own times, with ocular poems which, when written down on paper, take up the shape of triangles, spires and other geometrical figures. We might add the experiments conducted in hexameters and other quantitative metres conducted by Sidney and his friends. Writers took a lighter attitude towards literature than is compatible with Matthew Arnold's dictum about a necessary high seriousness or indeed with the development of a serious literary profession. George Puttenham defends these high jinks as 'the convenient solaces and recreations of mans wit', and argues, taking his case to extremes, that in the ultimate scale of things everything is equally trifling, even 'all the profoundest artes and studies among men'. If he had to choose, he preferred 'courtly trifles' to 'scholastical toyes'. It is possible to defend games as a necessary training-ground for more serious work, exercise in the manipulation of words and music, education in the many familiarizations which must occur before a man has the dexterity for his best work.

And certainly we can have little complaint with a group system which produced the poetry of Wyatt, Sidney, Donne and their kind. But, all the same, the Court-group system was not conducive to the development of that sense of dedication to literature which is an indispensable requisite of the profession of letters.

The greatest difficulty about the system was that it created among courtiers and their imitators a strong aversion to print. Today it is usual to ask of an author not 'What has he written?' but 'What has he published?' The achievement of print, with the *imprimatur* that it implies of a recognized audience of publishers and critics, has become a rough guide to quality and permanence. But the Renaissance courtier would have been embarrassed, if not insulted, by the question. It would have seemed to him to introduce an irrelevant emphasis upon a relatively unimportant and at times discreditable aspect of authorship. Most courtly literature was intended for manuscript or oral circulation at Court. Edmund Molineux's comment about Sidney's *Arcadia* is typical: 'Few works of like subject hathe been either of some more earnestlie sought, choislie kept, nor placed in better place, and amongst better jewels than that was; so that a speciall deare freend he should be that could have a sight, but much more deere that could once obteine a copie of it.'[1] In time, of course, copies of different works got abroad: the copies of copies, memorized transcriptions, copies written down in the commonplace books of the time, and so on. And while transcription proceeded, no writer could possibly have said, and few seem to have cared, how many copies were in existence, nor how accurate they were. And ultimately some works found their way, as chance had it, into the hands of a publisher. There was no law of copyright; indeed, the idea of copyright in a coterie society, where literature was communally owned, was a contradiction in terms. Once a work reached a publisher, no matter how imperfect a copy it might be, the writer had no powers of intervention. Thus, courtly literature straggled into print, hobnobbing with all kinds of strange companions and with a catchpenny title on the cover. Henry Constable's *Diana* (1594) appeared in print, padded out quite shamelessly with 'divers quatorzains of honourable and learned personages, with no other

[1] Molineux was once secretary to Sidney's father. *Vide* his note contributed to Stow's continuation of Holinshed's *Chronicles*.

object than that of making up the volume'. In the same way Sidney's *Astrophel and Stella* in 1591 was augmented with 'sundry other rare Sonnets of diuers Noble men and Gentlemen', including Daniel, Oxford and Campion; the device was considered by Greville an insult and by Daniel a piece of smart practice, but everyone was quite powerless to stop the publisher. The best the courtier could do was to ignore print altogether.

There was a dilemma in this situation which the leading Court writers never solved. On the one hand, the Humanists and patriots among them knew perfectly well, from classical example, that literature was not an ephemeral art; on the contrary, the best works lasted for ever and brought permanent credit to the writer and his nation. They knew that it was no mere conceit that Shakespeare borrowed from Horace:

> So long as men can breathe, or eyes can see,
> So long lives this, and this gives life to thee.
> (*Sonnet 18*)

On the other hand, in practice and in defiance of Humanist theory, the Court writers never threw off a quasi-medieval humility about their own works, confined themselves to a narrow contemporary audience and ignored posterity almost altogether. Fulke Greville's consent for even a posthumous edition of his poetry was at best lukewarm: 'These pamphlets, which having slept out my own time, if they happen to be seene herafter, shall at their own perill rise upon the stage when I am not.'[1] And Greville is said to have burned the manuscripts of his plays rather than run risks of having them pried upon. His plans for an edition of Sidney's *Arcadia*, forced upon him by the possibility that Ponsonby or some other printer would produce a corrupt text, were troubled by the conviction that Sidney's pages 'were scribled rather as pamphlets, for entertainment of time and friends, then any accompt of himself to the world'.[2] From one point of view, Spenser's claim to have written a *Shepheardes Calender*

> That steele in strength, and time in durance shall outweare:
> And if I marked well the starres revolution,
> It shall continewe till the worlds dissolution

[1] *Poems and Dramas of Fulke Greville*, ed. G. Bullough (1939), I. 24.
[2] *Works of Fulke Greville*, ed. A. B. Grosart (1870), III. 20–21.

was an unexceptionable expression of hope in the best classical tradition. From another point of view, it was an act of braggadocio which no courtier would have the immodesty to commit.

Thus, although in many respects literature became a national art during this period, there were many limitations upon the establishment of anything worthy of the name of a literary profession. The amateurs of the Court and their satellites treated literature seriously enough; they forged a firm and unbreakable connexion between the literary art and a proper enquiry into human nature, into personal experience, into the things which make men human. But they were essentially amateurs unable to give writers, as such, the kind of status shared by other professional men, unable to give literature, as such, the undivided and dedicated attention and public place the art demands. And this ambivalence created endless difficulties for those who were seeking at this very time to establish through print a true profession of letters.

# IV

# The Renaissance Professionals

*What greater and more odious infamye, for on of my standinge in the Universitye and profession abroade, then to be reckonid in the Beacheroule of Inglish Rimers?*

GABRIEL HARVEY to SPENSER[1]

WHILE later writers have relied upon periodicals and printed books to help them to an audience, it must be said at once that during the Renaissance the printing trade was in its infancy and tightly bound in swaddling clothes of various kinds. Between 1500 and 1630 the total national book production, of new books and new editions, rose from forty-five a year to only 460, a figure we might compare with the total in 1960 of 23,783. Sharp increases in production did not occur until the Civil War created entirely new social conditions. For political reasons the authorities were markedly fearful of the power of the printed word, and kept the stationers firmly under control. By the regulation of 1586, for instance, all published books had to be approved by the Archbishop of Canterbury or the Bishop of London. For most of the period, no printing presses were tolerated outside London, except those operated under special dispensation by the universities of Oxford and Cambridge and by the Flemings of Norwich. The stationers willingly, for the most part, co-operated with the

[1] E. J. L. Scott, ed., *Letter-Book of Gabriel Harvey, 1573–80* (Camden Society, Second Series, XXXIII, 1884), pp. 59–60.

régime; indeed, State control suited their 'scarcity economics'—it paid the stationers to have various trade agreements regulating the output of books and defending themselves against interlopers. In any case, illiteracy in the total population was widespread, more so in the provinces than in London and the Home Counties.

An edition of any book was limited by law, except by special dispensation, to an impression of 500 copies, and 250 was the usual size. There was no law of copyright protecting authors, and it was the custom for the writer to sell his work outright for a standard fee, usually about £6. 10*s*., but occasionally rather more, up to about £20. Even if the writer produced a best-seller, he received no further reward unless, at the publisher's discretion, he received a fee for any revisions required for a later edition. Many writers tried to augment their earnings by proof-reading or by writing pamphlets, at £2 or so a time, for political causes of the day. Without patronage a literary profession, of any kind, would have been impossible. The writer was usually given complimentary copies which he delivered to selected patrons in the hope, at the least, of a gratuity; a dedication to a particular nobleman might earn an additional £2 or £3, and some books might be subsidized much more generously or lead to some kind of position in the entourage of the patron.

The main object of courtly patronage, as far as print was concerned, was translations, handbooks, historical compilations, and works of piety and controversy, and the function of printed literature, according to Eleanor Rosenberg, was to 'popularize learning', 'raise the cultural level of England', and provide 'a learned ministry and an enlightened ruling class'.[1] The best-sellers of the age, besides the Bible and Prayer Books, were books like John Norden's *Pensive Man's Practice* (1584), which exceeded forty editions by 1627, Michael Sparke's *Crumbs of Comfort* (?1623), which reached forty-one editions by 1650, and Arthur Dent's *Plain Man's Pathway to Heaven* (1601), twenty-five editions by 1640. In verse, too, significantly, the best-sellers were of a similar kind: the Sternhold-Hopkins Psalter (1549), which reached forty-seven editions by 1600, Thomas Tusser's *Good Points of Husbandrie*, seventeen editions between 1557 and 1620, Robert Southwell's *Saint Peter's Com-*

[1] *Leicester, Patron of Letters* (New York, 1955), p. xvi.

*plaint*, fifteen editions between 1595 and 1636, and William Hunnis's *Seven Sobs of a Sorrowful Soule for Sinne*, fourteen editions between 1581 and 1636. The courtiers and their satellites, as well as the traditionally pious middle class, readily bought this kind of book.

Now and then this didactic trade produced a great book for which posterity has been ever grateful: Sir Thomas Elyot's *The Boke named the Governour* (1531), Roger Ascham's *The Scholemaster* (1568), Richard Hooker's *Laws of Ecclesiastical Polity*, Sir Francis Bacon's *Essays* (1597–1625), Robert Burton's *The Anatomy of Melancholy* (1621) and Sir Thomas Browne's *Religio Medici* (1642). And there were the great translations, the Authorized Version of the Bible, and work by North and Florio and others. But in the main homely and rather humdrum piety ruled the day. When Sir Thomas Bodley refounded the university library at Oxford he refused to have on his shelves what he called 'idle bookes, & riffe raffe', terms that apparently included virtually the whole of English poetry and drama, for in the 1605 Catalogue there are only three books—a 1561 edition of Chaucer, a 1554 edition of Lydgate's *Fall of Princes*, and Puttenham's *Arte of English Poesie* (1589)—which might be described as belles-lettres in English.

Like modern poets, then, but for different reasons, Renaissance writers could not look upon the printed-book market as lucrative. The only really satisfactory commercial proposition lay in the broadside street ballads and their prose equivalents. In 'rhythmedogrell plaine' the street ballad, a cross between a modern newspaper and popular sheet music, spread the news of the latest London murders, scandals, disasters and controversies, far into the provincial greenwoods, killing off incidentally the local oral ballads which were the last flowering of the medieval order. It was hawked by the hundred by professional hucksters, like Out-roaring Dick of Essex, who earned, according to Henry Chettle's *Kind Hart's Dream* (1592), as much as 10s. a day, better than the pay a College Head could earn in a fortnight. This was profitable merchandize: when the cupboard of the Stationers Company was checked in 1560 it was found to contain only forty-four books, but 796 ballads. And street ballads and pamphlets were often made to serve political purposes, so that this kind of literature was subsidized by the authorities.

Greene, Nashe, Dekker, Munday and many other Elizabethans profited from the opportunities presented to them by pamphlets which sold at a penny or halfpenny a time, and were worth to the writer £2 or £3 a time. Very few writers attempted to earn a living from books themselves, which sold at about *6d.* each. Thomas Churchyard is the most conspicuous instance: his sixty books in fifty years brought him in about £10 a year. Most writers only turned to print as a means of supplementing their income, especially when, like Ben Jonson, their funds ran low. And most writers, it must be said, only reached hard covers once in a lifetime.

All this helps to provide an additional explanation for the concentration of talent at Court. Apart from the public theatres, as we shall see, there was no satisfactory way in which a writer could capitalize his genius and win a reasonably secure livelihood except by interesting the Court. But to say this is not to deny the growing importance of print. If we can put aside for the time being the opportunities presented in the public theatre, the printed-book market offered, in potential at least, three things essential to the establishment of a literary profession and especially attractive to writers who wanted to devote their lives to writing. The money offered, though meagre, was a straight professional return for literary services, and there were many writers who sickened of the servility and flattery expected of the literary aspirant. Secondly, the printed book by its very nature reached a much larger audience than manuscripts and at much less expense; the wider audience, and the potential patronage it implied, offered greater security than the favour of one or two men. Thirdly, writers realized that through print they had the opportunity of reaching posterity, and thus achieving a more substantial fame than the applause of their own contemporaries; and this motive became the stronger the more a writer was acquainted with classical precedent.

The publishers were ready to print courtly literature. Belles-lettres at worst presented them with titles which had a catch-penny, snob appeal; at best with titles which sold surprisingly well. Shakespeare's *Venus and Adonis* ran to twelve editions between 1593 and 1637, Sidney's *Arcadia* to twelve between 1590 and 1633, Marlowe's *Hero and Leander* to eleven between 1598 and 1637, and the anthology, *The Paradise of Dainty Devices*, at least ten editions between 1576 and 1606. After all, these volumes on the bookstall cost *5d.* or *6d.* each, and though this was only the price of a can of canary, only the wealthier sections of the community could afford to buy them. The lower classes confined themselves to halfpenny broadsheets as they did to halfpenny ale. This means that the market was not entirely dominated by the middle-class merchants and his apprentices whose tastes were limited so largely to pious didacticism. There was an audience, large enough, from within the courtly groups themselves, especially from the satellite and attendant gentry of the universities and Inns of Court, and all the others of less genteel status who were fascinated by the manners of the Court. Even the courtiers themselves were not averse to buying books from the stalls or receiving complimentary copies from the authors.

Print, in fact, made possible a form of collective patronage. This was an obvious desideratum for the writer who wanted to devote his life to literature. Lifelong patrons were few and far between; indeed, patronage was occasional rather than permanent, and limited in amount, particularly for the writer who had little else to offer by way of service except his writings. The patrons who were prepared to reward purely literary services were relatively few, and their names occur over and over again in so many different volumes that we must infer a limit to the burden of patronage they would have been prepared to accept. In 1593 George Peele wrote an *Ad Maecenatem Prologus*, in which he complains

> . . . other Patrons have poore Poets none,
> But Muses and the Graces to implore. . . .

Sidney and Walsingham are gone. Why do not the poets of today follow Chaucer, Gower and Marlowe to the grave?

> And leave this Center, barren of repast,
> Unlesse in hope Augusta will restore,
> The wrongs that learning beares of covetousnes,
> And Courts disdaine, the enemie to Arte.[1]

This kind of complaint becomes quite common in the 1590's when, owing to the increasing poverty of the Crown, patronage

[1] *The Honour of the Garter*, in D. H. Horne, ed., *Life and Minor Works* (New Haven, 1952).

of all kinds was in short supply. At about the same time one comes across, more frequently, the kind of distaste for the whole system voiced, for instance, by Joseph Hall in his satires (1598):

> O age well thriven and well fortunate,
> When ech man hath a Muse appropriate,
> And shee like to some servile eare-board slave
> Must play and sing when, and what he would have.[1]

Too much need not be made of these complaints. The difficulty was that, as time went on, there were more writers competing for courtly attention, and that, in any case, the essence of the system was that only the best should be favoured while the others, eliminated for all kinds of faults, from political tactlessness to the failure to be sufficiently versatile, fell by the wayside.

In these circumstances, print offered a way forward, and a way out of difficulties, by collective patronage. In his *Challenge* (1593), Thomas Churchyard printed fifteen different pieces, each of them with a separate dedication. He must have thought this a good idea, because in the same book he advertised his next work as 'twelve long tales for Christmas, dedicated to twelve honorable Lords'. The device was not new. Spenser in 1589 had dedicated the *Faerie Queene* to the Court at large, writing as many as sixteen dedicatory sonnets to influential Privy Councillors and Court ladies, with an extra omnibus sonnet to all the other 'gratious and beautifull Ladies' whom he had not named earlier. If Spenser could do this with a work as important as the *Faerie Queene*, the example was worth following and improving upon. John Davies of Hereford prefaced his book on handwriting with thirty dedicatory sonnets, as well as omnibus sonnets to the 'intire body of the Kinges Maiesties most honourable Privie Councell', the University of Oxford, 'all the right noble Nobilitie of England', and 'all the right Honourable Earles & Lords of Scotland'. Even more promiscuously, Henry Lok dedicated *Sundry Christian Passions* (1593) to fifty-six different patrons, and added other sonnets to 'the Gentlemen Courtiers in generall', 'the Honourable Ladies and Gentlewomen attendants in the Court', and 'all other his Honourable and beloved friends in generall'. The practice was imitated by Michael Drayton, Thomas Drant, Gervase Markham, Barnabe Barnes and Joshua

[1] *Virgidemiarum*, Book VI.

Sylvester, who, shamelessly, dedicated his *Epistle Consolatorie* to 'all the noble Sidneys and semi-Sidneys'!

As a by-product of this practice, some poets, like Daniel, were prepared to pay for private editions intended for presentation to special patrons, and some printers were prepared to ask writers to contribute to the cost of publication of books intended directly for patronage. In the end, the dedication market became a racket. Dekker describes in his pamphlet *O per se O* how some authors privately printed a stock of books with the dedication page left bank, to be filled in later by hand, thus enabling the same book to be submitted to many different 'sole patrons':

> And thus to give bookes now's an occupation,
> One booke hath seaven score patrons. . . .

But patrons in time became wary and turned a blind eye upon publications of which they had no prior knowledge, and Henry Peacham in his *Truth of our Times* (1638) warned would-be dedicators that 'if thou gettest but as much as will pay for the binding and strings, thou art well enough'. This particular development of collective patronage was indeed hazardous; in a later age, in different social conditions, it appears again in the guise of subscription patronage. For the Renaissance writer, other lines were more useful: in particular, the special advantage print possessed of advertising a man's talents to the widest possible field. Court writers who did not normally seek print were prepared to try one book to advertise themselves in this way.

Edmund Spenser's *Shepheardes Calender* is a case in point. Previously he had circulated poems only in manuscript, keeping discreetly his patrons' susceptibilities in mind: he told Harvey, in a letter dated October 1579, that he had not sought print, 'least by over-much cloying their noble eares, I should rather gather a contempt of myself, or else seeme rather for gaine or commoditie to doe it, for some sweetnesse that I have already tasted'. But now the time was ripe for the furtherance of his career by the publication of a manifesto of his ability. 'Whiles the yron is hote, it is good striking, and minds of Nobles varie, as their Estates.' The *Calender* is very much a manifesto, displaying all this resourceful poet's many talents of metrical and linguistic virtuosity. We might well find Shakespeare's *Venus and Adonis* a similar poem, written at a similar stage in his career and by a writer who appears to have been little interested in print at other times.

But the writer who went to market with his wares, for whatever reason, ran the risk of becoming a butt. Passing beyond the bounds of polite manuscript circulation brought one into company with the red-nosed fiddlers, the ignorant ale knights, the 'frye of wooden rhythmours', the 'reakhellye route', and the 'uncountable rabble', terms used by courtly people to deride the homely balladists and pamphleteers who were the mainstay of the printed-book trade. This is the basis of Gabriel Harvey's alarm that his *Verlayes* might be published by Spenser and then hawked at Bartholomew Fair or Stourbridge Fair by a ballad-monger crying

> I pray you will you see any freshe new bookes? Looke, I beseeche you, for your loove and buie for your moonye. Let me yet borrowe on crackd groate of your purse for this same span new pamflett. I wisse he is an University man that made it, and yea highly commendid unto me for a greate scholler.[1]

Suppose I am mistaken for the writer of broadside ballads! 'You have of the Wits,' snorted Sir John Daw in Jonson's *Epicoene*, 'that write verses, and yet are no *poets*: they are Poets that live by it, the poore fellowes that live by it.'[2] It was a two-edged joke: Jonson himself, like so many other writers, was one of the poor fellows that lived by poetry, if indirectly, and only a fine distinction differentiated him from the poetic entertainers he derides. And hence a very real dilemma for the writer who sought print. If he did not print, perhaps the right people would never discover he was a poet; if he did, the right people might suspect he was no gentleman. For the professional the achievement of print ultimately became an economic necessity; for the aspirant to courtly promotion the avoidance of print was a social desirability.

Some courtiers protested against this stigma of print. George Puttenham, for instance, argued that since

> . . . so many noble Emperours, Kings and Princes have bene studious of Poesie and other civill arts, and are not ashamed to

[1] *Loc. cit. supra.*
[2] II. iii.

> bewray their skils in the same, let none other meaner person despise learning, nor . . . be any whit squeimish to let it be publisht under their names, for reason serves it, and modesty doth not repugne.[1]

But, significantly, he was himself so 'dayntie of his doings' that he withheld his name both from his manuscript poem *Partheniades* and from his printed essay on the *Arte of English Poesie*. Faced with a stigma they could not shift, writers tended to elaborate all kinds of conventions to bypass it.

One way out was for the poet to cloak his identity behind anonymity, a pseudonym or initials. A familiar instance is Spenser's adoption of the name *Immerito*, as an addition to the smoke-screen thrown across the *Shepheardes Calender*, by his supposed friend, E.K., whose identity is also concealed. Francis Davison obscures from view the authors in his miscellany, *The Poetical Rhapsody*, under the labels *Anomos* and *Anonymoi*. Other pseudonyms in common use were Anon, Anonimus, A.W. (Anonymous writer), Ignoto, Incognitus, Immeritus and their variants. Some authors, in bashful jocularity, used pseudo-foreign names, William Warren becoming 'Guillam de Warrino' and Bartholomew Young 'B. Giouano del M. Temp'. Others, like Roger Bieston, Richard Robinson of Alton, and George Marshall, obscure writers with little cause for this kind of bashfulness, revealed their names only in acrostics. As for the initials, there is no more unrewarding task than attempting to identify the initials appended to Renaissance writings, for there can be no guarantee of their genuineness. Some were arbitrarily selected from the alphabet, as George Gascoigne on one occasion chose F. I. And some authors sent their work abroad *sans* name, *sans* pseudonyms, *sans* initials:

> Go, bastard Orphan! Pack thee hence!
> And seek some stranger for defence!
> Now 'gins thy basenes to be known!
> Nor dare I take thee for mine owne;
> Thy levity shall be descried![2]

Naturally, when such works were sent to a patron, the author emerged very quickly from his shell of anonymity.

If, however, the author could prove that he was publishing

[1] G. Gregory Smith, ed., *Elizabethan Critical Essays* (1904), II. 23–24.
[2] Barnabe Barnes, *Parthenophil and Parthenophe* (1593?).

old stuff, the stigma of print appears to have been diminished. Presumably, it was recognized that the printers would eventually get hold of even the most private work, and that therefore it was only a venial offence to save them a year or two. Francis Davison, the anthologist, for instance, assured his readers that his own poems were written 'most of them sixe or seven yeares since', that his brother Walter was 'not 18 yeeres olde when hee writt these Toyes', and that a third poet in his anthology, Anomos, had written '(as appeareth by divers things to Syr *Philip Sidney* living, and of him dead) almost twentie yeers since'.[1] Davison ingeniously combines here an assurance of decorous delay and an alibi on the grounds of youth with, tipping his hat to Sidney, an appeal to the reverence due to antiquity.

The commonest formula for excusing oneself for self-advertisement was that of a reluctant surrender to the insistence of friends. 'Write for the stage,' Jonson has Ovid Junior retort to Ovid Senior in *Poetaster*,

> I am not knowne unto the open stage,
> Nor do I traffique in their theaters.
> Indeede, I doe acknowledge, at request
> Of some neere friends, and honorable Romanes,
> I have begunne a poeme of that nature. . . .[2]

Friends sometimes exonerated the writer from all blame by publicly taking the responsibility upon their own shoulders, and it is curious to find such confessions given prominence by the publisher among the prefatory material. Writers seemed to help each other out with this kind of service, as George Turberville supported George Gascoigne. One might have imagined that the publication of religious material would not have required from the writer this kind of defence. But it was 'at the motion of some wel-deserving friendes' that Barnabe Barnes committed to the 'publique tipographicall theatre of general censure' his *Divine Centurie of Spirituall Sonnets*, and Archbishop Matthew Parker's *Psalms* were finally published only when 'frendes requests' persuaded the writer to release them from private circulation. The subject itself does not seem to have been decisive. The nearer a man was to Court, the more reluctant he appears to

[1] H. E. Rollins, ed., *A Poetical Rhapsody* (1932), I. 6.
[2] I. ii.

have been to seek print, however unexceptionable the subject.

The writers overflow with protestations of modesty. William Warner described his *Albions England*, an historical work of considerable size and inherent pretension, as 'a thriftles trauell which the request of Friends did importune me to performe, and I with small or no fancie do now publish'. Thomas Churchyard apologized for his first collected edition by adopting the title *Churchyardes Chippes*, so that he should 'beguile no man with better opinion than the substaunce it selfe doth import'. John Dickenson preferred to parade his humility in mottoes: *est labor in minimis*, or *brevissima, gratissima*, or *est aliquid levibus depingere seria nugis*. This is a humility of a different kind from the modesty conventional with medieval writers, who believed that everything worth saying had been said a long time ago. While the courtiers did not choose to print their work, these minor writers had to defend themselves from the charge of pretentiousness. Ulpian Fulwell deals directly with this charge in a work aptly called *The Arte of Flatterie* (1579) by admitting that he is not the 'meetest man to take this charge in hand', and expressing the hope that his own inadequate performance would 'call the fine force of writers that now swarme in England, to leave off the current handling of Venus Pageants (wherein they shew their excellency) and prosecute this'. Edward Hake, a Mayor of Windsor, hits the nail on the head: it was embarrassing that 'we should cloye the worlde with to many bookes of weake handling: especially, whiles the learned travailes and profitable labours of worthye writers are fayne to keepe the doore (as I may terme it) or, which is more, lie buried in silence'.[1]

All this explains why publishers had a motive stronger than mere snobbery in emphasizing the social status of writers, and indeed of their desired audience, on title-pages and elsewhere. The writer must not be mistaken for an ignoramus 'neaver enstructed in any grammar schoole, nor atayning to thee paringes of thee Latin and Greek tongue'.[2] Almost any claim to gentility sufficed: 'Robert Green Master of Arts', 'Thomas Lodge of Lincolnes Inn, Gentleman', 'Christopher Tye, Doctor in Musyke, and one of the Gentlemen of hys Graces most honourable Chappell', and

[1] *Newes Out of Powles Churchyarde* (1579), 'To the gentle reader'.
[2] Richard Stanyhurst, *Aeneis* (1582), ed. E. Arber (1880), p. 10.

so on. When Michael Drayton became an Esquire, about 1605, the title of rank in one edition was given a whole line of print to itself. William Hunnis, George Gascoigne, Barnabe Googe and others printed facsimiles of their coats of arms. It was important that readers should understand that anthologies like *The Phoenix Nest* (1593) were 'built up with the most rare and refined works of Noble men, worthy Knights, gallant gentlemen, Masters of Arts, and brave Schollers'. In addition to the catchpenny appeal of the declaration, the publisher was protecting the reputation of his authors. So, too, the audience was elevated, being addressed as 'all courteous gentlemen, readers, scholars and whosoever else affects the studie of poetrie', or in similar terms. The façade wears a little thin when John Grange dedicates his *Golden Aphroditis* (1577) to the 'Courtelike Dames and Ladie-like Gentlewomen', a phrase which reads as if the dames were not of the Court but would like to be, and the gentlewomen were no ladies, and thinner still when Richard Johnson addresses his *Nine Worthies of London* (1592) to 'the gentlemen readers, as well prentices as others'. Nor is the façade limited to prefatory dressing-up. John Grange gives his poems titles like 'A valiant yong Gentleman . . . bewayleth his former life in this order', 'A Gentleman seeing his brother desirous to goe to the seas, wrote these verses', 'The Description of the love of a Gentleman and Gentlewoman', and so on *ad nauseam*. One of Arnold Bennett's characters describes the popular newspaper of his day as written 'by errand-boys for errand boys'. These Renaissance writers would have liked to give the impression that their literature was written by gentry, for gentry, and about gentry. The necessity to follow what must have become in time a well-worn gambit persisted for several generations and complicated, to say the least, the endeavours of the writer exploring the professional possibilities of print.

And unfortunately the printed-book writers had yet another obstacle to overcome. Underlying many of the quotations above is a certain moral hesitation about the value of the imaginative literary arts, lyric poetry, drama and so on, in which the Court excelled. Even the courtiers themselves seem dubious about these kinds of literature outside the limits of the intimate circles for which they were primarily intended: maybe the art is too frivolous to deserve the permanence of print. This reluctance is connected with the religious thought of the day which *faute de mieux* we have labelled puritanism. Before a radical protestantism set itself up in opposition to the Church and the Court, 'Puritanism' was a line of thought as fashionable among leading intellectuals and politicians as, say, Marxism or Freudianism has been in our own century. Burghley and Leicester, Sidney and Walsingham, and many others, were committed, one way or another, to the sterner code of public morality which the Puritans advocated. They had the support, particularly, of the mercantile classes of the country, especially in London, the Home Counties and East Anglia, the areas which ultimately proved the strongholds of nonconformity against the royalist west and north. This region, with its relatively high standard of literacy and its plentiful bookstalls, was also the backbone of the printed-book market, and it was therefore inevitable that the publishing trade should be sharply affected by the first impact of puritanism; the interests of the Court and the middle classes coincided in the various measures taken to secure a higher standard of morality in all printed matter.

The Puritan objection to all fiction was descended from centuries of scholastic theology, from Tertullian, Jerome, Boethius, Augustine, and Gregory, who were convinced that at best it was a waste of time and folly in the eyes of God. Why cultivate sheer vanities when life was short enough and there were many other activities more profitable for the soul? Even the great classical writers had to be defended in terms of weight, length and gravity, rather than other qualities. But songs and sonnets, plays and pastorals, the finest products of the Renaissance, were too slight to be defended in the same way. In the reign of Henry VIII bishops like Miles Coverdale, critical of popular ballads, wrote psalms in the hope that they would replace 'naughty songs of fleshly love and wantonness', so that 'women sitting at their rocks, or spinning at their wheels . . . young men also that have gift of singing, musicians and courtiers' would be better occupied 'then with *hey nony nony*, *hey troly loly* and such like phantasies'.[1] The basic criticism here of all courtly poetry, which was very much concerned with fleshly love and sometimes even with adultery (Sidney's Stella was, after all, another man's wife), was maintained in the reign of Elizabeth by Archbishop

[1] *Goostly Psalmes and Spirituall Songes* (*ante* 1539), preface.

Matthew Parker, psalmists like Thomas Sternhold and Robert Holland, and John Hall, a member of the Worshipful Company of Chirurgeons, who published in 1565 an anthology entitled *The Courte of Vertue*, a direct counterblast to the Courts of Venus. As a result, the psalm was a form of poetry cultivated not only by churchmen but by courtly writers like Wyatt, Surrey, Sidney, the Countess of Pembroke, and later Milton.

The censorship was a convenient weapon for preventing the publication of such courtly literature as was deemed immoral. In 1599 the censors ordered the destruction not only of satires with political implications, like Joseph Hall's *Virgidemiarum* and Middleton's *Sixe Snarling Satires*, but also Marlowe's translations from Ovid, which were considered to be too lascivious. The bishops were supported by the Lord Mayor and Aldermen of London, among whom, certainly after 1570, there was a Puritan majority, and various measures were adopted, including steps to outlaw the public theatre, to the embarrassment, as we shall see, of Shakespeare and his colleagues. At various times the Privy Council itself came down in favour of Puritan legislation, so that the Court presented the extraordinary spectacle of condemning in public aspects of the very Humanism which it was its policy at other times to foster. In 1582, for instance, it was decided that the 'lascivious' and 'heathen' classical poets should no longer be read in schools, and Christopher Ocland was commissioned to supply innocuous Latin verse, in praise of the Queen, in lieu. Sidney's *Defence of Poesie* (the title, like Puttenham's *Apologie*, indicates that a battle was in progress) is considerably weakened by the contradictions in his views. In sympathy with Puritan sentiments, he had no hesitation in contemning the public theatre, the street ballads, the bawdy sonnets and all the productions of the ragged rhymers. But he was unable to defend in public the courtly alternative, 'that Lyricall kind of Songs and Sonets', because in practice it was equally offensive to public morality. He fell back on the insistence that good poetry was *utile et dulce*, upon classical and Biblical precedents, and advocated forms of poetry, like the epic poem and the play constructed on classical models, of which at that time English Literature had few examples. This kind of defence was important, in the long run, in directing the attention of writers towards the kinds of writing which stimulated the establishment of a literary profession, but in the short term it had the effect of leaving the Puritans in full possession of their targets in the printed-book market, deepened the reluctance of the courtiers to provide any kind of Aunt Sally in print, and darkened the outlook of would-be professional writers.

Donne once expostulated, 'I will have no such Readers as I can teach.' His view is typical of the courtly writer to whom the *dulce* of literature was more important than the *utile*. But the publisher and the printed-book writer could not dismiss didacticism so lightly: not only the censorship but a large and influential section of the public demanded that each book should provide its money's worth of didactic value. And hence all kinds of pressures. A historian like Richard Stanyhurst makes a point of assuring his readers that

> . . . in perusing this historie, you shall find vice punished, vertue rewarded, rebellion suppressed, loialtie exalted, hautinesse disliked, courtesie beloved, briberie detested, iustice imbraced, polling officers to their perpetuall shame reprooved, and upright governours to their eternall fame extrolled. [1]

Such a book was clearly safe for the grocer's sons and apprentices. The translators for their part were able to follow medieval precedent in finding hidden allegorical meanings in Virgil and concealed moral purposes in Ovid. Thomas Peend gravely declared that the real purpose of his *Hermaphroditus and Salmacis* was the exposure of the 'fylthy lothsome lake of lust', which takes the 'strengthe from lusty men', and of the 'mad desyres of women, theyr rage in folysh fits'. Horace, said Thomas Drant, 'was excellent good in his time, a muche zelous controller of sinne, but chiefly one that with sharp satires and cutting quippies, coulde wel displaie and disease a gloser'.[2] But Drant does not seem to have been too sure that this claim would entirely satisfy his audience, and to please them better he appended to the same volume the *Wailings of the Prophet Hieremiah*. Arthur Golding, who translated the whole of Ovid's *Metamorphoses*, insisted that

> With skill, heede and iudgement, this worke must be read,
> For else to the Reader it standes in small stead.

[1] Dedication to Sir Henry Sidney, printed before his contribution to Holinshed's *Second Book of Chronicles* (1586).

[2] *A medicinable Morall* (1586), 'To the reader'.

But as one of his descendants, L. T. Golding, has pointed out, 'Golding was apparently dissatisfied by his failure to impress Elizabethans with the fundamental ethical purpose that he saw in the *Metamorphoses*, for he never again translated a classic that in any degree bordered on the immoral or improper. In fact he did not translate any other classic for ten years, and at that time he did the unexceptionable work of Seneca'.[1] It is a complex story, because side by side with genuine Puritans like Golding there were others who were only concerned with erecting a moral façade about their work. And hypocrisy is an exhausting burden for a professional writer to carry.

Love poetry was particularly difficult to defend or conceal. All else failing, it could always be represented as a public confession of folly. When George Gascoigne divided his poems into 'Flowers, Hearbes and Weedes', in response to criticism of his morals by the Court of High Commission, he called them 'a myrrour for unbrydled youth, to avoyde those perilles which I had passed'. The sham of this kind of façade was exposed by William Averell's suggestion that those who were shocked by his *Charles and Julia* should burn it by the candle with which they read it. On a smaller scale, we are almost in a modern world where newspaper proprietors expose lurid vice for Sunday reading under the pretence of performing a public service.

The young soldier, Arthur Broke, gives the game away. His preface is uncompromising enough:

> And to this ende (Good Reader) is this tragicall matter written, to describe unto thee a coople of unfortunate lovers, thralling themselves to unhonest desire, neglecting the authoritie and advise of parents and frendes, conferring their principall counsells with dronken gossyppes, and superstitious friers (the naturally fitte instrumentes of unchastitie), attemptyng all adventures of peryll, for thattayning of their wished lust, usyng auriculer confession (the kay of whoredome and treason) for furtheraunce of theyr purpose, abusyng the honorable name of lawefull mariage, to cloke the shame of stolne contractes, finally, by all meanes of unhonest lyfe, hastyng to most unhappye deathe.[2]

This is the right anti-papal note which would flatter the preju-

[1] *An Elizabethan Puritan* (1937), p. 55.

[2] *Romeus and Iuliet* (1563), in P. A. Daniel, ed., *Originals and Analogues*, I (New Shakespere Society, 1875), preface.

dices of the mercantile paterfamilias. But the poem, *mirabile dictu*, was the version of *Romeus and Juliet* that inspired Shakespeare's tragedy of star-crossed lovers. If the paterfamilias had read beyond the preface, he would have found that in the poem Romeus is declared 'free from fowle desire', Juliet refuses 'wanton love' and an 'unlawfull sute', and Friar Lawrence is 'not as the most . . . a gross unlearned foole', but a doctor of divinity, a man of beauty and wisdom, beloved and honoured by all, who in the end

> . . . was discharged quyte, and no marke of defame
> Did seeme to blot or touch at all the honor of his name.

Far from condemning the lovers, Broke confesses

> I graunt that I envie the blisse they lived in:
> Oh that I might have found the like, I wish it for no sin . . .
> Of shyvering care and dred I have felt many a fit,
> But Fortune such delight as theyrs dyd never graunt me yet.

At the end the lovers are given a stately tomb,

> Lest that length of time might from our myndes remove
> The memory of so perfect, sound and so approved love.

It is sad that such a book should have had to be dressed in such hypocrisy for the bookstalls. The reverse happens nowadays, of course, when an unexceptionable book is often given a lurid cover.

If the consequences of the Puritan onslaught on fiction had been limited merely to obliging writers to construct ingenious moral façades, it would not have mattered very much. But there were more insidious effects. A whole general condition was created which made it difficult for writers to exploit in print the very forms of art which flourished best in courtly society. On top of all the other difficulties, this was the last straw. Just as writers like Lodge and Marston ultimately abandoned the theatre and turned to more respectable ways of earning a living, Lodge as a physician and Marston as a priest, so other writers, browbeaten by opposition, reached the stage of publicly retracting their work and resigning from their ambition to write imaginative fiction. George Gascoigne, after the *Posies*, wrote only didactic verse of a reformative character or didactic prose like his *Droome of Doomes Day* and *A Delicate Diet for daintie-mouthde Droonkardes*. Lodge followed his resignation from the theatre, in 1589, with a resignation from poetry in 1596, when he decided to cleanse himself from the 'leprosie' of his 'lewd lines' and to employ his pen thereafter only for the 'comfort of the faithfull'. And though he lived on until 1625, the author of *Rosalynde* and *Phillis* restricted himself to medical treatises, translations from Seneca and Josephus, and a summary of du Bartas. There are many other instances. George Turberville sums it up in his farewell to poetry at the end of his *Tragic Tales:*

> Wherefore, goe (wanton) trusse up all your trash
> Fancy farewel, to graver gods I goe,
> Then love and Venus, cleane my handes I wash
> Of vayne desires that youth enrageth so.
> Vertue doth farre surmount such filthy vice:
> Amend my mates, or els you know the price.

It is a strange epilogue for those who contributed, if only in a minor vein, to the golden poetry of the Renaissance.

Most writers who appeared in printed books turned their backs upon courtly forms and concentrated upon didactic works of piety. New kinds of book adapted to the market were invented. Moral miscellanies appeared, full of 'godlie and compendious discourses' on Biblical subjects, from William Hunnis, Abraham Fleming, and ladies like Anne Wheathill and Elizabeth Grymeston. Geoffrey Whitney pioneered the 'emblem' book, in which symbolic pictures were accompanied by versified moralization. There was a brisk trade in the chapbooks and broadsides written by repentant sinners or by those about to be executed. In parody of the secular Petrarchan fashion, centuries of divine sonnets were published by Henry Lok, Barnabe Barnes and others. There were plenty of Biblical abridgments, the 'digests' of the day, and compendia of good advice, like Edmund Elviden's *Closet of Counsels*. And educational romances appeared like John Partridge's *Plasidas*, which were the forebears of the later encyclopaedias of moral and political science. But none of this is much remembered nowadays, for it lacks the deep imaginative concern with human nature which distinguishes literature from other forms of human knowledge.

It is little wonder that the Renaissance writer who ventured into print, with the stigma of social impropriety on one cheek, and the stigma of moral folly on the other, should present, on the whole, such a blushing picture. These were no times to establish a literary profession through print. Only a cultural revolution, involving a complete revision of the relationship between writers and their audience, could effect any significant change. The printed-book audience was potentially the best of the day, ranging as it did from the courtiers at one end of the scale through the satellite gentry, the university and Inns-of-Court men, and the churchmen, to the solid mercantile public at the other. But in practice the printed word was circumscribed with so many non-literary considerations, of religious, political and economic kinds, that literature in our sense, remained, in all essential respects, confined to the Court and its environs.

# V

# Taking Root

*I have found no evidence that the taste of the Court was particularly good. I am inclined to think that the practice of writing to sell in the open market did more good than harm. The most frankly commercial type of literature, the drama of Marlowe, Shakespeare and the rest, includes much of the greatest work.*

C. S. LEWIS, 1958[1]

THE open market, then, in the period before the Civil War had its limitations. There was a great variety of books on the stalls, but most of them were pious and didactic: handbooks of information, conversation manuals, courtesy books, books of aphorisms, similes and flowers of rhetoric and history, condensed histories, self-teachers, mercantile manuals, travel handbooks, guides to Godliness, diligence and thrift, books about the domestic arts, about hunting and other sports—the list is quite exhaustive. In addition, there were certain categories intended for entertainment rather than instruction: jest-books, romances, wonder stories, *novelle* imported from Italy, and so on. But the *dulce* is quite outweighed by the *utile*, and the imaginative writer who was concerned with the qualities which turn mere books into literature had very little footing in the market of the time.

Except in the theatre. By a combination of special circumstances which require explanation, the theatre provided the first fruitful soil in which a profession of letters took root. The truth

[1] *English Literature in the Sixteenth Century excluding Drama*, p. 63.

is that the theatre managed to avoid that dichotomy between the literary interests of the Court and the literary interests of the man in the street, which, as we have seen, proved an insuperable obstacle to the establishment of a literary profession in the printed-book market. In the theatre there was a happy union of interests which gave writers, on the one hand, assured status and security, and on the other hand, broadly-based public support. Paradoxical though it might seem, it was the Court which sponsored and fostered a thoroughly popular and commercial theatre.

The popular drama of the Middle Ages had disintegrated by Shakespeare's time. All over Europe, the Mystery Cycles had passed away, coming to an end in Freiberg in 1528, in Paris in 1548, in Milan in 1565, in York in 1569 and in Coventry in 1591. It is said that the last performance in England took place in Kendal in 1604. Ancillary forms of drama, like the saint's plays, the paternoster and creed plays, and the older forms of morality, were also in decline. Like his colleagues, Shakespeare knew something of the old medieval religious drama: the Porter in *Macbeth* has stepped straight from the *Harrowing of Hell*, Hamlet refers to players who 'out-herod-Herod', and in some of the earlier plays there are descendants of the devils, personifications and fools of medieval drama. In all kinds of ways the Elizabethan theatre remained indebted to its predecessor and shared common attitudes about, for instance, open-air staging, conventions of gesture and delivery, contemporary costuming, music, songs, dancing, effects, trapwork, machinery and so much else. But the old drama itself was dead. And the typical actor ceases to be the gildsman, amusing himself as an amateur on the Feast of Corpus Christi, and becomes the travelling professional entertainer, a man usually of some education and social status, perhaps the servant of a noble house or the product of the royal choir schools. Instead of local communities producing their own drama, professional players through the sixteenth century set up the rudiments of an entertainment industry, bringing metropolitan drama to the towns and villages. And all this was part of the revived interest taken in drama during the Renaissance. Drama was an obligatory activity for the schoolboy and the courtier; it was an essential part of school curricula, and was encouraged, like other arts, at the universities, at the Inns of

Court and in noble houses. The Court had its Revels, and in all the centres satellite upon the Court there was inevitably an equivalent.

The typical dramatist ceases to be some obscure member of the Church and the gilds, and becomes a courtly gentleman. The pre-Shakespearean dramatists we know about—Thomas Norton, Thomas Sackville, Thomas Watson, John Heywood, Nicholas Grimald, William Gager, Nicholas Udall, Thomas Kyd, Christopher Marlowe, John Lyly and others like them—were of this class. The plays they wrote reflect their classical education: *Gorboduc* imported from Seneca the classical Chorus and Messenger and the device of liberally sprinkling the text with the learned aphorisms known as *sententiae*; *Ralph Roister Doister* imported from Plautus stock characters like the parasite and the elderly gull or *senarius*, and the device of patterned dialogue, with successive lines or half lines of exactly the same length, known as *stichomuthia*. These elements mingle with importations from Italy, like the dumbshows, and things native, like trapdoor apparitions, horrific properties and mock requiems, to make the Tudor interlude a curious patchwork quilt. But even in a play like *Gammer Gurtons Nedle*, written by a Cambridge don about the Cambridge countryside, as a relaxation from things academic, the native elements are never strong enough to make us feel that the Wakefield Shepherds and the York Noah are just around the corner. Drama was being written, promoted and played by people nearer the top of the social tree.

This trend was reinforced by Puritan objections to the theatre in London. The city authorities were increasingly hostile to all drama played in public places, like the innyards. They believed that drama, like all other fiction, was intrinsically worthless, only acceptable at all when set in a didactic mode, as for the City's own shows and pageants. It was inevitable that Puritans should be horrified by the growth of an entertainment industry, especially in vicious and unhygienic places like innyards, where strong drink was available and where the prostitutes were accustomed to make their assignations. Doubtless something like the complete prohibition of 1642 would have occurred much earlier if the players had not had the support of the Court. Puritan writers like John Field could not understand why a nobleman with Puritan sympathies, like Leicester, should keep his own troupe of players. And doubtless Leicester, whose company was formed in 1559, was unable to explain the contradictions inherent in a courtier who was both Puritan and Humanist. At any rate, treading carefully, the City Council proceeded first against those who were not protected by the Court, who had popular rather than courtly roots. In 1571 'all fencers, bearewardes, comen players of enterludes and minstralles wandering abroade' were declared to be vagabonds and therefore liable to immediate arrest and imprisonment. Players who wore the livery of a nobleman were exempt from this act; the result was that the city was cleared of all players except the more courtly groups. Leicester's men at this time sued their patron to be retitled, quite formally, as 'household Servants and daylie wayters' without any increase in stipends or other benefits. In other words, the professionals of drama became dependent upon a connexion with the Court which was far from tenuous.

In 1574 further city statutes limited the number of plays permitted in innyards: the innkeeper had to bind himself to keep order, a percentage of the takings had to be given to the poor, and no plays at all were allowed on Sundays and Holy-Days, traditionally the most profitable. The response of the liveried companies to this regulation was the building, from 1576 onwards, of their own theatres in localities where the Council had no direct authority. But this further step towards professionalization was attended by the forging of even stronger links with the Court. The patron was continually called upon to protect the new playhouses from their enemies. The city was still able to prohibit theatrical performances, like other kinds of public meeting, in the interests of public health, and there were sufficient plagues and threats of plagues to hurt the players hard. Sometimes intervention was necessary at the highest level, from the Privy Council or the Queen herself. In November 1581 the Privy Council interceded with the Lord Mayor so that players might resume their performances, to relieve their want and to enable them to rehearse for Christmas entertainments at Court. In 1583 the Queen took over the patronage for a time of Leicester's players. Indeed, in time it became the fashion for all the companies to describe themselves as 'Her Majesty's Servants' for their London seasons. Ultimately, after the accession of King

James, all the companies placed themselves under the protection of a member of the royal family. The Puritans remained hostile until the outbreak of the Civil War gave them the opportunity to close down all theatres, a veto that remained in force until the Restoration. All through the period, then, from 1571 to 1642, it was not popular support alone which kept the theatres open and the dramatists busy, but essentially the patronage of the Court.

It was a lucrative profession. Quite apart from earnings in the playhouses and on tour, the players were occasionally called upon to give special performances before the Queen and the nobility; when they did they boosted their takings from a single performance from about £6, the average day's 'house' at the Globe in 1600, to £35. And sometimes plays or masques were specially commissioned by the Court, earning the playwright alone anything between £5 and £30. Sometimes other courtly services were required: in 1604 Shakespeare's company were commanded to close down their theatre and to present themselves at Court as supernumerary grooms, specially to impress a visiting Spanish envoy, earning a gratuity of £20 a man. As elsewhere at Court, it paid the man of the theatre to be versatile. Writing plays (worth in the normal run about £6 apiece) would not have provided a comfortable living in itself; it was better to be an actor, too, for even hired actors earned 6*s.* a week, and by 1635 leading players commanded as much as £180 a year. Then there were other possibilities in housekeeping and shareholding. Some players certainly retired rich. Edward Alleyn became a prominent London gentleman and patron of the arts, wealthy enough to spend £10,000 on Dulwich College. Shakespeare retired to Stratford as an esquire with his own coat of arms, to become a leading citizen of the town. These are outstanding instances, but there is no doubt that a career in the theatre was economically an attractive and viable proposition.

Hence the gentility of the dramatic writers of the age, who were every bit as much courtly gentlemen as public entertainers. Christopher Marlowe, the writer of horrific plays which were extremely popular in the innyard and other theatres, was also a classical scholar, translator of Lucan and Ovid, and an agent in courtly service with Sir Thomas Walsingham. Thomas Kyd, author of the *Spanish Tragedy*, possibly the most popular of all Elizabethan plays, was an agent with Essex and the translator of

Garnier, the French Senecan then popular at Court. John Lyly, the writer of the most popular plays performed by the children's companies, was at different times secretary to the Earl of Oxford, M.P. for Aylesbury, and clerk controller of tents and toils at the Revels Office. Ben Jonson, the first literary professional to call his writings 'works', at different times served Sir Robert Townshend, Lord Aubigny, Sir Robert Cotton, and Sir Walter Raleigh, was a Privy Council agent at the time of the Gunpowder Plot, and received pensions from King James and King Charles. George Chapman was Sewer in Ordinary to Prince Henry and the writer of royal masques. Cyril Tourneur was a diplomat and agent in service with Sir Edward Cecil. And so on. Shakespeare himself, before he attached himself to Lord Hunsdon's players, appears to have had a period of courtly service in the retinue of the Earl of Southampton. All the playwrights inevitably had some kind of connexion with the Court. Players and playwrights were the Lord Chamberlain's servants, the Lord Admiral's servants, the Queen's servants, the King's servants and so on, and whatever the power of 'the box', their financial rewards in the playhouses, whatever the power of commercial impresarios like Philip Henslowe, their courtly status was of primary importance.

Even in the playhouses themselves, the players seem to have been more concerned with the approbation of the courtly patron than with the mass of the audience. Hamlet certainly advised his players to have care for the opinions of the 'Judicious', 'the censure of the which One, must in your allowance o'reway a whole Theater of others'. Neither the dramatists nor the business managers showed much respect for the 'understanders', the poorest clients, who paid a penny to stand in the yard, exposed to all weathers. These were the youths that thunder and fight for bitten apples (Shakespeare, *Henry VIII*, V. iv), the grounded judgments fit for sweeping the stage and gathering up the broken apples for the bears within (Jonson, *Bartholomew Fair*, Induction). Much more important, in financial and other ways, were the spectators in the galleries, who paid twopence for a seat and an extra penny for a quiet position and a cushion. And even more important than the 'public rooms' were the private, the 'twelvepenny' or 'Lords' rooms, of which there may have been four in most theatres, each seating a fair number (Cranford

Adams suggests thirty-six) of special patrons, who were allowed to mingle freely with the players, before and during the performance.

Nor is there much indication that the richer customers became less important as the playhouses established themselves. On the contrary, in the seventeenth century there was a marked trend towards coterie drama catering specially for an *élite* few. When Shakespeare's company opened the Blackfriars in 1609, and Henslowe's followed suit with the Whitefriars, later known as Salisbury Court, in 1610, these 'private houses', with their successors like the Cockpit and the Phoenix, rapidly became much more profitable than the 'public' houses like the Globe and the Fortune. And yet they were much smaller, seating only a couple of hundred spectators, compared with the thousands who could squeeze into the Globe. In 1625 the average takings from a performance at the Blackfriars were £15. 15*s*., compared with £6. 13*s*. 8*d*. at the Globe. Seats were more expensive and more comfortable, and the theatres were covered not open, artificially lit and specially equipped with facilities for satisfying the growing taste in splendid spectacle which was being nourished by the courtly masque. The Civil War accelerated the trend. The result of the Puritan period of prohibition, from 1642 to 1660, was that the public playhouses completely disappeared, while the private houses one way and another survived. By all kinds of devious formulae—private parties, musical evenings, drama schools and so on—Sir William Davenant and others kept the taste for drama alive before private audiences, and the royalists exiled in France developed their interests in the French theatre. Meanwhile, the public playhouses fell into disuse and were pulled down—only the Red Bull was still standing at the Restoration—and worse, a whole generation grew up which had no experience of, and therefore no taste in, theatrical entertainment. There seems to be an inevitable progression from the private theatres of James I to the coterie theatres of Charles II.

And yet the Elizabethan theatre was firmly based upon the popular support of the butchers, bakers and candlestick-makers. Without this broadly-based patronage, dramatists could hardly have advanced beyond the Court masque and the academic, neoclassical play which one found at the universities. Shakespeare and his fellows were faced with a heterogeneous audience to satisfy, and they could well afford to ignore extreme tastes of any kind. *Hamlet* and *King Lear* were not written for the people whose favourite verse was provided by psalmists like Sternhold and Hopkins, nor for Puritans who regarded the theatre as anathema. On the other hand, plays were not written to satisfy the academic requirements of a courtier like Sidney, who, before he had had a chance to see Elizabethan drama at its best, committed himself in the *Defence of Poesie* to neo-classical standards which were alien to England. If there had not been middle-class Londoners capable of digesting Shakespeare's high poetry, there would have been no public playhouse at all. And if the Court had agreed with Sidney, neither Elizabeth nor James, nor Hunsdon the Lord Chamberlain, nor Effingham the Lord Admiral, would have bothered to keep the companies alive and safe through so many years of Puritan opposition. It would seem that Shakespeare's audience followed a *via media Anglicana*, in drama as in religion, a middle course between the overintellectualized standards of the academic Humanists and the 'bread and circuses' of the bull- and bear-baiting rings. Prince Hamlet would have nothing to do with drama which was 'overdone' or with the contrary kind which came 'tardy off'. The dramatist's aim was a play which could be performed with success in any of the places where his company might be called upon to play. Some public plays were originally written for a special Court performance: Leslie Hotson suggests that *Twelfth Night* is one of these. Others were originally written either for the public or the private playhouse and then called to Court: *Macbeth* and *The Tempest* are examples of these. Most plays could be produced anywhere—at Court, in the playhouses, in noble houses, on tour—with very little change either in content or in staging. And this very fact, I would suggest, augured well for the establishment of a literary profession.

The point is worth a critical digression. So many Elizabethan and Jacobean plays look like pot-boilers, designed, as Jonson would say, 'to please not the cookes taste but the guests'. To take Marlowe's plays as an example, there is plenty of material to send the groundlings shuddering home: prisoners beating out their property brains against the bars of their cages, nunneries and armies demolished *en masse*, devils and fireworks *ad lib.*, and knockabout farce as full of custard as any pie. And the texts we have represent only a genteel version of the stage original; certainly, the printer of the 1592 *Tamburlaine*, for instance, expurgated many elements that were 'of some vaine-conceited fondlings greatly gaped at, what times they were shewed upon the stage in their graced deformities'. Yet there is no reason to believe that more educated tastes were at all averse to blood and thunder; in fact, they revelled in it, to judge from horror plays like *Progne*, produced at Oxford in 1566, and *Roxana*, produced at Cambridge in 1592, and all the other pseudo-Senecan gruesome thrillers staged at the universities and the Inns of Court in the name of tragedy. But there is other stuff in these plays, such stuff as dreams are made on, dreams of fabulous wealth, infinite knowledge, unlimited power. Marlowe's heroes reach for the Moon and by divine dispensation have the Moon brought within their grasp. The plays are about what happens to them then. What the respectable London tradesman made of these egocentric, erotic Giant-the-Jack-Killers (the word is C. S. Lewis's) is not recorded. They outraged every bourgeois sympathy, if the spectator had had time or breath to consider seriously the implications of the story in which he was caught up. But the airy dreams and the earthy farce and horror were so closely married together that the question did not arise. And the fame of Aeneas, the power of Tamburlaine, the wealth of Barabas, the knowledge of Faustus, and so on, were examples of Elizabethan ambition; no other writer quite conveys the exhilaration of boundless horizons, the heady ambitions of the day. Sometimes Marlowe merely takes to extremes a contemporary dream, and leaves the implications in the air to disturb the sangfroid of those who were committed to realizing the dream. Tamburlaine achieves universal and absolute power, but Marlowe leaves open the question whether he were a tragic hero or a villain. Can spiritual ambitions be realized in a material context even on the vastest scale? In other plays, however, Marlowe takes his extreme hypothesis a stage further towards a solution: Faustus becomes a tragic hero precisely because Marlowe emphasizes the waste of spiritual effort confined to tawdry material satisfactions. In both kinds of play, Marlowe writes for different levels of attention, engaging the interest of his whole audience, in different degrees of air and earth.

Shakespeare's first plays do not differ much in kind from the academic plays of a young university wit. *The Comedy of Errors* is an exercise after Plautus, *Love's Labour's Lost* a courtly masque, the early histories royal chronicles discussing the divine right of kings, and *Titus Andronicus* Shakespeare's contribution to Senecan horror. The funny men of the early plays, Holofernes and Armado, Launce and Speed, are funny because they are pedantic, or pretentious, or stupid, the very flaws that university men found amusing. Like Jonson's early comedies, these plays sparkle with the wit of a university-trained man writing for university-trained men, and the fact that neither Shakespeare nor Jonson went to a university is beside the point. But although Shakespeare continued to set his plays in courts and noble houses, and to interest himself in courtly themes, his work in the public playhouses seems to have broadened his appeal. Without changing his general approach—Malvolio is the descendant of Armado, Dogberry of Dull, Hamlet of Romeo, Rosalind of Julia—he widened his drama to embrace in human content the whole globe. But he avoided the fatal divisions of attending to mutually incompatible levels of attention simultaneously. Falstaff is not in the play to amuse the groundlings and galleries while the serious drama goes on over their heads. Falstaff, the arch rationalist, has as much to contribute to the study of a true prince as Hotspur or any of the noble characters. Similarly, the clown in *Antony and Cleopatra* is not there, as it were, to work the comic shift; he is the symbol of everyday human life, coming to terms with experience in his homely way, while Queens die. Behind this growth in Shakespeare is a new, and English, definition of tragedy and comedy, based upon an increasing knowledge of what men deeply care about, what men need to reconcile themselves with, and rise above, the limitations of life, whether they are princes like Hamlet, the complete Renaissance nobleman, or cripples like Caliban, the slave by nature and instinct. All this is too vast a topic to embark on here. My point is that Shakespeare was both a courtly gentleman and a public entertainer, and that the combination of both roles, made possible by the distinctively happy status of the theatre in London at the time, is at least one element in his greatness.

And similarly with other writers. Ben Jonson's attitude towards the theatre might hardly seem to have commended him to public playhouse audiences. No other writer of the time so defended academic standards, condemning his colleagues' rejection of the Unities, their love for creaking thrones and nimble squibs, their 'concupiscence of dances and antics', and much else. No other writer was so content with stories which are so rudimentary, concerned with themes—very often the debunking of solemn city humbugs by university men—which are hardly likely to commend themselves to a middle-class audience. And yet no other filled his plays with so many delighted references to the architecture of the 'thronged round', or with so much colour and rowdy nonsense from contemporary London. At his best, Jonson has in balance the full range of taste of his mixed audience.

Webster and Tourneur, and other horror writers, designed plays which, again, had different levels of appeal. They deal with a distorted society, taking to extremes the hypothesis that ambitious dogs are reasonable to eat dogs, and that the hindmost gets what he deserves when he is caught by the Devil. Suppose a world, they said, in which love was always, or nearly always, lust, in which Man was no more than a clever animal, in which loyalty and friendship were meaningless terms compared with self-interest and survival: what then would happen to 'human values'? At one level this was what the man-in-the-street Londoner imagined contemporary Italy to be; at another, this was the kind of world, in his moments of despair, which the courtier imagined England to be. And the hero of the play is invariably a secret agent, that familiar figure of the time, the man whose job it was to manipulate events to suit his patron. It is all of a piece: the action that hurtles along at breakneck speed, the poetry that gets beyond the melodrama to the human tragedy inherent in the nightmare, and the stopping of the show on occasions to exploit a fashion parade of costumes or to deliver a homily about natural history. In a sentence, the plays of the time were homogeneous, because they were written for homogeneous audiences by writers who could confidently anticipate the public response craved for by all literary professionals, mass popularity strengthened by the support of the intelligentsia. It is rare in literary history for writers to enjoy such a happy combination of circumstances.

One final word must be said about the influence of the Court upon staging practices. There are so many popular elements contributing to the evolution of the Globes and Lyceums, from the Mystery stages, the bear rings, the innyards, the *théâtre de foire*, and so on, that we tend to forget the contribution of the Court. This was precisely why in the nineteenth century literary historians were apt to assume that the Elizabethan stages were bare, bleak places, scaffolds devoid of furniture, scenery and colour, anonymous except for the poetry that set the scene for the spectator's imagination. Knowing this picture to be quite false, a few modern critics have veered to the opposite extreme of representing these stages as highly decorated and luxuriously appointed, the wonder of Europe. The truth, probably in between these extremes, is that the playhouse became more and more splendid as the years went by, more lavish in spectacle, richer in properties and settings, better equipped with effects. There is a big difference between the 'ragged foils' by which Agincourt is represented in *Henry V* and the colourful, carpeted processions of *Henry VIII*, between the apparatus and equipment available at the Globe in 1599 and the Blackfriars in 1609, between the makebelieve nights of *Romeo and Juliet* and *A Midsummer Night's Dream* and the quasi-realistic nights of Jacobean drama, from *Macbeth* onwards, in which the flickering torches and sudden lights in close-shut, murderous rooms seem to be indispensable parts of the play in their own right. The incentive towards greater spectacle came from the example set by the masques and shows of the Court Revels and Progresses. Left to his own resources, the street player might well have been content with the simplest apparatus, his scaffold and booth, his trapdoor to Hell, his cresset for lighting. But the player involved with courtly drama had to march with the times. Perhaps the 'picture stage', the eventual goal of the trend towards the spectacular, destroyed the best values of the theatre; but for the moment, the theatre, at this happy juncture of history, provided a fertile meeting-point for so many ideas and influences, and at this point a literary profession was first established.

All the things necessary to a literary profession were here: a theatre in which, in Yeats's phrase, the spoken word was sovereign, a theatre indeed of high poetry; a dramatic art which held high national prestige; the coming together of many vivid minds dedicated to a common calling; writers like Shakespeare, Fletcher, Ford, Middleton, Massinger and others who were primarily men of the theatre and who hardly concerned themselves with other things, and others, like Marlowe, Jonson, Dekker, Marston, Thomas Heywood and so on, who if not full-time professionals of the theatre at least devoted a major part of their lives to the serious pursuit of the art; above all, a system of rewards and a balanced audience which ensured that writers were reasonably free to devote their lives to intrinsically literary interests. All this, plus a ready acceptance of the shared basic premise that the job of literature was the imaginative exploration of human values. In the theatre two elements fused which the Renaissance had tended to divide: the theatre brought together a wide public (which elsewhere had been fed, by and large, with unimaginative material) with truly literary material (which elsewhere had been reserved, by and large, for a narrow public).

We have already seen why nothing equivalent to this fusion could have occurred in the printed book market. This is not to say that writers in print, especially the neo-classical humanists, did not attempt to fashion a happier social status for themselves. But these writers, working against the tide of things, were apt to conclude, as Milton did at an early stage in his career about the kind of literary status he hoped to achieve, that

> *Fame* is no plant that grows on mortal soil,
> Nor is the glistering foil
> Set off to th' world, nor in broad rumour lies
> (*Lycidas*, 78–80)

They consoled themselves, as Daniel did, with the thought that perhaps 'after times' would understand and give them their proper value. Of all these writers, perhaps the career of Edmund Spenser describes most fully what they wanted and why they failed. Like most young men, Spenser achieved his first reputation by the circulation of poems in manuscript. He had followed the *carrière ouverte aux talents* to Court, *via* a scholarship at Merchant Taylors' School and a sizarship at Pembroke College, Cambridge. His brief sojourn with the genteel Spencers of Northampton had proved somewhat unprofitable, and in 1578 he had attracted the attention of Leicester and served him as an agent and secretary. To this early period of his life belong the poems which E.K. mentions in the Epistle to the *Shepheardes*

*Calender*, but which have not survived manuscript circulation: 'his Dreames, his Legendes, his Court of Cupide, and sondry others'. It was a good beginning, but Spenser was very ambitious, and the *Shepheardes Calender* was deliberately published in 1579 as a manifesto of his ability.

His literary success was immediate. I doubt if even Pope or Byron or Auden so conspicuously rocketed to early fame. He became the 'new poet', 'the miracle of wit', the 'rightest English poet that ever I read', 'our principall poet', the man everybody was talking about. Five editions were produced by 1597, as fair a success as a writer could wish in the market of the time. And he seems to have been read as much by middle-class Londoners (the book was after all an almanac of didactic value containing many fables and homilies of wide appeal) as by the courtiers and their satellites. But whether Spenser was satisfied with the new social status accorded him is much less certain. In 1580 he was appointed private secretary to Lord Grey in Ireland, and there he occupied a number of posts in the Civil Service: Clerk of Degrees and Recognizances in the Irish Court of Chancery, Commissioner of Musters in County Kildare, Clerk of the Council in Munster, and ultimately Sheriff of Cork. He was able to lease the abbey and manor of Enniscorthy in County Wexford and to acquire other houses elsewhere. But it is usually assumed from his remarks to Leicester in the dedication of *Virgils Gnat* (published in 1591, but written some time before 1588, probably in the early 1580's) that he was disappointed with his fortunes:

> Wrong'd, yet not daring to expresse my paine,
> To you (great Lord) the causer of my care,
> In clowdie teares my case I thus complaine
> Unto your selfe, that onely privie are. . . .

Some writers have inferred that, like the gnat in Virgil's poem, which was crushed and then exiled in spirit to a waste wilderness for having dared to warn a shepherd of an approaching danger, Spenser was virtually banished to Ireland for his rashness in circulating in manuscript *Mother Hubberds Tale*, to warn against the marriage of Elizabeth to the Duke of Alençon. However this may be, it is clear that the initial move to Ireland was a valuable promotion for which the poet had every reason to be grateful and that what irked him was Leicester's failure, for some reason, to follow up with further promotion which would have brought Spenser home to London. Leicester may have been wise to keep his protégé, with his extreme Puritan enthusiasms, at a safe distance from Court, but the poet was increasingly frustrated by a second-best career in Ireland.

After Leicester's death and with the incentive of a new patron in Raleigh, Spenser made a fresh bid for preferment by publishing the *Faerie Queene*. But neither the first three books in 1589, nor the second three published in 1596 under the aegis of yet another new patron, Essex, yielded the promotion Spenser wanted. After some delay, he won a pension of £50 a year, which gave him a comfortable living, but there was to be no transfer from Ireland and no relief from the heavy responsibilities, in times of war and political discontent, which beset him as an agent of the Crown. He made the best of things, settling down with a new wife and building up his own literary circle, in which the most prominent figure, besides himself, appears to have been Lodowick Bryskett, but his bitter disappointments seem to have soured him and to have driven him to break with the normal literary ambitions of the courtly satellite. In fact, he becomes more and more outspoken in his criticism of courtly literature. In poems like *Colin Clouts Come Home Againe* he condemns as a fool the poet who goes to Court, and he specifically rejects the love poetry written by the 'vaine votaries of laesie love'. He was no longer content to let his poems take a courtly course through manuscript circulation, but set out to print everything he could, old and new. True, he continued to show some respect for the stigma of print. He allowed Ponsonby to take the blame for the publication in 1591 of the *Complaints*, some poems having been 'disperst abroad in sundrie hands, and not easie to bee come by, by himselfe'. Ponsonby also made himself responsible for the publication of the *Amoretti* during the poet's absence overseas. Spenser himself put forward a moral pretext for the publication of the *Fowre Hymnes*: the necessity 'at least to amend, and by way of retractation to reforme', the Hymns to Love and Beauty, many copies of which were 'scattered abroad', poisoning young men and women with their 'affection'. But an index of Spenser's real attitude is provided by his second thoughts about *Mother Hubberds Tale*. Before 1589 it never crossed his mind that the poem should be printed; his sole audience was the Leicester group. But after 1589 he decided that the political satire would interest a larger audience, and he was prepared to rewrite it specially for what appears to have been a middle-class public. More and more he seeks to write for those who would be interested in 'meditations of the worlds vanitie, verie grave and profitable'.

Moreover, though he was a practised writer of courtly songs and sonnets, his real ambitions clearly aimed at higher ideals. The *Shepheardes Calender* was a pastoral eclogue in a classical form, and it was published with all the bravado of an annotated text, as if it were a classical text indeed. One recalls in modern times an analogous situation when T. S. Eliot published his *Waste Land* complete with notes. There is a claim about literature here which is to be found in the critical theory endorsed by courtiers like Sidney, but not present in their own creative work. Other pastorals and satires followed. The *Faerie Queene* itself is a romance, after Aristo and Tasso, of epic dimensions. And all these poems are intended to last for ever; they are not intended to be confined to the transient pleasures of courtly communication. Spenser expresses the hope that the Faerie Queene will 'live with the eternitie' of Elizabeth's fame, and in the dedicatory sonnets associates his own name with that of Virgil, suggesting that his poetry too 'immortalizes' and 'eternizes' his patrons. He tells the Countess of Pembroke that the *Ruine of Time* is 'speciallie intended' to eternize the renown of the Sidneys. He sees himself, in short, as a national poet commemorating national heroes and preserving the records of his civilization for future generations. This is the Humanist conception of literature. E.K. has a few words on the subject in the argument to the October eclogue in the *Shepheardes Calender*: the poet was

> . . . in all ages, and even amongst the most barbarous alwayes of singuler accounpt and honor, and being indede so worthy and commendable an arte: or rather no arte, but a divine gift and heavenly instinct not to bee gotten by laboure and learning, but adorned with both: and poured into the witte by a certain ἐνθυσιασμὸς and celestiall inspiration, as the Author hereof els where at large discourseth, in his booke called the English Poete.

In this book, which is unfortunately lost, Spenser presumably endorses Sidney's views, which in their turn endorsed Horace's, that '*orator fit, poeta nascitur*'. The theory would not itself have astonished any of the courtly writers of Elizabeth's time, although perhaps Wyatt and his colleagues of Henry's reign might have raised an eyebrow or two. What was surprising was that Spenser sought to establish this kind of poetic identity and status through print. Of course, as the son of a London tailor who shared so many of the political and religious sympathies of the mercantile middle classes, Spenser was not frightened of the printed-book public. And in his work he reveals the capacity to entertain different audiences at different levels of attention. As Sir John Harington, his contemporary, says about the advantages of allegorical writing, 'the weaker capacities will feede themselves with the pleasantnes of the historie and sweetnes of the verse, some that have stronger stomackes will as it were take a further taste of the Morall sence, a third sort, more high conceited than they, will digest the Allegorie'.[1] In the *Faerie Queene*, at a first level there is a romantic story, imaginative, sensuous, and exciting. At a second level, there is the moral or religious lesson, particularly acceptable to the middle-class citizens who bought the book as an encyclopaedia of morality —Spenser was nearly twice as popular as his nearest rival, Michael Drayton, and four times as popular as Shakespeare, as a source for sayings to annotate in commonplace books, according to the evidence in Robert Allot's anthology of quotations, *England's Parnassus* (1600). At a third level, there were historical and personal identifications, and many other subtleties, available only to an educated and informed mind.

But when all this is said, Spenser is a long way from achieving the fusion of a wide public and imaginative material which his more fortunate colleagues in the theatre enjoyed. The printed-book public lacked the fusing intimacy of the playhouses, lacked numbers, and lacked the strength to give the writer any kind of security or independence. Without these things there was not enough homogeneity in his audience, or indeed in his own aims, to give Spenser the chance of cementing together groups with disparate tastes. At one level, the *Faerie Queene*, for instance, is about a Fairyland where anything might happen on the next heath, in the next forest, in the next castle, where Good prevails

[1] *A Briefe Apologie of Poetrie*, preface to *Orlando Furioso* (1591), in G. Gregory Smith, ed., *Elizabethan Critical Essays* (Oxford, 1904), II. 203.

over Evil, as it does in a juvenile adventure story, but the real point lies in the impossible task set the hero, the seductiveness of his adversary, the excitement of the pursuit. At this level the whole poem is a kind of expanded conceit, an extravagant, outrageous, incredible metaphor of the individualist taking arms against a sea of troubles. What happens at this level of attention when the moral allegory, insisting upon the invulnerability of the hero's morals, resolves the crises of the plots, like a *deus ex machina*, to protect Good from any suggestion that Evil may be victorious? At another level, the poem is a lesson in which Good is destined to overcome Evil, and the whole point was the invulnerability of virtue and the inevitably corrupting consequences of vice. What happens at this level of attention when the poet, carried away by the excitement of the story (and Spenser confessed to Raleigh that many 'adventures are intermedled, but rather as Accidents, then intendments'), paints the vices in an attractive or seductive light, and the virtues as astonishingly imperfect? This kind of question inevitably arises where the writer seeks to address different audiences simultaneously, and it was to be a hundred years before the printed-book public was sufficiently homogeneous to release the writer from these problems.

But if Spenser did not succeed himself, he pioneered a trail in which other men were interested, and none more than the man who regarded him as his 'teacher', John Milton. Like Spenser, the young Milton circulated his poetry only in manuscript. In the first twenty-nine years of his life, he only printed the Latin lines, *Naturam non pati senium*, which were privately and anonymously published at Cambridge in 1628, and the epitaph, *On Shakespeare*, which was prefixed without a name or even initials to the Folio edition of 1632. Neither of these ventures, the one for a university press, the other a genteel commendation, incurred any courtly stigma. Young Milton had nothing to gain from print. He was under no economic compulsion to augment his income, which, though modest, was adequate enough to make possible the luxury of a grand tour, something Spenser could never have afforded. There was no need to advertise his talents. Unlike Spenser, he was not attracted to any form of social promotion then available: he rejected any idea of a career in the Church, the High Church of Laud, and although his political instincts are discernible at an early age, he showed no anxiety to serve under King Charles. When Henry Lawes, the Court musician, put in his way the opportunity of preferment under the patronage of the Countess of Derby and the Egerton family, he wrote two masques, but made no attempt to pursue the advantage, although the Countess had helped many poets, including Shakespeare, Donne, Marston, Jonson, John Davies of Hereford, and Spenser, and although she lived at Harefield, only ten miles from his home at Horton. We can only conclude that he had no ambitions at all at Court.

Yet there are all the indications that he could have lived a happy life as a courtly satellite. He was susceptible to feminine charm; dainty and fastidious, like Donne, he went visiting, took an interest in the theatre, cultivated music and swordsmanship, and like any courtier, evaporated his thoughts in verse. Like Sidney he paraphrased psalms. Like Donne he exercised his wit with puns, word play and conceits. He tried his hand at songs and sonnets, elegies and other Renaissance forms, and his verse was occasional, prompted by day-to-day events, a birthday, a death, a book read, a jubilee, a vacation exercise. Perhaps he was more learned that the average courtier, and wrote with greater fluency and frequency in Latin and Italian, but superficially at any rate he belonged to the courtly order of things. In his heart, however, Milton saw writing as a dedicated trade. In his teens he had begun to condemn the 'triming' and 'toys', the exercises of mental agility and wit which occupied so much courtly time. He regarded poetry as, potentially, an art of high seriousness, devoted not to the entertainment of a few friends and patrons but to the service of the nation itself. He denied himself a courtly career, as he rejected all other personal indulgences, so that he might prepare himself for the writing of national epic. As he himself said

> . . . he who would not be frustrate of his hope to write well hereafter in laudable things, ought him selfe to bee a true Poem, that is, a composition, and patterne of the best and honourablest things; not presuming to sing high praises of heroick men, or famous Cities, unlesse he have in himselfe the experience and the practice of all that which is praise-worthy.
>
> (*An Apology*, 1642)

This ideal involved him in an encyclopaedic programme of reading unattempted even by Spenser, intensive study that left him few idle hours. It was an unrewarding apprenticeship, as Milton himself complains in *Lycidas*:

> Alas! What boots it with uncessant care
> To tend the homely slighted shepherds trade,
> And strictly meditate the thankles Muse,
> Were it not better don as others use,
> To sport with *Amaryllis* in the shade,
> Or with the tangles of *Neaera's* hair?

There is nothing equivalent in his life to the *Shepheardes Calender*. When *Comus* was printed in 1637, Milton made no attempt to seek patronage through the poem; he sent away copies only to personal friends like Sir Henry Wotton. The publication was anonymous, and truly so: for many years very few people knew the identity of the author, and the printers treated it with scant respect, binding up some copies with the *Poems* of Thomas Randolph, 'that the Accessory might help out the Principal'. In fact, one must believe that the publication was Lawes's idea: the poem was so lovely 'and so much desired, that the often Copying of it hath tir'd my Pen to give my severall friends satisfaction'. In the following year *Lycidas* was printed, decorously as part of a memorial volume for Edward King, a collection of elegies by a group of Cambridge contemporaries, half of them in Latin. Milton's contribution was printed modestly above his initials at the end of the volume. Once again he sent copies to his friends, but not to potential patrons; and once again, despite his accents of militant Protestantism, which must have been congenial to the London Puritans, he made no attempt to address a middle-class audience. He was interested neither in the Court nor in the printed-book market.

This situation was radically transformed in the early 1640's. The first agent of change was his journey to Italy, where he experienced an entirely new relationship of writer and audience. At this time every Italian writer of note—statesmen, churchmen, lawyers, doctors, scientists, geographers, philosophers, antiquarians, poets—belonged to one or other of the learned academies of *literati*. In Rome alone there were fifteen such societies: this city of 110,000 inhabitants supported over 450 resident writers who found, whatever their specialism, a common platform and medium of communication in the academy. The Italians had never heard of this young Englishman, but they invited him to their meetings, and among Gaddi's *Svogliati* and Coltellini's *Apotisti*, Milton's recitations of his Latin prose and verse earned high praise. The impact upon the poet was quite transforming. Henceforward, on the one hand, Milton saw himself as an international figure with an international audience, the man who had talked with celebrities like Galileo, Grotius, Manso, Frescobaldi and so on. On the other hand, his Protestant nationalism was stirred: he started looking for glory and honour very much this side of the grave, as the writer of work which would elevate in international opinion the literature of his country, as Homer and Virgil and Tasso had elevated theirs:

> What the greatest and choicest wits of Athens, Rome, or modern Italy, and those Hebrews of old, did for *their* country, I, in my proportion might do for *mine*; not caring to be once named abroad, though perhaps I could attain to that, but content with these British Islands as my world.
>
> (*Reason of Church Government*, 1641)

Soon after his return to England, Milton became involved in political pamphleteering in defence of his friends. Thus, his views about the value of print began to change. The first three pamphlets which he published in 1641 were anonymous, and as late as 1644 his tract *Of Education* appeared without his name or initials. His name was first advertised only in reply to a personal attack. These early pamphlets were intended for a private rather than a public audience; he intervened as a friend to help the Smectymnuuans against Bishop Hall. But it was not long before he was proud to have his name 'openly avowed'; far from a shame, he accounted it a virtue to appear in public in his true colours, refusing to snipe at his enemies from the hole and corner of anonymity. But he refused to think of himself as a middle-class pamphleteer like Dekker. He had no desire to address the people, the 'herd confus'd', the 'miscellaneous rabble'; his audience was the new intellectual *élite* thrown up by the social revolution, the new Parliament and the Assembly of Westminster. Besides these intellectuals, he thought, too, of sympathetic minds abroad and of posterity. To make sure he reached the right people, he sent out complimentary copies *ex dono authoris*, and made use of his friends on their travels as postmen. Marvell once tracked down Bradshaw with a pamphlet Milton was most anxious the great man should read, and Henry Oldenburg, off to the Continent, invariably took with him a supply of Milton's latest. He sent copies also to Patrick Young, Keeper of the King's Library at St. James's, and to John Rous, Bodley's Librarian at Oxford, not only because they were sympathetic intellectuals, but because the library was a 'temple of perpetual memory'. In these ways Milton built himself an academy of his own:

> I feel myself not as if in a forum or law-court, surrounded only by one people, whether Roman or Athenian, but as if, with nearly all Europe listening, and as it were seated together before and criticising . . . an aggregate of all the meetings and conventions of the gravest men, cities, and nations.
>
> (*Defensio Secunda*, 1654)

At the height of his fame, when tracts like the *Pro Populo Anglicano Defensio* (1651) were translated into several languages and made available in dozens of editions all over Europe, this audience was not a dream but a reality; and this to Milton was the profit of print. He was not interested in commercial rewards; he refused the financial recompense offered him by the grateful Council of the Commonwealth, though he might have made more money than his friend Morland, to whom the Council paid £700, with the right of all profits, for a single book. He had no reason, of course, for financial anxiety. His capital, in money, investments and property, amounted to about £4,000, and he was paid a salary, at first £288 a year, as Secretary for the Foreign Tongues after 1649. But even in less prosperous times Milton insisted his pen was not for hire: he was dedicated to higher things altogether.

But all this brought home to Milton the value of print. When he came to publish his poetry he again thought of his audience as an 'academy'. There was not much time available during the Civil War for thinking of poetry, but in 1645 he did publish a collected edition of his poems. Before Jonson, no author would have dreamed of committing an act of such braggadocio, but times had changed. In Humphrey Moseley, Milton found a publisher genuinely interested in imaginative literature, and who had experience in handling the work of poets like Waller,

Davenant, Crashaw, Shirley, and Carew. True, the edition goes through the forms of paying respects to the stigma of print, including publishing personal notes by friends like Wotton, but the canon is presented with care, and the book is actually prefaced with a portrait. It was a bad portrait, and Milton amused himself by writing rude lines about it, but formerly portraits had only been included in posthumous editions of poets like Shakespeare and Donne. The innovation is a significant indication of a changed attitude to print. When *Paradise Lost* was printed in 1667 there was no vestige remaining of the Renaissance stigma, no apology for appearing in print, no prefatory matter of any kind. But Milton had not modified in any way his refusal to be considered as a commercial author. Although he was considerably impoverished by the Restoration, losing his pension and money invested in Commonwealth securities, he sold the book and copyright of his great poem for a mere £20. Once more the complimentary copies interested him far more than the cash returns. According to the agreement with the printer, Samuel Simmons, 1,300 copies from each of the first three impressions were to be 'retaild off to particular reading Customers', while as many as 200 were to be delivered to the author. Over 13 per cent of the total impression, in other words, was reserved for Milton's 'academy'. Milton was exploring a system of communication which ultimately developed into 'subscription patronage' during the Augustan age.

There is no evidence that the poet was other than satisfied by this 'fit audience, though few'. General sales of his books proceeded well enough to serve as a means to the main end of addressing the intellectual *élites* of Europe. Before long *Paradise Lost* was translated into French, Dutch, German, Italian, and Latin. In his old age the poet was not 'eyeless in Gaza', without friends or honour. On the contrary, as Aubrey reveals, he was much visited 'by the learned, more than he did desire', and foreigners came to see the 'house and chamber where he was born' and 'mightily importuned him to go into France or Italy'. Milton wanted to establish a place for the writer which gave him classic status while he was still alive; doubtless, it gave him joy to discover that he was the first English writer to be granted this kind of status. As his material prosperity declined—he lost property in the Great Fire and there were other adversities—he printed more and more of his work, but with the pride of an Augustan like Dryden or Johnson, secure in his contemporaries' respect, rather than apologetically like the Elizabethans. Pride in his own status made him unearth old manuscripts and print everything: an *Accedence Commenc't Grammar*, a *History of Britain*, the treatise *Artis Logicae*, and most significant of all, the *Epistolarum Familiarum Liber Unus*, comprising private letters and youthful essays which had been preserved, single-mindedly it seems, for forty-two years. Like Pope, he was sure that discriminating readers of his own and later ages would be interested in his letters and *juvenilia*, and of course he was right.

All the Renaissance values that he had once accepted and even admired became *anathemata*. Late in life he not only rejected the ballad-singers, the 'millinery-hucksters' of verse, and the scandalous anthologies (*Songs and Sonnets*, in the end, became collections of indecent poems which were banned and burned by the Commonwealth), but he openly condemned, or at best damned with faint praise, the best Renaissance poetry and drama. One of his attacks on King Charles in *Eikonoklastes* was based on the report that Charles was a 'more diligent reader of Poets than of Politicians'; it was shameful that the King should express affection for his wife 'in strains that come almost to sonnetting', and the King relied too much on the 'polluted trash of Romances and Arcadias':

> . . . the vain amatorious poem of Sir Philip Sidney's *Arcadia*: a book in that kind full of worth and wit, but among religious thoughts and duties not worthy to be named, nor to be read at any time without due caution.

Worse, the King had apparently adopted Shakespeare as the 'closet companion of these his solitudes', the very poet whom Milton had himself so honoured in 1630. Even 'feigning' Spenser does not escape a passing sneer. In controversy, of course, Milton went to extremes; but even his more studied opinions reveal that in rejecting the monarchy he also went a long way in condemning the forms and modes of courtly literature. Masques, for instance, he now deplored as contributing to the 'debauching of our prime gentry'. Rhyme he now declared 'no necessary Adjunct or true Ornament of Poem or good Verse . . . but the invention of a barbarous Age, to set off wretched matter and lame Meeter',[1] and Elizabethan tragedy, he concluded, was now of 'small esteem, or rather infamy . . . hap'ning through the Poets error of intermixing Comic stuff with Tragic sadness and gravity; or introducing trivial and vulgar persons . . . brought in without discretion, corruptly to gratifie the people'.[2] These neo-classic accents reveal how far Milton had travelled in his career as a writer from his courtly starting-point.

Once the writer had assumed the mantle of a national bard, and the function of a leader in determining the pattern of a nation's deepest imaginative life, it was impossible for him to remain within the courtly system. Milton was one of many writers who came to reject the limitations imposed upon literary professionals by the attitudes of the Court. During the seventeenth century the whole courtly system withered away. A new society was to devise means, through subscription patronage and otherwise, whereby writers could live prosperously, often on the rewards of only one book, set themselves up with squirearchal status, and from a position of security actively influence and responsibly lead the nation's thinking. Milton lived and wrote without the benefits of this patronage system, which re-created in so many ways the relationship of writers and their audience in Augustan Rome. But he contrived by other means to occupy very much the same position in society as was later adopted by Pope and Swift and Fielding. Thanks partly to the special conditions obtaining in the Elizabethan and Jacobean theatre, and partly to the pioneering work of writers like Spenser and Milton, a literary profession in this country had begun to take root, and the changed social conditions which followed the Restoration of 1660, and even more the 'Glorious Revolution' of 1688, enabled growth and consolidation in the century that came after.

[1] *Paradise Lost* (1674), preface on 'The Verse'.
[2] *Samson Agonistes* (1671), preface on 'Tragedy'.

# VI

## Prose, Print and the Profession

*An author ought to consider himself, not as a gentleman who gives a private or eleemosynary treat, but rather as one who keeps a public ordinary, at which all persons are welcome for their money.*

HENRY FIELDING[1]

BEFORE the Civil Wars literature was essentially the art of amateurs; it was predominantly either oral or committed to manuscripts; it was chiefly poetic or dramatic. After the Civil Wars, gradually but quite unmistakably, print triumphed, prose dominated, and a genuine literary profession became possible. Inevitably war brought a great increase in the output of printed matter, carrying news, journals and controversial essays and disquisitions upon the conflict. The public which had long bought books of piety and devotion now became the target for writers enlisted in the various political and ecclesiastical campaigns of the times. From the war journals derived new literary media like newspapers and periodicals. These in their turn fathered new kinds of literary form, like the essay and the biography, and ultimately the novel. These provided fresh outlets for writers to whom print became the normal, and in time entirely respectable, medium of communication with any audience, and prose the normal language of professional literary expression.

There was an expanding circle: the more books, the more

[1] The opening words of *Tom Jones* (1749).

booksellers, the more readers, the more books. Whereas in the Elizabethan period booksellers were scarcely to be found outside London and the university cities, by 1775 there were 150 in the provinces and 200 in the capital. Whereas in the Elizabethan period libraries were not to be found outside the noble houses, colleges and churches, by 1800 every town of any size had its own circulating library, a small town like Southampton, for instance, having one with 7,000 volumes. More and more people could read silently in their own homes; more and more people could afford books and felt the need for them. All this volume of activity became the means of supporting a large number of full-time writers, including some whose ambitions reached higher than journalism and who were able to demand from the reading public proper professional rewards and proper professional esteem. It was at last a golden age.

After the triumph of print the victory of prose was perhaps predictable. As we shall see, the theatre, which in Shakespeare's day had been the greatest hope of a literary profession, changed its course and direction: the written word gradually ceased to be sovereign, became subservient to other arts in a growing entertainment industry, and as a result ceased to interest literary men. At the same time poetry lost its unique pre-eminence. There were as many poets as ever: F. W. Bateson has calculated that between 1600 and 1700 the country had one poet in every 61,200 souls, between 1700 and 1800 one poet in every 58,900 souls, and between 1800 and 1900 one poet in every 63,800 souls, a ratio which remains, despite the rise of print, reasonably constant.[1] The poets led by Dryden and Pope were as important as they had ever been: their work was discussed and criticized in the coffee-houses as enthusiastically as Elizabethans ever argued about poetry in their courtly salons; and for the first time poetry was accepted in the neo-classical eighteenth century as the literary art best suited for national statements of dignity and decorum—epic, translation, satire, commemorative ode, and didactic commentary. All the same, writers now invented and developed other media of imaginative expression: the essay, the sermon, the speech, the letter, each transformed into important means of art in this age.

Christopher Caudwell suggests that poetry, the mnemonic

[1] *English Poetry* (1950), p. 259.

art, is essentially the 'language of collective speech and public emotion', while prose is essentially the language of business, conversation, private letters and teaching; that is to say, the private language of one man with another. From this point of view, the more 'private' literature became, the more important, as an art, prose became. Further, the 'Augustans' of the eighteenth century, the squires and merchants who came to dominate society, were men of business, conversation, letters and teaching. Just as the prevailing mood of the Enlightenment in the new age emphasized in language the qualities of plainness, succinctness, clarity and explicitness, and in life and living the scientific, mathematical, common-sense approach, so in literature it stressed the useful and the didactic. The Augustans demanded a particular balance, between fancy and fact, between imagination and judgment, between dignity and common sense, between fiction and truth. This demand produced a new set of values for poetry; it also induced a new flood of prose. Hence, the biographies and biographical collections, essays learned and occasional, sermons, critical editions and criticism, articles, handbooks, anthologies, encyclopaedias, even dictionaries, and in the end, when Puritan suspicions about the value of fictitious literature had been relieved by ingenious formulae combining fiction and truth, the novels. And thus, for the first time, to put beside the roll of the poets, a roll of prose authors, numbering among them the first genuine professionals of letters: Johnson, Defoe, Richardson, Fielding, Smollett, Sterne, Goldsmith, as well as Gibbon, Burke, Bunyan, Pepys, Locke, Swift, Addison, Steele, Berkeley, Adam Smith, Hume, Chesterfield, Junius, Boswell.

As we have seen, the book-buying public of the seventeenth century had reading tastes which were almost entirely serious, and indeed grave. It had serious theological, philosophical and political interests, and the impact of the Civil Wars deepened these interests and greatly increased the demand for literature which served them. The story of the development of the arts of prose in the eighteenth century is an account of the mellowing and widening of tastes which retained their pristine gravity. In order to establish any kind of literary profession the writers left frivolity to the theatre and to manuscript poetry, and came to terms with the public's insistence upon truth, usefulness and gravity.

The newspaper originated in London in 1620, developed during the Civil Wars, and by 1720 was a national institution, any town of size having its own local journal. By this time the first periodicals were well established, developing from sectional features in the newspapers. Book notices, for instance, started appearing in newspapers about 1646. By 1668 a special journal, the *Mercurius Librarius*, served as a trade paper advertising the term catalogues of the London booksellers. In stages notices became abstracts, then critical notes with an account of the quality of the author, and finally reviews, literary and dramatic criticism in the modern sense. By the 1690s there were journals called the *Athenian Mercury*, the *Works of the Learned*, the *Compleat Library or News of the Ingenious*, which were wholly devoted to book reviews and to accounts of learned discoveries from many countries. Soon there were journals for all kinds of subjects: periodicals devoted to a single general essay-commentary, like the *Weekly Entertainer* (1700); others, like Daniel Defoe's *Weekly Review* (1704), which contained an account of the activities of a political club; others devoted to specific kinds of social reform, like the *Night-Walker*, which tackled the problem of prostitution, and the *Observator*, which tried to clean up politics; there was even a house journal, the *General Remark*, launched by a fire insurance firm. At first serious commentary was varied only by personal satire and concomitant ribald jests; later, general journals were devised, like the *Monthly Miscellany* (1707), which concerned itself with a variety of topics ranging from history and philosophy to poetry and music, printing poems and attempting to involve the readers in discussion.

The market for the miscellany gave Steele and Addison their opportunity, with the thrice-a-week *Tatler* (1709), the daily *Spectator* (1711), which at one time reached a circulation between 3,000 and 4,000, and then the *Guardian* (1713). The 'essay', an omnibus term which might be used to refer to any of the articles in these periodicals, was in origin a serious dissertation upon topics of national interest; but its limits were so vague that writers could indulge themselves, as in a potpourri, with whatever ingredients pleased the taste of the cook and the guests. What the audience wanted, it seems, was a survey of contemporary life, written from a moral viewpoint, combining erudition and criticism with wit and humour, and the great eighteenth-century essayists, mixing imagination with their reporting, gave them just that. And there were dozens of imitators, like *Titt for Tatt*, and the *Female Tatler*, 'by Mrs. Crackenthorpe, a Lady that knows every thing'. In time a marriage between the periodical and the miscellany produced the magazines, originally repositories or digests of articles which had already appeared in the weekly, tri-weekly or daily journals: the *Gentleman's Magazine* (1731) leads to the *Monthly Review* (1745), and then to Smollett's *Critical Review* (1756).

All this activity in the periodical market not only provided writers with a means to a living, and a medium of seriously and increasingly imaginative expression, but also enhanced the status of writers themselves, since literature became a matter worthy of serious critical discussion in a national forum. Another development which helped the writers establish a new status was the saleability of literary editions. The very fact that authors writing in English should be considered important enough to merit the labours of an editor in the preparation of a reprint was itself an accolade of historical importance. Before the Renaissance, English literature was not accorded this kind of esteem. Henry VIII, as a patriotic nationalist, encouraged modern editions of Anglo-Saxon authors, if only to forge links between the Reformed Church and the ancient Church in Britain. But the only relatively modern author to receive attention was Geoffrey Chaucer, first edited by William Thynne in 1532 and then by Stow in 1561 and Speght in 1598. Seventeenth-century reprints were plain texts, seldom well prepared, with no commentary apart from, occasionally, a biographical preface. No genuine edition of an English author appeared until a hundred years after Speght, until Patrick Hume honoured Milton by treating him as akin to a classical author, in his edition of 1695. Hume was not interested in poetry, nor did he have very much curiosity about the writer's social context, but he thought Milton needed an explanatory edition like those provided of classical authors in schools. Thus, he explains, 'the texts of sacred writ relating to the poem are quoted; the parallel places and imitations of the most excellent Homer and Virgil cited and compared; all the obscure poets rendered in phrases more familiar; the old and obsolete words with their originals explained and made easy to the English reader'. Other classical scholars turned their attention to Milton, notably Richard Bentley, Pope's 'slashing Bentley', and by 1749 the first variorum edition had appeared, Thomas Newton's, based on a scientific collation of earlier texts.

Other authors received similar attention, notably Shakespeare, first edited by Rowe in 1709, and then in turn by Pope, Theobald, and Samuel Johnson in 1765. Spenser, Waller, and Samuel Butler were also edited by scholars; in time the whole field of literature was worked over, and literature and scholarship became working partners. Augustan nationalism and neo-classicism thus combined to give English literature a more serious status. Antiquaries, for the first time to any important degree, turned their enquiries towards English authors, seeking to discover and preserve the best work of the past. The first general poetic anthology produced in this country was Elizabeth Cooper's *The Muses Library* (1737)—'a general collection of almost all the old valuable poetry extant, now so industriously enquir'd after, tho' rarely to be found, but in the studies of the curious'. The idea was taken up in the following year by Thomas Hayward's *British Muse*, and then by hosts of imitators. By 1744 Dodsley had begun his mammoth task of reprinting old plays from the Elizabethan and Jacobean periods.

Another indication of the demand for serious, useful books is provided by the popularity of handbooks and encyclopaedias. It is significant that John Campbell, the man dubbed by Johnson 'the richest author who ever grazed the common of literature', earned his income, well over a thousand pounds a year for many years, entirely from contributions to vade-mecums like the *Modern Universal History*, the *Biographia Britannia*, the *Political Survey of Great Britain*, and similar encyclopaedic best-sellers. This is the age which made 'heavy' literature like encyclopaedias, and even dictionaries, commercial propositions. No earlier age had tried to define the English language in dictionary form. Samuel Johnson pioneered this typically Augustan pursuit in his great work of 1755, although he had predecessors of kinds in Bayle's *Dictionnaire Historique et Critique* in 1697 and Nathan Bailey's dictionary of 1721. Typically, too, it was in the eighteenth century that the *Encyclopaedia Britannica* (1771) first saw light, together with its predecessor, the *Cyclopaedia or Universal Dictionary of Arts and Sciences*, associated with the immortal name of Ephraim Chambers.

Perhaps the prose form which most appealed to Augustan writers, which gave them and their audience the best opportunity to combine and bring together in one stream useful fact and imaginative adventure, was the biography. This art had its origin in the medieval saints' lives and royal chronicles, in sixteenth-century translations of classical biographies, and in the antiquarian movement of the Renaissance, which produced, on the one hand, the life stories of great patriots, useful in encouraging nationalism, and on the other, the life stories of pious churchmen, useful in ecclesiastical controversy. From these beginnings the Augustan biographers, from Izaak Walton to Samuel Johnson, evolved an art which was both objectively historical and subjectively imaginative. Biographies became popular in the market in collections which were, at first, seriously historical and academic. When Bishop Fuller published his *History of the Worthies of England* in 1662, he aimed at a scholarly and accurate account of the great men of each county, taking the trouble to check and evaluate his sources, and to find original sources in public offices, private manuscripts and elsewhere. True, he was apt to be rather unselective in his subjects, to be as much waylaid by a prodigious sleep-walker as by a prodigious Lord Chancellor, and his style is freely entertaining, with a countryman's love of proverbs and anecdotes, but the whole is primarily a serious history of some value still. Other collections, like Edward Phillips's *Theatrum Poetarum* (1675), William Winstanley's *Lives of the Most Famous English Poets* (1687), and Gerard Langbaine's *Account of the English Dramatick Poets* (1691), are still of interest to the literary scholar, collecting as they do in one set of covers what was known in these times about our early writers. These serious collections led to formal national collections, like Curll's *Memoirs British and Foreign* (1711–15)—obituaries for the year, of which Arbuthnot remarked to Swift: 'They added a new terror to death', and then the *Biographia Britannia* (1747–66), and ultimately in the next century the *Dictionary of National Biography*.

While the serious collections multiplied, devoted to subjects as varied as saints and poets, physicians and painters, great ladies and great seventeenth-century Frenchmen, there was a growing market for collections not quite so respectable: the lives of travellers, gamesters, courtesans, murderers and so on.

The lapsing of the censorship in 1694 explains how even serious biographies were spiced with much that was scurrilous, and how it was possible to publish libellous biographies of all kinds, even of prominent figures like Marlborough and Walpole. But the interest of the public was not restricted to the enjoyment of mere political satire; behind the popularity of the scandalous biographies was a contemporary flair for what has been called 'the higher truth of pure scandal', the anecdote perhaps, true or false no matter, which illustrates the character of the subject better than whole chapters of fact. The great biographies seem to begin when painstaking scholarliness and the ear for revealing anecdote combine in one writer, the whole satisfying that 'common curiosity about our neighbour' which accepts the scurrilous and the salacious without in the least affecting a general insistence that such enquiry is morally useful. Biography was Johnson's favourite literary art, because 'it is that which is most eagerly read and most easily applied to the purposes of life'.

The discovery and establishment of the novel, a form invented in the eighteenth century, illustrates again a gradual blending of truth and fiction, fact and imagination. The novel, indeed, is such an all-in-all that literary historians have always had great difficulty in defining exactly what a novel is, and still more what a novel does. Many have concluded that this is not a distinctive genre at all, but a kind of blanket word covering all kinds of lengthy, and not too unorganized, prose fiction. It seems to have been a highly flexible mould, into which all kinds of imaginative creations have been poured; nevertheless, novels first became popular because they were assumed to be true—the usefulness of their truth was their first justification.

Proust suggested that 'in art there is no such thing as an originator, a precursor . . . for everything is comprised in the individual, and each man takes up the continuous effort of art, or of literature, on his own account'. Certainly, as far as the novel is concerned, so many different individuals contributed so many different elements that it is quite impossible to say, precisely, here is where the novel begins, here is the first novel. The novel does not seem to arrive as a whole until all the accumulation is complete, and by then, oddly, it already seems an old art, seems to have been on the scene for 200 years, in some incomplete and partial form, before it can be exactly identified. The only thread the different elements had in common appears to have been a concern to develop from truth to fiction, from historical account to imaginative adventure.

The name itself comes from the Italian *novella*, collections of fairly short stories made familiar to English audiences from the time of Elizabethan story-books, like William Painter's *Palace of Pleasure*. These stories were frequently based upon true events, and were accepted by the English public, and by dramatists who made plays from some of them, as true-life accounts of the lurid passions and crimes excited under the hot skies of a Latin climate. Another predecessor of the novel is the romance, a yarn of chivalry, passion and the marvellous, of which there is a long line of descent from Sir Thomas Malory to Aphra Behn. Once again, the appeal of the old legends, the Arthurian for instance, was that everyone believed them to be true; in fact, there are still zealots today who would be offended by any suggestion that they were not substantially based upon true history. Whatever their wild improbabilities, romances possessed for eighteenth-century readers the fascination of real events. Another predecessor is the travel story, something which purported to be true, no matter how inevitably laced with the fiction to which all homecoming voyagers are prone; here again there is a line of descent from the medieval Mandeville to the Elizabethan Hakluyt, and so to fictional travels like *Pilgrim's Progress* and *Robinson Crusoe*. Then there is an element which the novel borrows from true-life biography, the following through of a life-history. And also an element deriving from the rogue-history, originally a true account of the travels and adventures of some kind of social outcast or rogue: this is the particular element developed by Cervantes, and carried on in such works as Nashe's Elizabethan *Unfortunate Traveller* and Defoe's *Moll Flanders*. And something, too, from the philosophical fictions of Utopia, works like Sidney's *Arcadia* and Lyly's *Euphues*, stories of idealism, perhaps, but full of discussion of contemporary society and its ills. Above all, the novel borrowed the discursive range of the essay; most early novels are prolonged essays set in story form, discussions of ethics and morals and politics. The novel is concerned with all the things men do: their actions, characters, motives, morals, philosophies, social settings, conversation, inclusively everything—and nothing seems fictional even when it is.

The eighteenth-century novelists seem to have stumbled across the novel, almost accidentally, when they were pursuing other ends altogether. It was a long time before novelists consciously thought of the novel as a separate art-form, and just as long before their audience thought of it as fiction rather than truth. Daniel Defoe, for instance, had been writing for forty years before he attempted a novel. He was a shrewd journalist who saw in novels, as in other works like his *Journal of the Plague Year*, a means of selling fiction as if it were fact. The novels were, in fact, an extension of his news reporting. In his *Review* he had already blended with the news startingly new features, like a personal advice column (Defoe was probably the first Evelyn Home in journalistic history), a Family Instructor, gallows revelations by the infamous Jack Sheppard, and a *Mercure Scandale*, 'a weekly history of . . . vice and debauchery'. The same flavour of advice, instruction and saucy revelation attends his novels. *Robinson Crusoe* is not essentially an escape story about far-away places; it is the story of a struggle for survival, exotic only in its setting, by a man who is entirely practical in his outlook, facing the facts of life in minute detail with the reasoning, down-to-earth realism of the London tradesman. *Moll Flanders* is not essentially an escape story from the seamy side; it is the story of a struggle for survival by a woman who is so practical and realistic in her outlook that her first thought after a broken *affaire* or marriage is to tot up her pounds, shillings and pence, and see how she stands. Defoe insists, with an entirely straight face, that *Moll Flanders* was 'Written from her own Memorandums', even if 'the style of the famous lady we here speak of is a little altered; particularly she is made to tell her own tale in modester words'. The novel opens, matter of fact:

> My true name is so well known in the records or registers at Newgate, and in the Old Bailey, and there are some things of such consequence still depending there, relating to my particular conduct, that it is not to be expected I should set my name or the account of my family to this work. . . .

It ends, circumstantially:

> My husband remained there some time after me to settle our affairs, and at first I had intended to go back to him, but at his desire I

altered that resolution, and he is come over to England also, where we resolve to spend the remainder of our years in sincere penitence for the wicked lives we have lived.

WRITTEN IN THE YEAR 1683

The matter, then, was true, useful and revealing, good for Everyman's money. And the style, what has been called 'an honest-to-God Dissenter's market-place utterance', was right for Everyman, too; as Defoe says himself, 'If any man were to ask me what I should suppose to be a perfect style or language, I would answer, that in which a man speaking to five hundred people, of all common and various capacities, idiots or lunatics excepted, should be understood by them all, and in the same sense in which the speaker intended to be understood.'

If Defoe saw the novel as an extension of journalism, Swift saw in its verisimilitude a convenient vehicle for satire. *Gulliver's Travels* (1726), published two years after Defoe's last, may not be quite a novel, although it compounds a travel story, a biography, a rogue-history, a romance and a philosophical disquisition. Nevertheless, Swift made his work look as much like a novel as he could, taking pains to impress upon his readers the authenticity of the geography and the credibility of the detail. He had written satire, vehement criticisms of contemporary society, in other forms, in verse and in prose pamphlets, many years before he discovered in the novel form the best means of impressing his ideas upon the widest possible public. The novel came late, too, in Samuel Richardson's life. Here was a London printer whose sole literary skill was an aptitude for writing letters. In his late forties he joined the Society for the Encouragement of Learning, where his colleagues persuaded him to compile a book of 'familiar letters', a handbook on letters for various occasions. His Low Church interest in public morality encouraged him to turn the letters into vehicles of moral advice, to a fictional daughter in a country town who was being courted by a subaltern. While engaged in this task, he realized that groups of such letters could, in fact, tell a story, and make the basis of a realistic novel, 'a new species of writing, that might possibly turn young people into a course of reading different from the pomp and parade of romance-writing, and, dismissing the improbable and marvellous, with which novels generally abound, might tend to promote the cause of religion and virtue'.[1] Hence *Pamela*, and its successors.

Henry Fielding did not turn to the novel until at the age of 33 he had abandoned a career in the theatre for a career in law. To support himself, he undertook some journalism, as an editor and pamphleteer, and in due course came across Richardson's first novel, which so infuriated him by what he conceived to be its hypocrisy and false values that he wrote a brief parody of it which appeared in 1741 under the title of *Shamela*. This did not apparently satisfy him, presumably because it did not provide enough scope to give Richardson a sufficiently positive reply; at any rate, he followed the parody with a more constructive protest, a novel about Pamela's brother, *Joseph Andrews* (1742). Others followed, drawing still more deeply and realistically upon his own experience, as a barrister and later as a magistrate, with the criminals and outcasts of London society, aiming like Richardson 'to promote the cause of virtue, and to expose some of the most glaring evils, as well public as private, which at present infect the country'.

The first novelists, then, were social reporters, commenting like the journalists and pamphleteers and essayists upon the true life about them, basing their journeys into fiction upon hard fact. Swift appended maps to convince his readers that Lilliput and Brobdingnag actually existed in the southern seas as yet unexplored. Smollett prefaced his novels with covering letters vouching for the authenticity of the documents which by chance have come his way and which he has decided in the public interest to publish. The teller of the tale in an eighteenth-century novel tends to use the first person singular, tends to be a vivid and authentic *I*, rather than some less credible omniscient narrator; he tells what he knows from his own experience to be true, lacing his talk with whatever historical, philosophical, literary or homilectic disquisitions please his fancy, the whole adding up to a personal, solidly realistic view of life. Unlike the romances, the novels were not compounded of what the Puritans called 'lies and foolishness'. The joy of the novel, then, was the same as the joy of the biography, but salted to taste by the ancillary joys associated with essays, real-life letters, true travel stories,

[1] Letter to Aaron Hill, Sir Walter Scott, *Biographical Memoirs of Eminent Novelists* (1834), III. 30.

histories and other forms. The novel is not a thing apart, but a form of literature which derives inevitably from, and remains integrally interconnected with, the host of the other prose forms in this age of prose.

In contrast with the wealth and variety of opportunity open to the writer of prose in the world of print, writers at this time found drama increasingly limited and disappointing. Indeed, the reason why the novelists, in particular, were given their opportunity at all, the reason for the quite extraordinary heterogeneity of novels, the variations in their content discernible from the very beginning of their history, is connected with the failure of drama. The imaginative functions exercised by the theatre in Shakespeare's day, the outlets then given to writer and audience alike, were taken over, in all their variety, by the new art.

Over the period between 1660 and 1740 the theatre gradually ceased to attract, interest and reward literary men. This is a paradox, because it is also true that in the same period the dramatic arts established themselves in the affections not only of cliques in London but also of the general public all over the country. It would seem with the growth of the theatre there was a concomitant decline in its literary qualities.

As we have seen, the public theatres had been declining for a generation before the Civil Wars. The restrictions imposed by the Commonwealth régime accelerated the trend, so that when theatres were legally reopened in 1660 they were very much the private domain of the courtly set. Royal decree ensured that friends of the Court held a monopoly: only two licences were permitted, to William Davenant, using the theatres at Salisbury Court and Lisle's Tennis Court, later the Duke's, and Thomas Killigrew, using the Red Bull and Gibbons's Tennis Court. The royal patent granted in 1661 lasted Davenant and Killigrew, and their long line of successors, until the repeal of the act in 1843. Throughout this period 'straight' drama was confined to the theatres operated by the two patent companies, originally known as the Duke's and the King's, which ultimately built successive rival theatres at Drury Lane and Covent Garden. The only halls outside the reach of the monopoly were theatres in the provinces, of which in the early years there were none at all except the Smock Alley theatre in Dublin, and new houses in

London which were built to stage opera, pantomime, and other musical or semi-musical entertainments exempt from the law. The 'words' of the dramatists were thus made sovereign in two theatres alone, and by definition new forms of drama were devised to eliminate dependence upon a literary text.

The dramatists of Restoration times, even more so than in Shakespeare's day, were usually courtly men. The founder of the 'heroic' tragedy most esteemed at the time was Roger Boyle, first Earl of Orrery (1621–79). The founder of Restoration comedy, Sir George Etherege (?1635–91), was a squire from Oxfordshire who became the friend of courtiers like Buckingham, Rochester, Buckhurst, and Sedley, and who served his king as envoy to the Diet of the Empire at Ratisbon. The most prolific playwright of the day, John Dryden, was a Northamptonshire squire who married the daughter of the Earl of Berkshire and became the Court's Poet Laureate and Historiographer Royal. William Wycherley, author of *The Country Wife*, was a Shropshire squire who was introduced at Court by the King's mistress, Barbara Villiers, Duchess of Cleveland; he served as a naval officer and would have been royal tutor if he had not blotted his record with an unfortunate marriage. Sir John Vanbrugh was a courtier in the Renaissance tradition: after serving the King as a soldier and as a secret agent, he attracted the attention of the Duke of Marlborough and the Earl of Carlisle, and ultimately became Clarencieux King at Arms, the royal architect who helped to design Blenheim, Castle Howard, and Greenwich Hospital, and Comptroller of the Board of Works. The greatest of them all, William Congreve, was a Staffordshire squire who became a favourite at Court, especially with the Duchess of Marlborough, and who was rewarded, like any Renaissance aspirant to social security, with various courtly sinecures, becoming Commissioner for Licensing Hackney Coaches at £100 a year, Commissioner of Hawkers and Pedlars, Searcher of the Customs, and Secretary to Jamaica at £700 a year.

The actors, too, retained all the social status accorded them in the days of Elizabeth and James; indeed, if anything, their status was higher. There was no social stigma of any kind to prevent young wits like Thomas Otway, George Farquhar, and Nathaniel Lee from openly selecting acting as a career. Indeed, many of the actors of the time had been trained at courtly schools either in France or in Sir Balthazar Corbier's Academy in the time of Cromwell. More strikingly, women were accepted on the stage for the first time. When French actresses were imported to the stage of a Jacobean public playhouse in 1621 it is recorded that the conservative audience were so incensed that they pelted them off with 'pippins'. By 1661 French precedent was at last accepted here. True, a large number of the first actresses were, or became, the mistresses of courtly patrons, some of Charles II himself. And Restoration dramatists were not slow to exploit sex in a way not open to Shakespeare and his colleagues, and the Earl of Rochester has the dubious distinction of producing the first nude show in the history of the English theatre. But the salaciousness of Restoration comedy is balanced by the intense sexual idealism of Restoration tragedy (there were nearly as many tragedies written as comedies), and, improbable though it might seem, remembering the amours of mistresses Gwyn, Barry and the others, the acting profession was genteel and respectable according to the values of the times. The audiences also tended to be predominantly genteel, paying admission prices ranging, at the Dorset Garden theatre (1671–1706), from 4*s*. in a box to 1*s*. in the upper gallery. The theatre was no more than a fashionable resort for the fashionable set, something akin to the pleasure gardens and balls.

The term 'comedy of manners' did not exist until it was coined by Charles Lamb, as late as 1822, but Restoration comedies were limited very much to courtly manners. The current term in use was 'genteel comedy': Restoration men were proud of the gentility and civilization of their times, and recoiled from the 'lowness' and 'barbarousness' of the Jacobeans. 'Who should act genteel comedy perfectly,' asks Horace Walpole, 'but people of fashion that have sense? . . . Etherege, Congreve, Vanbrugh and Cibber wrote genteel comedy because they lived in the best company.'[1] Comedies were always set in the resorts of the coteries: the drawing-rooms and boudoirs, Hyde Park and Covent Garden, the Royal Exchange and Mulberry Gardens. The themes invariably concerned themselves with the humorous contradiction between civilized and natural values: the civilized man substituting sense and good breeding for barbarian feeling and denying his own needs in the process; the fool who tries to

[1] Letter to the Countess of Ossory, June 1787.

play the coterie game, but is overcome by passion; the outsider who apes his betters and gets the rules of the game irretrievably confused; the dolt who does not even know the game exists. This is a limited theatre, with a limited range of humour, and the best dramatists usually found that they had exhausted its possiblities in a few plays written before they were thirty. They spoke of themselves as being imaginatively limited: Etherege, for instance, confessed that 'I have been so used to affectation, that without the air of the court, what is natural cannot touch me'.[1]

If Restoration comedy was attenuated, the heroic tragedy of the times was even further removed from the broad perspectives of the Elizabethans. By convention, tragic characters were nearly always of noble birth, possessed of virtues and vices on an epic scale, suffering magnificently in accord with the contemporary taste for spectacular scenic grandeur. 'None but the brave deserves the fair', comments Bonamy Dobrée, 'and naturally, the more wonderfully brave the hero, the more virtuously fair must the heroine be.'[2] It is a world of incredible superlatives, designed specifically, as Hobbes reveals, 'to raise admiration, principally for three Vertues, Valour, Beauty and Love'.[3] Augustan critics tend to be unhappy about their Tragedy: Johnson said of Addison's *Cato* that it was 'a poem in dialogue rather than a drama, rather a succession of just sentiments in elegant language than a representation of natural affections, or of any state probable or possible in human life'.[4] Tragic writing tends to be self-consciously and ostentatiously florid, stuffed with metaphors which in verse less deliberately sublime Augustan writers treated with reserve. It is a highly idealized form of tragedy tailored to the aspirations of the coteries. Certain qualities, of concentration, detachment and nobility, recommended them to the taste of the day, but the limitations have not helped these plays to survive for later generations.

During the decades in which the courtly coteries dominated the theatre, drama remained essentially an amateur art in which

[1] Quoted in B. Dobrée, *Restoration Comedy, 1660–1720* (1924), p. 60.

[2] *Restoration Tragedy, 1660–1720* (1929), p. 20.

[3] Preface to *Homer's Odyssey* (1675), in J. E. Spingarn, ed., *Critical Essays of the Seventeenth Century* (Oxford, 1908), II. 68.

[4] *Lives of the English Poets*, G. B. Hill, ed. (Oxford, 1905), II. 132.

professional writers could not thrive and the poorer gentlemen, like George Farquhar, starved in garrets. But from one extreme, after 1700 the theatre rapidly proceeded to another extreme. As long as courtly influence survived good writing of a kind was possible in the theatre, even if only by amateurs. With the decline of the power of the Court, aristocrats, especially the younger set, were no longer so fully occupied as before in courtly life, with its many obligations and conventions; they were no longer servants of a dynasty which expected from them day-to-day involvement in its fortunes and duties. On the other hand, they were not generally expected to have any other kind of occupation: gentlemen did not work for a living. Remarkably, they became even more idle and less serious than they had been at the Court of Charles II: much more committed to the pleasure principle. The fashionable patrons of the theatre, after 1700, were less intellectual, less prepared to accept drama which required any kind of mental effort, more ready to relax into passive entertainment. With such an audience, Congreve's *Way of the World*, the finest comedy of the period, was a failure from the first night, ending Congreve's interest in all original play-writing.

As the theatres became larger and more popular, spectacle, bombast and presentation quite overcame the sovereignty of the spoken words. Successive dramatists testify to the changing scene. George Colman the younger sings:

> Let your Shakespeares and Jonsons go hang, go hang!
> Let your Otways and Drydens go drown!.
> Give us but Elephants and white Bulls enough,
> And we'll take in all the town. . . .[1]

Garrick was aware of a split in tastes, suggesting that the pit relished satire, the boxes wit, the gallery humour, and the 'gods' 'hornpipes and Hearts of Oak'.[2] Jephson in similar words suggested that the pit wanted sublimity, the boxes polished sentiments, the gallery nature, and the 'gods' 'processions, bustle, trumpets and fighting'.[3] As always happens in this kind of free competition, uncontrolled by patrons, the lower tastes ultimately

[1] *New Hay at the Old Market* (1795).
[2] Epilogue to Murphy's *All in the Wrong* (1761).
[3] *The Count of Narbonne* (1781), prologue.

prevailed, and the audience called the tune: in the word of Monk Lewis,

> Give us Lightning and Thunder, Flames, Daggers and Rage;
> With events that ne'er happened, except on the Stage.[1]

Power in the theatre passed from the writer to the actor. The leading stars became more important and autocratic, some of them serving as actor-managers. The theatre became a place which exploited acting personality, and dramatists were forced increasingly to write plays for particular players. Gagging and ad libbing became more prevalent: indeed, some dramatists, resigned to the inevitable, seem to have inserted stage directions like 'A great deal more of this stuff'. Outside the monopoly houses drama was rapidly submerged by hornpipes, equestrians, dancing dogs and other performing animals, tumblers and wire-dancers, along a road leading to the circus and to vaudeville. Even at Drury Lane and Covent Garden the theatre moved away from literary drama towards its future of a mass entertainment industry.

Whether all this was ultimately good or bad for the theatre is not in question: drama is a hybrid art, and there is some difference of opinion about the nature of the sovereignty of the written text. But from the point of view of the literary playwright, all this growth was a retrogression. In the early part of the eighteenth century, despite the aversion to play-writing of literary leaders like Swift and Pope, many literary men, among them Addison, Steele, Fielding, Thomson, and Young, played a not unimportant part in the theatre. Later the men of letters disappeared, almost entirely, and plays were written by hacks who were prepared to meet the needs of particular companies. Such a writer might earn from his company as much as a thousand pounds for a play, exclusive of the additional two hundred earned from publishing it. Despite these rewards, the men of letters turned to the closet theatre, to private readings in drawing-rooms, and lost touch with the physical stage. By the early nineteenth century those writers like Keats and Shelley who still attempted drama produced completely unactable plays (though Coleridge, an exception, did reach the boards of Drury Lane, once, with *Remorse*).

[1] Epilogue to Holcroft's *Knave or Not?* (1798).

Quite apart from the vulgarization of drama, writers were also deterred by its sentimentalization. As the theatre became noisier and more spectacular, the effort was also made to make it more moral. There was an inevitable reaction to the sexy frankness of Restoration Comedy when men like Dryden, Cibber, and Congreve were ready to agree that frankness had become licentiousness and 'ordure'. The Society for the Reformation of Manners, founded in 1692, employed spies to report on plays. The chief voice of the reaction was the Puritan, Jeremy Collier, whose book *A Short View of the Profaneness and Immorality of the English Stage* (1697) ran into two editions in three weeks. 'The business of plays', he said, 'is to recommend virtue and discountenance vice . . . 'Tis to expose the singularities of pride and fancy, to make folly and falsehood contemptible, and to bring everything that is ill under infamy and neglect.' His arguments were extraordinarily effective. Committed to the neo-classical principle that drama was *utile et dulce*, the dramatists could not deny their responsibility as moral teachers. Collier believed Shakespeare too guilty to quote as a precedent, and the dramatists perforce agreed, since they, too, tended to think of him, for all his genius, as an untrained barbarian. When Collier argued that Latin writers were less smutty than ours because we failed to obscure obscenity with ambiguity, dramatists were unable to give the lie to an argument so outrageous; they had said so often themselves that the best genteel humour was subtle and unobvious. At any rate, Collier won the day, even if his aim denied the possibility of art at all: he essentially wanted the theatre to portray life not as it was but as it should be, to describe a sham world in which virtue is always rewarded and vice always punished, the world, in fact, of the Goodies and Baddies of modern juvenile fiction.

At first the pressure of the moralists induced merely hypocrisy in the writers. A good instance occurs in Cibber's play *Love's Last Shift*, where the hero spends four acts as an utter rake, only to discover in the last that the woman he has been seducing with such outrageous success is the wife whom he abandoned eight years before! Vanbrugh coolly suggests in a preface that 'the business of comedy is to show people what they should do by representing them upon the stage doing what they should not'. But ultimately the necessity to make all plays morally conformist undermined the right of the imaginative man to look at life as it really was. Despite idiosyncratic protests against the trend by writers like Goldsmith and Sheridan, the theatre moved steadily towards the escapist world of *East Lynne*. George Lillo's *The London Tragedy* (1731) reveals which way the wind was blowing. This play is about the tribulations of an apprentice tempted by gold and a wicked woman:

> In artless strains, a tale of private woe.
> A London prentice ruined is our theme.

Lillo took to extremes the notion that tragedy is useful because it teaches, and inferred that 'the more extensively useful the moral of any tragedy is, the more excellent that piece must be of its kind'. Why write therefore about princes and sceptred chiefs, when it would be more universal to describe the boy next door? At the time the theatre had become so corrupt that this kind of argument met with only the mildest of criticisms, like Pope's gentle suggestion that perhaps the play had 'a greater elevation of language than was consistent with the characters and the situation'.

Vulgarization and sentimentalization were mighty deterrents to the man of letters who wanted to explore reality through his imagination. But the final blow fell, the last hope went, when Walpole passed the Licensing Act of 1737 and imposed upon drama the censorship of the Lord Chamberlain. Although literary comedy and tragedy were in decline, the writers still had opportunities in political satire. Anti-Whig writers like Henry Fielding in his *Historical Register, or the Life and Death of Tom Thumb the Great* (1730), had discovered a vein of fantasy which was popular and imaginative. Fielding himself had written potboilers for the public taste, comedies and farces and ballad-operas. The titles speak for themselves: *The Modern Husband*, *The Old Debauchees*, *The Pleasures of the Town*, *The Intriguing Chambermaid*, and so on. But it was the political satire which retained his interest in the theatre (he was for a time manager of the Little Theatre in the Haymarket). In this he could play a public role useful to his Opposition friends, Lyttelton and Pitt, and satisfy the ambitions which later impelled him to undertake the public duties of a Bow Street Magistrate and made him one of the first reformers of the Metropolitan Police. But Walpole and his friends could not tolerate this platform for the opposition, and suppressed this kind of freedom. Fielding immediately abandoned the theatre and started a new life as a lawyer.

Fielding's defection was a symbol of the times, like Congreve's before him. The theatre was prosperous enough to provide a living wage, and more, for the writers who were prepared to write to formula. This apparently was not enough. Between Fielding and George Bernard Shaw, a century and a half later, hardly any literary men or women took more than a passing interest in the theatre. It is not surprising that this century and a half is also the period of English drama most barren of great or even good plays. Whether the theatre gained anything by its neglect of the writers is another matter; sufficient here merely to note that the professionals of letters, Shakespeare's heirs, sought outlets elsewhere.

The poets did not suffer the disaster that befell the dramatists; nevertheless, they had to come to terms with a new social context. The change came gradually and not abruptly. In the Renaissance tradition of the Stuarts, Charles II encouraged poetry. The leading poets of the Restoration were courtiers—the Earl of Rochester, the Earl of Dorset, Sir Charles Sedley, Sir John Denham, Sir William Davenant and others. These, like every Renaissance courtier, gathered their satellites, the Wallers, Shadwells, and Godolphins. Indeed, it was probably true that until the reign of Walpole almost every statesman wrote verse. Court patronage continued on Elizabethan lines, with the award of sinecures and the like, and with the expectation that poets would serve in capacities other than the purely literary. Addison's poem, *The Campaign* (1704), earned him the post of Commissioner of Appeal in Excise, one of a string of appointments which ultimately took him to the position of Secretary for Ireland and a pension of £1,600 a year. But as the printed word became a major social force, patrons expected their protégés to devote more and more time to *non-poetic* literary services, in other words to serve as political journalists and propagandists.

Much depended upon the individual nobleman. The Earl of Dorset patronized Waller, Sprat, Dryden, Butler, and Wycherley, expecting from them only poetic and courtly service. The Earl of Halifax patronized Prior and Addison, but expected them to help him not only as poets and diplomats, but also as propagandists. To the Earl of Oxford, Defoe and Swift were primarily useful as propagandists, while Walpole's only act of purely literary patronage was a pension to Edward Young: his other protégés were all journalists. The Court itself seems gradually to have lost interest in poetry: Queen Anne seems to have read nothing but books of piety and official documents, while George II is reported as saying, in an appropriately gutteral accent: 'I hate bainting and boetry. Neither the one nor the other ever did any good.' On the other hand, while the Court lost its power and its influence, the statesmen who inherited power found it increasingly difficult to reserve sinecures for writers. In the new parliamentary system voters had become important, and all too often voters had to be bought. In short, the Renaissance system of patronage broke down.

But the leaders of Augustan society continued to prize poetry. Indeed, there was something compulsive about their interest. When Hobbes remarked that 'readers of poesie are commonly persons of the best quality',[1] he was testifying to the deep respect for the art which, after the Renaissance, even upstart aristocrats were bound to feel. In this neo-classical age, an age which called itself Augustan because it aspired to the standards of Augustan Rome, poetry was esteemed as the medium of expression for the highest human aspirations, as the repository, in epic and other serious verse, of quintessential national qualities. Poetry was indispensable to Augustanism, to the culture which produced the great palaces and the portraits, the *beaux* and the *rococo*. But individual patronage along Renaissance lines was no longer possible; and manuscript circulation, the means whereby individual patrons had been connected with the intimate circle of the poet's friends, had lost its primacy in the machinery of communication. On the one hand, poetry retained its special gentility, its status as the civilizing literary art *par excellence*; on the other hand, poetry had to come to terms with machinery of communication dominated by print and prose. Literary professionals whose talents were chiefly poetic faced a subtle and complex problem.

Now that authors were generally unable to think of themselves

[1] *Homer's Odyssey* (1675), To the Reader concerning the Vertues of an Heroique Poem.

as gentlemen giving, to use Fielding's words, 'a private or eleemosynary treat', and began to think of themselves as keepers of 'a public ordinary, at which all persons are welcome for their money', the question was whether writers could accept the failure of outworn systems of patronage and yet still achieve a respectable literary career, with the standards appropriate to a proper profession. The poets were most sensitive to the changing times, but all writers were involved in this general crisis. Dependence upon the printed-book market, after all, brought writers perilously near Grub Street. Their battle for an all-round independence is now the main theme of this story.

# VII

## The Profession Established

*My inducement to it is not love nor desire of fame, but the want of money, which is the only motive to writing that I know of.*

SAMUEL JOHNSON[1]

*Knowledge has no value or use for the solitary owner: to be enjoyed it must be communicated. . . . Glory is the reward of science, and those who deserve it scorn all meaner views. . . . It was not for gain that Bacon, Newton, Milton, and Locke instructed and delighted the world.*

LORD CAMDEN[2]

WRITERS began comparing England and the English with Augustan Rome about the middle of the seventeenth century. The term was applied to Cromwell by Waller in 1654, to Charles II by Dryden in 1660, to the English language by Atterbury in 1690, and to English literature by Oldmixon in 1712. For Defoe and Gay, London was Augusta. The comparison between imperial Rome and the London of 1700 was natural: both cities had about half a million inhabitants, were approximately the same size, were capital cities aware of themselves as centres of commerce and empire, and were each proud in particular of their literature. The name Augustus was handled by nationalists in much the same way as the name Arthur in the

[1] *Works*, ed. Hawkins (1787), p. 362.
[2] In the House of Lords debate on copyright, February 1774.

reign of Henry VII by those who wished to find and fashion links between Tudor England and the greatness of the legendary King. Much play, for instance, was made of the fact—one of his few assets—that George II had been christened Augustus. It was important that a new national image should be fashioned, in the arts as in every other aspect of life, and it was natural that the builders of the new civilization that followed the Civil Wars should turn, like other Europeans, to classical examples and styles.

The 'Augustanism' which resulted owed its particular flavour to the balance of forces, frequently contradictory, which created the new, post-Revolution society. It reflects a marriage between the 'squirearchy', the landed gentry who effectively brought an end to Stuart power, and the merchants of London and other towns who were busy establishing the country's pre-eminence in commerce. On the one hand, this was the age of the Agrarian Revolution, of a steady increase in the nation's wealth from systematic farming and efficient estate management, of the gentry to whom a country seat was indispensable, and who were as likely to express themselves in the new country pursuits—landscape gardening, foxhunting, angling, cricket—as in politics and the arts. On the other hand, it was also the age of the urban rationalists, of the Royal Society's foundation, of the establishment of great financial institutions like the Bank of England and Lloyd's, of the pioneering of new industries under the leadership, particularly, of independent-minded mercantile nonconformists, who were beginning to find the leisure and the need for cultural expression. Country common sense and urban rationalism combined well, had much in common. But the squires had an aristocratic taste for majesty and grandeur, while the merchants inclined to the utilitarian and to plain matters of fact, so that the alliance between them, while real, was based as much on compromise as on identity of interests.

The arts of the day reflected, on the one hand, the straightness, plainness and clarity to be expected of the Enlightenment and of a mercantile class which prided itself upon its common-sense, and on the other hand, the dignity, decorum and heroic sense of a new ruling class conscious of itself as a new aristocracy and anxious to fit the part. It is thus the age of Wren's straight lines, squares and circles, buildings that had the 'lucidity and completeness of a mathematical equation', and the age, too, of Hawksmoor and Vanbrugh and vast Palladian mansions worthy of the heroes for whom they were intended. It was the age not only of Purcell and Handel and the exact harpsichord (to be superseded in the latter half of the eighteenth century by the piano), but also of heart-stirring pomp like *Rule Britannia*, *Hearts of Oak*, and *God Save the King*, and such extraordinary events as noblemen's and gentlemen's musical breakfasts. It was the age not only of painters who could scientifically reproduce old masters, or who like Hogarth could produce direct and witty social satire on canvas, but also of Reynolds and the great portrait painters who could demonstrate in every picture that their subjects were indeed gentry of substance and quality. The age of Hobbes and Locke, of a theoretically egalitarian materialism, was also the age in which aristocratic gentility was cultivated, almost as a mystique. The punctilio with which the fop dressed himself or took coffee, the devotion to rococo ornamentation, and the exquisiteness of polished heroic couplets are different aspects of a general insistence that while a man ought to be lucid and rational, he should not thereby become vulgar and barbarian. The Royal Society wanted to encourage 'a close, naked way of speaking; positive expressions, clear senses; a native easiness; bringing all things as near the Mathematical plainness, as they can: and preferring the language of Artizans, Countrymen, and Merchants, before that of Wits, or Scholars'.[1] But, significantly, John Dryden, F.R.S., one of the members of the sub-committee which prepared this famous declaration, insists elsewhere that the poets at least could not be mean: ' 'Tis true, that to imitate well is a poet's work; but to affect the soul, and excite the passions, and, above all, to move admiration. . . . a bare imitation will not serve. The converse, therefore, which a poet is to imitate, must be heightened with all the arts and ornaments of poesy'.[2] And Johnson is thinking of language at once subtle and gracious when he talks about the achievement of 'that comprehension and expansion of thought which at once fills the whole mind, and of which the first effect is sudden astonishment, and the second rational admiration'.[3] These Augustans needed their

[1] Thomas Sprat, *History of the Royal Society* (2nd edn., 1702), pp. 111 ff.
[2] W. P. Ker, ed., *Essays* (Oxford, 1900), I. p. 113.
[3] *Life of Cowley*, G. B. Hill, ed., *Lives of the English Poets*, I. p. 2021.

imagination delighted at the same time as their rational judgment was challenged: they became adept in combining and fusing impulses which seem to lead them in opposite directions.

With the same capacity for balance and reconciliation, the Augustans attempted a solution of the problems and contradictions peculiar to the establishment of a literary profession. On the one hand, writers wished to retain the status and esteem accorded the leisured amateurs and the freedom to write according to the laws of writing. As Lord Camden suggested in the Copyright debate in 1774, writers aspired to immortality, to the permanent fame which might be bestowed upon them by posterity, to the idea that literature brought benefits to the community which were far from transient and ephemeral. On the other hand, writers had to live, to find means whereby they could please and be rewarded by the contemporary society about them; some writers had ascetically modest needs, others were caught up in the expensive social behaviour of their friends and needed more than subsistence expenses. The problem was to ensure a competence which left the writers reasonably independent, free not only to write but to write as well as they were able. Towards the end of the period Goldsmith was able to boast that writers—he was dealing with poets but his remark applies equally to other literary men—'no longer depend on the great for subsistence; they have now no other patrons than the public'.[1] But the road to this point was difficult and complicated.

All too often the establishment of a literary profession has been attributed to the energies and achievements of a rising middle class. Quite apart from the difficulty that throughout British social history there always has been a rising middle class, the term is particularly inappropriate when applied to the eighteenth century: it is a modern term, involving a different concept from what Joseph Butler had in mind when in 1740 he commented upon 'the enlarged middle rank of people'. Instead of seeing a distinct class occupying the social strata between the nobility and the commonalty (those whom Defoe described as 'the meer labouring people who depend upon their hands'), eighteenth-century observers saw a number of differentiated, ranks, orders, or degrees: the lesser gentry, the clergy, the merchants and traders, the farmers, and the various kinds of

[1] J. H. Lobban, ed., *Selected Essays* (1915), p. 65.

professional men were all distinct. The calculations of Nicholas Hans indicate that the nobility and gentry were still the largest group: of 3,000 notable men detailed in the *Dictionary of National Biography*, 'the *élite* of the Eighteenth Century', 735 were baronets, squires, and gentlemen of independent means, 609 were clergymen, Church or Dissent, 436 merchants and traders, 239 farmers, and 144 members of the medical profession (there were even fewer teachers and lawyers, and all the other professions, including the artists, added together made up only 65). Moreover, the different degrees included only a relative few who sponsored and supported cultural activities. Every gentleman tried to acquire a library; but as often as not books would be bought in bulk, at an auction or sale, indiscriminately as to contents provided the bindings were impressive enough; and sometimes empty shelves were filled up with wooden books. One remembers Pope's lines:

> His Study! With what Authors is it stor'd?
> In Books, not Authors, curious is my Lord;
> To all their dated Backs he turns you round:
> These Aldus printed, those Du Sueil has bound.
> Lo some are Vellum, and the rest as good
> For all his Lordship knows, but they are Wood.
> (*Moral Essays, IV*, 133)

Literacy, and the right kind of literacy, develops unevenly in this century. Where one might expect a steady expansion in the educational opportunities provided, there is a mid-century slump: Winchester had only eight commoners in residence in 1751, compared with 93 in 1737; in the latter half of the century entrance numbers at Eton dropped from about 500 to 230; Oxford and Cambridge slumped in prestige and numbers. At the same time nonconformist academies move from strength to strength and one is quietly aware that, somehow, more and more educated, cultured women are making their mark in society. The only fair conclusion is that the new literature of the period, like the other arts, was supported by an alliance of interests between minorities in all the degrees and ranks aspiring to literacy.

Certainly, the contemporary centres of literature, the coffee-houses and clubs, were frequented by representatives of many different degrees. The first coffee-house in this country was opened in 1657: by 1708 there were three thousand of them in London alone. In houses like Will's and Buttons' the writers met their first audience of friends and acquaintances, sometimes informally, sometimes formally as a 'club'. In the Rainbow originated the Society for the Encouragement of Learning (1735), which aimed at instituting 'a republic of letters for the promoting of Arts and Sciences'; in the Bedford originated the Society for the Promotion of Arts, the forerunner of the Royal Society of Arts and Crafts; in the Chapter, the favourite of booksellers, originated London's best circulating library, with a subscription of only a shilling a year. In these houses, and in taverns which emulated them, the writers rubbed shoulders, in an egalitarian context, with their patrons, whether they were noblemen or squires or parsons or merchants or professional men. Besides Johnson, the ten members of the King's Head club (1763) included three physicians, two scholars, a bookseller, a divine, a magistrate and a West India merchant. In the next few years new members were added from the politicians, the gentry, and the other arts and professions: a society in which Johnson mixed in socially equal terms with Burke and Fox, Reynolds and Garrick, Percy and Gibbon, Windham and Stowell. This club, perhaps the most famous of them all, had its eminent predecessors in the Kit-Kat, which Jacob Tonson the bookseller founded at the Fountain Tavern to bring together the Whig aristocrats, politicians and writers, including Steele, Addison, and Congreve, and its Tory rival, the Brothers, founded by Bolingbroke with Swift, Pope, and Arbuthnot. It is the mark of the literary societies of the age that membership was entirely heterogeneous, including politicians, diplomats, lawyers, theologians, scientists, physicians, surgeons, actors, and so on, besides the poets and other writers. This heterogeneity is representative of the reading public as a whole.

It was a public friendly to the writer's aspirations. In this age for the first time Parliament took action to define and defend the rights of authors to their literary property. In an attempt to curb the traditional prerogative of the stationers, as early as 1642 the House of Commons had attempted to ensure that 'the printers do neither print nor reprint anything without the name and consent of the author', but the measure was ineffectual. It was not until 1709 that the Act for the Encouragement of Learning first defined copyright: thenceforward, works already published were under copyright cover for a further twenty-one years, and new works were covered, for the author or his assignee, for an initial period of fourteen years, renewable for a further fourteen if the author were still alive; various fines for infringement were imposed. The Act was far from perfect: it limited by legislative means the argument that authors had a natural right to perpetual copyright; it gave no protection against Dublin or the pirate publishers in London who printed with impunity under the name of a bankrupt. But it gave the writers the power to bargain edition by edition, to hold back the outright sale of a copyright until the most profitable moment. The Act remained in force until further, more generous measures were passed in 1774, 1814 and 1842. The way was clear for better rewards for the authors: Gay received £400 for the copyright alone of the *Beggar's Opera*, £1,000 for his *Poems*, and £1,200 for his *Polly*; Goldsmith received £500 for each of his plays, and 800 guineas for his eight-volume *Natural History*; Mrs Radcliffe £500 for the *Mysteries of Udolpho* and £800 for *The Italian*; and so on to the really grand returns—£4,500 for Robertson's *Charles V* and £6,000 for Hawkesworth's account of the South Sea Expedition.

This growing strength of the writers rested upon the prosperity of the printed-book trade which served an increasing number of readers throughout the country. In time the publishers became the most important patrons of the literary profession. The traders of Little Britain and Paternoster Row included a few who developed their own literary taste to the point of identifying and encouraging the writer whose abilities showed promise: Dryden owed much to Jacob Tonson, Pope much to Bernard Lintot, Fielding much to Andrew Millar, Johnson much to Robert Dodsley. The more enlightened booksellers joined together in partnerships to publish some of the more expensive works, as Tonson and Lintot combined forces for the first collected edition of Steele's *Dramatic Works*. Grouped together in organizations like the Printing Conger (1719), the New Conger (1736), or the Chapter (the group which published Johnson's *English Poets*), they were a much more effective body of patronage than, for instance, the Society for the Encouragement of Learning (1736–48), which under the Duke of Richmond and a management committee a hundred strong, attempted co-operative publishing independently of the professional book-sellers and went badly bankrupt. On the other hand, there were disreputable booksellers like Edmund Curll and Ralph Griffiths, of the kind Roger North condemned in 1744 when he wrote: 'They crack their brains to find out selling subjects, and keep hirelings in garrets, at hard meat, to write and correct by the groat; and so puff up an octavo to a sufficient thickness, and there is six shillings current for an hour and a half's reading, and perhaps never to be read or looked upon after.'[1] Worse, some of the best rewards awaited those who became 'Scribblers for a Party': between 1731 and 1741 Walpole spent £50,077 on political propaganda, and an obscure hack like Arnall earned £10,997 in four years. This was the Grub Street, successfully turning out rubbish to demand, that Pope anathematized in the *Dunciad*. And these were the hacks, James Ralph in 1758, and Guthrie in 1762, who pioneered the use of the term *Author by Profession*, only to bring it into disrepute.

It was a complex scene: a golden age, supported by a new wide public patronizing the increasing number of booksellers and circulating libraries throughout the country, but also a hard and commercial age. There was fierce competition for a market which had its limitations. A normal edition numbered only 2,000. Books were still expensive: a duodecimo volume cost 2*s*. 6*d*. or 3*s*., an octavo 5*s*. or 6*s*., a quarto or folio 10*s*. or 12*s*., and Bibles on royal paper £5. At a time when schoolmasters earned an average of £12 a year, labouring men 8*d*. to 1*s*. 6*d*. a day, labouring women 4*d*. to 1*s*. a day, and Johnson calculated that it cost him £30 a year to live, there was an economic ceiling to the aspirations of the trade. Remarkably, despite the growth of periodicals and magazines and the new literary media pioneered by them, once the book trade had adjusted itself to the more modest demands of the reading public after the Civil Wars, there was relatively little increase in the number of new books published each year: the figure remains constant at rather under 100 from 1666 to 1756, and only rises sharply after 1790. The periodicals and the books, the men of genius and the hacks, the would-be professionals and the genteel dilettantes were in competition in a limited market; there was a much greater variety of

[1] *Life of the Hon. and Rev. Dr. John North* (1744).

opportunity offered, just as the reading public were interested in a much wider field of interests, but security for the writer was hard to find, and security with a proper measure of independence was harder still. The dedicated writers, who believed in literature as the art of imaginative enquiry, were heavily outnumbered on the one hand by the drudges and hacks, some acquiring fortunes, others labouring for a pittance, and on the other hand by the amateurs, the country parsons and minor gentry, who flooded the publishers with their poems, and sermons, and other offerings. Yet there is a discernible line of progress in the establishment of a literary profession, detailed best perhaps in the careers of successive leading writers. The two extremes, the amateur like Waller uninterested in rewards and the journalist like Defoe struggling with his integrity for the sake of rewards, finally come together, stage by stage in the careers of writers like Dryden and Prior, until with Pope, Fielding, Johnson and their successors there is an accord and a balance, tenuous perhaps but viable at last.

Edmund Waller, as far as form and style are concerned, was the first Augustan poet: Dryden confessed that 'unless he had written, none of us could write',[1] and Percival Stockdale, his biographer in 1772, affirmed the common view that 'his works gave a new era to English poetry'. Nevertheless, his attitude towards the social context of poetry is almost indistinguishable from that of the Renaissance courtly poet. Indeed, he lived the life of a courtly poet. He served under Cromwell and Charles II as a member of Parliament, a commissioner for trade, and dramatic censor. He wrote occasional verse about a naval victory, a royal visit, a birthday, a new park, a new play, a card-game: in many ways he was what Douglas Bush called him, 'a fluent trifler, the rhymer of a Court gazette'. Further, he was a rich man who inherited a large estate and who made two prosperous marriages: he had no incentive to become a paid professional. Though some of his poems were sold by the 40,000, in unauthorized print, before he was 18, and though his published speeches after the Restoration sold by the 20,000, he did not seek print for his poetry until he was nearly 60. He wrote manuscript poems 'only to please himself, and such particular persons to whom they were directed'; 'they pass'd up and downe

[1] William Walsh, *Dialogue concerning Women* (1691), preface.

through many hands amongst persons of the best quality'. While he was in exile three unauthorized editions of his work appeared in 1645, but even political poems, like *A Panegyric to my Lord Protector* and *To the King of his Navy*, were not intended for print. Although he took an interest in the book trade, and was one of those, with Hobbes, Cowley, and Sir Robert Howard, whom Dryden met in discussions at Henry Herringman's bookshop at the Blue Anchor, his attitude towards print for his own poems was one of courtly disdain. His publisher in 1664 claimed that he had been unwilling to print since the pirate editions of 1645, because readers of a 'confined understanding' 'admire most what they least comprehend'; better then to sell them pirated poems, 'as the Turks hang old rags, or such like ugly things, upon their fairest horses, and other goodly creatures, to secure them against fascination'! Here, then, was a genuinely leisured amateur, modest and without literary pretension, unwillingly acquiring a large and national audience through print, and discovering to his surprise that he was a literary figure of substance and influence.

At the other extreme, Daniel Defoe needed to write, to earn a living and to fulfil himself. The son of a butcher, by the time he was 30 he had failed in his first vocation as a hose factor, despite the fact that he had married a well-endowed girl from the mercantile class, and had become a liveryman of the city. Bankrupt on the large scale of £17,000, he was compelled to turn his education and literary skill to professional account. From youth he had dabbled in verse, particularly of a religious kind; he was thus able to attract the attention of the Whigs, particularly Halifax, and served them as a journalist. He became prominent for his pamphlet defences of King William, and won a national reputation with his essay in verse, *The True-Born Englishman* (1701), which sold over 80,000 copies and in four years passed into nine genuine and twelve pirate editions. Thereafter, this remarkable man became one of the most prolific authors in history: he has over 350 items of print to his credit, even excluding the journalism—sixteen volumes of political verse, over twenty-five books, and a wide variety of religious, political, economic, social and historical tracts. It was apparent to his contemporaries that this effort was more than a mere exploitation of a talent to earn a living: he lived for his writing. As John Dunton remarks, 'By his printing a poem every day, one would think that he rhimed in his sleep'; and 'It is hard to leave off when not only the itch of inclination, but the necessity of writing, lies so heavy upon a man'.[1]

Thanks to his patrons, Defoe secured positions in a Glass Duty office and a brick factory; he changed his name from its original form of Foe; he invented a family coat of arms and motto (his grandfather had some pretensions to the status of a country gentleman, but Defoe was in no sense an *armiger*); in short, he tried to rise in the world. To his credit, ultimately he paid off all his debts, but for a long time his security was vulnerable. With the Tories in power, he was pilloried and gaoled for the pamphlet, *The Shortest Way with the Dissenters*, in 1703. Hard beset at this time, with six children to provide for, to secure his release he had to come to an agreement with the Tory, Harley. Defoe was not so disloyal a turncoat as he might seem; he was essentially a non-party radical rather than a Whig, and Harley was a moderate. All the same, Defoe had to serve in whatever capacities his new patrons thought fit. Quite apart from journalistic work as editor of the *Review*, he acted as a secret agent, particularly in Scotland in the troubles that followed the Union. With the return of the Whigs to power, Defoe found himself in trouble and in prison again: keeping in favour with the Tories had led him to co-operate not only with Harley but also with more extreme politicians like Godolphin and even the Jacobite Bolingbroke, and this Defoe's old friends would not stomach. He was forced once more to come to some accommodation, and this time the price was that he should secretly edit, in the interests of the Whigs, the Jacobite journal, *Mist's Weekly*, and the Tory High-Church periodical, *News Letter*, taking the sting out of them. Unsuspected by the Tories, Defoe managed to fulfil this strange duty for eleven years. As long as he was free to write, he does not seem to have bothered himself unduly about political affiliations, and he regarded nothing in his record as personally perfidious. On the contrary, he was single-heartedly dedicated to print. His career, however, is far from the true professional ideal.

What with his family and his debts, Defoe's standard of living

[1] Quoted in Bonamy Dobrée, *English Literature in the Early Eighteenth Century* (Oxford, 1959), p. 34.

did not improve, nor a reasonable measure of independence from the politicians come his way, until he was nearly 60, until, in fact, he struck upon the novels, which began in 1719 with *Robinson Crusoe*, five of them ending with *Roxana* in 1724. There followed other best-sellers: ghost stories, rogue stories, a *Journal of the Plague Year*, a *Tour Through the Whole Island of Great Britain*, *The Complete English Tradesman*, *A Plan of English Commerce*, and so on. His actual cash returns are not known, but *Robinson Crusoe* ran into three editions in the first four months and made the publisher a profit of over £1,000. He was thus in a position to strike better bargains over the later work, especially as the other novels also sold well, *Moll Flanders*, for instance, reaching four editions in eighteen months. He certainly earned enough to buy an Essex estate for his daughter Hannah, and he bought himself a property at Stoke Newington, where he had stables, orchards and a four-acre garden. There he lived the life of a 'Squire in Town', producing works like *The Complete English Gentleman*, and *Augusta Triumphans*, a paean of joy for the new Augustan commercial society he saw springing up round him, enjoying at last the dignity, independence and rewards that had been denied him so long. He remained short of funds and died, untypically of a lethargy, most typically in hiding from a creditor during a spell of temporary financial embarrassment. But his last dozen years gave him a taste of the security and status at which he aimed all his long literary career. Social conditions were not yet ready to free this kind of writer, not from the hardships and struggles which he accepted as inevitable, but from the indignity of having to surrender his integrity in so many ways to the exigencies of politics.

Dryden seems to stand between the two worlds of Waller and Defoe: he shared Waller's social status and leisured courtly life, and yet he devoted himself to literature almost as voluminously as the professional, even though he thus acquired with his friends the reputation of a 'drudge'. As a result, there is a better balance in his career, more security and at the same time more independence. On both sides of his family there were small landowners, and all his life Dryden had a small private income from the rents of the Northamptonshire estate at Blakesley. Like many of his degree, he went to Westminster School and Cambridge, and later augmented his income by working as a clerk—he was known as 'the Squire' to his colleagues—in the service of Thurloe, a position secured for him through the agency of Sir Gilbert Pickering. He had had poems published as a schoolboy and as an undergraduate, an elegy for a dead friend, an introduction to a volume by a colleague. But he was 28 before he turned his attention to serious writing; at this age his friend Francis Gifford introduced him to Henry Herringman, the publisher, and Dryden earned a little money by writing prefaces to Gifford's translations, 'advertisements to the reader' and the like, and then the *Heroick Stanzas*, his eulogy of Cromwell. At first he merely seems to have been attracted by the means of extra income, but it is significant that unlike many of his degree he made no attempt to secure a political post: he seems to have quietly decided that his future career lay with writing. He abandoned his office job and lodged with Sir Robert Howard with the relationship of poet and patron, writing further political eulogies for Charles II and the Earl of Clarendon.

In 1663 he took two further steps forward. He married Lady Elizabeth Howard, daughter of the Earl of Berkshire and Sir Robert's sister, thus cementing his connexions with the courtly set; the lady also had a dowry of £3,000 which was paid over the years in instalments, providing useful private income. And Howard, who owned a quarter interest in Killigrew's company, introduced him to the theatre and he began to write plays which were produced at Court, thanks to the interest of the Duchess of Cleveland, as well as in the public playhouse. In the first difficult years he had his private income, and the patronage of Howard and his father, to insulate him from the rigours of the printed-book market. By 1667 he had achieved success, in printed poetry with *Annus Mirabilis*, and on the stage with *Secret Love*, which much impressed the King. By the following year he had been made Poet Laureate in succession to Davenant, he had a contract to write three plays a year for the King's Company, in return for a twelfth share in the company, and, the mark of fashionable success, he kept an actress, Anne Reeves, as his mistress. As laureate he had a salary of £200 a year, with an annual butt of canary wine. As company playwright he earned between £300 and £400 a year. When a year or two later he was made Historiographer Royal as well, his income, including his own rents, but excluding his wife's means, reached nearly £700 a year. He was wealthy enough to lend money to the King, £500 a time. The way was smoothed for a M.A. degree. The Earl of Rochester became his special patron. The winds were set fair for this rising man of letters.

But there were difficulties: none as fierce as those which harrassed Defoe, but Court intrigues, including an occasion when he was beaten up by hired thugs in Rose Alley, that made him sometimes wish for the quieter life of a don, a schoolmaster or a parson (there were rumours at one time that he was to be made President of Magdalen College or Provost of Eton). Further, income from the theatre was irregular, especially when company funds were needed to rebuild a playhouse burned down in a fire, and an impecunious exchequer frequently allowed his pension to fall into arrears. His complaints to Rochester reveal that at times his feelings were bitter: 'A quarter's allowance is but the Jesuit's powder to my disease; the fit will return a fortnight hence. . . . I only think I merit not to starve. . . . 'Tis enough for one age to have neglected Mr. Cowley and starved Mr. Butler.'[1] But he had sufficiently varied sources of income to weather the various storms, and he was never driven to Defoe's shifts. He retained throughout the dignity and status of a courtly writer, however professional, a man with means and friends.

Dryden's response to adversity was to explore a new line of writing. As a prose pamphleteer he was not successful, but the King discovered his talent for satirical verse, and encouraged him to write both *Absalom and Achitophel*, which ran into seven London editions in two years, and *The Medall*. After difficulties with the King's Company, he switched to the Duke's. He changed publishers from Herringman to Jacob Tonson. He explored the possibilities of translation, contributing to Tonson's *Ovid's Epistles* (1680), and translating Maimbourg's *History of the League*, and later in the *Sylvae* excerpts from Horace, Lucretius, and Virgil. He contributed in 1684 to Tonson's *Miscellany Poems*. With *Albion and Albanius*, he experimented, unsuccessfully however, with opera. Dryden reveals in his adaptability an all-round professional attitude, comparable on equal terms with Defoe's or Johnson's.

[1] In a letter to the Earl, summer 1683, *Works*, ed., Sir W. Scott and G. Sainsbury (1882), XVIII, pp. 103 ff.

After the fall of James II, and the loss of the Court appointments, inevitable now he was a Catholic, Dryden intensified his endeavours in the theatre, although his best plays had been written and nothing else quite matched the success of *Marriage à la Mode*, and in print. He was helped by patrons like the Earl of Mulgrave, and Charles Sackville, the Earl of Dorset, who once left a £100 note under his breakfast plate. In his last years he was shrewdly commercial, writing epistles to plays by friends for the sake of a guinea or two, obliging a musical society with *Alexander's Feast* for £40, flattering a more prosperous kinsman with a poem which probably yielded £500, and in 1697 producing his grand edition of Virgil, complete with three separate dedications, in a handsome folio priced at five guineas or two guineas a copy and earning from this means alone £1,200. He exacted hard bargains from his publisher, Tonson, securing for the *Fables*, for instance, the fee of 250 guineas for 10,000 lines, to be made up to £300 when the book went into a second edition. Tonson grumbled at Dryden because he wanted fifty guineas for 1,446 lines of translation, when he had accepted from another publisher only forty guineas for 1,518 lines. And Dryden grumbled at Tonson on being paid in depreciated gold, demanding in future 'good silver'. There seems to have been an entirely satisfactory professional relationship between these two. But in all this commercial activity Dryden retained the attitude of the courtly neo-classical poet, who saw in literature something more valuable than a commodity, to be bought and sold by the thousand lines. Dryden's deepest ambition was for a Virgilian immortality. At times he lost heart: 'Why am I grown old in seeking so barren a reward as fame?' But his whole drive and devotion, throughout his life, no matter how commercial his relations with the theatre and the printed-book trade, came from a deep, indeed sometimes arrogant, conviction that literature was a great and noble social activity, conferring upon the nation an indispensable service and upon the writer a reputation which lasted far longer than the pounds, shillings and pence with which he kept himself and his family alive, in proper dignity, while he remained free to pursue his high profession. His good fortune was that he had money and influence behind him to help him hold to his ideal.

Matthew Prior was not so fortunate. At the point where Dryden felt safe enough to commit himself to a literary career,

Prior selected a political alternative, envying inadvisedly the life of the leisured amateur like Waller, and he lived to regret his choice:

> I ne'er was Master of the tuneful Trade,
> Or the small Genius which my Youth could boast,
> In Prose and Business lies extinct and lost.
> (*A Letter to Monsieur Boileau Despreaux*)

Prior's birth was humbler than Dryden's: his father was a joiner who had inherited a little property in town and married the daughter of a Staffordshire landed family, so that he claimed to be *generosus* and sported unscrupulously a coat of arms: Queen Anne and the Duchess of Marlborough, knowing this, never quite accepted Prior as a gentleman. After his father's death, he was enabled to complete his education at Westminster and Cambridge only through the patronage of the Earl of Dorset, who discovered him as a bar-boy reading Horace between the rounds. After his degree, Prior for a short time was a fellow of his college, lecturing in medicine, and he acted, too, as private tutor to the son of Lord Exeter. But his patron Dorset, and his school friend, Charles Montague, the future first Earl of Halifax, enabled him to follow a political career. He became secretary to the English Ambassador at The Hague, Gentleman of the King's Bedchamber, at a salary of £100 a year, chief secretary to the Lords Justices, undersecretary to the Earl of Jersey, commissioner of the Board of Trade and Plantations at £1,000 a year, and Member of Parliament. It was a brilliant start to a career in politics, but Prior had had to pay a price. It was through a Tory, Jersey, that Prior finally won a parliamentary seat. Prior himself had few political beliefs beyond a loyalty to William III, and when the King was prepared for the sake of stable government to sacrifice his old Whig ministers, he actually sat on the Tory examining commission and voted for impeachment of the statesmen responsible in Tory eyes for the unsuccessful Treaty of Ryswick: Somers, Orford, Portland, and his old friend Halifax. The Whigs never forgave Prior, and Halifax turned his attention to another protégé, Joseph Addison.

In time the Whigs had their opportunity for revenge. Prior was useful to the Government as a skilled negotiator: William III, for instance, had paid him a special award of 200 guineas for his work at Ryswick. The Tories in their turn came to negotiate a peace treaty with France, the treaty of Utrecht, equally unsuccessfully. When the Whigs returned to power in 1714 they promptly impeached the Tory Ministers responsible, and Prior—the treaty is sometimes called 'Matt's Peace' in tribute to his part in the making of it—found himself imprisoned for a year and debarred from political employment for the rest of his life. His old patrons, Dorset and Halifax, were now dead. His savings were minimal, because he had always lived from pay packet to pay packet and had spent extravagantly in keeping pace with the standard of living of his political and diplomatic friends. His writings alone saved him from destitution.

Prior had always claimed to be a 'poet only by accident'. Hence, he sought to emulate the leisured amateurs:

> Sedley, indeed, and Rochester might write
> For their own Credit, and their Friends Delight,
> Shewing how far they cou'd the rest outdo,
> As in their Fortunes, in their Writings too.
> (*A Satire upon the Poets*)

He wrote only occasional verse, smoking-room ballads, drawing-room riddles, and the like. But because he needed the extra income, he had never been averse to selling poems to a publisher, either to journals like *The Examiner*, or to professional editors like Charles Gildon or Jacob Tonson for publication in their Miscellanies (Tonson printed eighteen poems by Prior in his fifth miscellany in 1703–4). A few poems were published as special single-sheet folios. Others found their way into pirate print, Curll on one occasion publishing seventeen without authority. When the end came to his political career, Prior realized that his best hope of surviving with any dignity lay in capitalizing in an important way the poetic talent which he had previously put to remunerative work only desultorily. His solution was a subscription edition of his collected poems.

Subscription patronage was a system particularly appropriate to Augustan society. The essence of the notion was that a poet, or his agents, collected subscriptions in advance for a projected book, to be published on a worthy theme in a worthy manner. Half the money was asked for in advance, to provide an income for the poet while the book was written, and the other half was paid on receipt of the book. Alternatively, the poet came to an arrangement with a publisher whereby he was given a substantial number of free copies to sell to a list of subscribers while the publisher made his money in sales for the general public. 'Every person of quality', suggests Leslie Stephen, 'felt himself bound to promote such a laudable undertaking; the patron had been superseded by a kind of joint-stock body of collective patronage.'[1] Sometimes subscription tickets were touted in the parks and other public resorts: both Swift and Sterne were particularly successful in helping their friends this way. Sometimes the publisher would arrange to sell subscriptions on a commission basis to agents living in the provinces, or would insert advertisements in the newspapers. The whole system seems to have developed from the Elizabethan practice of multiple dedications. As early as 1552, John Foxe published his *Tables of Grammar* with eight privy councillors subscribing. Later, John Taylor, the Water Poet, published pamphlets by subscription, on one occasion securing as many as 1,600 patrons. As I have already suggested, John Milton was reaching forward to this kind of patronage, and the fourth, posthumous, edition of *Paradise Lost*, published in 1688 by Jacob Tonson, is one of the first genuine subscription editions recorded. From the list of over 500 subscribers to this work one can gauge the kind of support offered to the writer by the system: there were peers like Abergavenny, Cavendish, Dorset, Drumlanrick, Kent, Kingston, Lexington, Mordaunt, Middleton, Ossory, Pembroke, Somerset, and Worcester; writers like Atterbury, Dryden, Flatman, Southerne, Stillingfleet, and Waller; Somers, Howard, Betterton, Davenant's sons, L'Estrange, and other leading members of the professions; and all kinds of minor clergy and gentry. These lists repeat themselves throughout the eighteenth century. With this support it was often true that a writer could establish himself for life on the proceeds of one book.

The system was adopted by many authors, of prose as well as poetry. Dodsley's *Old Plays* was printed in 1746 for nearly 800 subscribers. There was a subscription collected edition of *The Tatler*, and Fielding produced his *Miscellanies* for subscribers. Fanny Burney earned £3,000 for a subscription *Camilla*. But the poets profited most. The Augustans liked their poetry printed

[1] *English Literature and Society in the Eighteenth Century* (1904), p. 87.

with a decorum proper to its high status. Most books of poetry, until about 1740, were folio in size, and for the rest of the century quarto was quite normal. It was only in the nineteenth century that poetry was reduced to its modern scale of octavo or duodecimo. Poetry was required in handsome books for handsome people, durably bound in a manner appropriate to the armorial bookplates affixed to the inner cover. Such expensive publications were naturally at home in the subscription market. Pope, as we shall see, made his fortune in this way. William Cowper's Homer sold at three guineas a time, with a subscription list of 700, earning the poet £1,000. Even an obscure and insignificant writer like William Mickle got nearly 600 subscribers for his *Lusiad* at a guinea each. Perhaps in time subscription print carried some kind of stigma: Johnson growled, 'He that asks subscriptions soon finds that he has enemies. All who do not encourage him defame him', and in 1751 Warburton, publishing a collected Pope, preened himself that 'the Editor hath not, for the sake of profit, suffered the Author's name to be made cheap by a *subscription*'. Doubtless, there were many snags: luxury bookselling has always appealed to those seeking to purchase culture with more money than taste. But for a poet with genteel aspirations, like Prior, subscription patronage offered a decorous half-way house between the amateurism he could not afford and the professionalism he abhorred.

Prior's subscription *Poems* attracted 1,445 subscribers, selling altogether 1,786 copies, in different sizes of volume, the largest attaining the regal dimensions of 36 in. by 12 in.; and the poet himself earned 4,000 guineas. The list of subscribers includes virtually all the nobility, even political enemies like Stanhope, together with writers like Pope, Swift, Congreve, and Steele, and 'hosts of Cambridge dons and Dorset vicars'. In the postscript Prior apologizes for his overt commercialism: 'I published my Poems formerly, as Monsieur Jourdain sold his Silk: He would not be thought a Tradesman; but ordered some Pieces to be measured out to his particular Friends. Now I give up my Shop, and dispose of all my Poetical Goods at once: I must therefore desire, that the Public would please to take them in the Gross; and that every Body would turn over what He does not like.' Prior's prose, his *Dialogues of the Dead* and *Essays upon Learning*, was printed only posthumously; but then, he died prematurely in 1721 without feeling the need to add to the income achieved by the poems. This was enough to enable him to buy Down Hall in Essex, reserve the services of the leading architect, James Gibbs, to redesign it on an Augustan scale, and to begin to lead the life of a self-made squire. Perhaps if he had dedicated himself, like Dryden, to a full-time literary career, his prosperity would have come much earlier in his life and his name may have mattered more than it does in the annals of English letters.

Prior still had some of the prejudice of an amateur to professional print. Alexander Pope had none: indeed, he followed and went beyond Dryden in making the printed-book market serve his own professional but entirely genteel ends. Denied a career in the professions or in politics because he was an invalid and a Catholic, from his earliest years as a child prodigy he devoted himself to the profession of letters. He needed to augment the small inherited income he received from property rents, and writing was the only route open to him: hence his lifelong single-mindedness. His poems, like Prior's, first appeared in magazines like *The Guardian* and *The Spectator*, or in miscellanies like Tonson's, which published his Pastorals in 1709, or Lintot's, which published *The Rape of the Lock* in 1712. His returns were at first only modest. Between 1712 and 1715 he earned £16. 2*s*. 6*d*. for his translation of the first book of Statius, only £7 for the *Rape*, £32. 5*s*. for *Windsor Forest*, £15 for the *Ode on St. Cecilia's Day*, £15 for a revision of the *Rape*, £32. 5*s*. for the *Temple of Fame*, and £10. 15*s*. for what he called a 'Key to the Lock'. He was cautious about appearing too commercial with Jacob Tonson: 'I shall be satisfied if I can lose my time agreeably this way, without losing my reputation. I can be content with a bare saving game, without being thought an *eminent hand*. . . . Jacob creates poets, as kings do knights, not for their honour, but for their money.' But he was shrewd, switching from Tonson to Lintot, sending the *Essay on Criticism* to an obscure bookseller called Lewis, in order to get the highest possible returns.

Pope's attitude at this time makes a remarkable contrast with that of his friend, Jonathan Swift. The Dean had little incentive to become a paid professional: as secretary to Sir William Temple he earned £20 a year, as a parson he earned first £100, then £200 a year (his income about the time he began to write in earnest), as Dean of St Patrick's he earned £700 a year. He lived the life of a parson-cum-squire in his little estate in Dublin, complete with its willow walk, grotto, and a stream straightened out, in the fashion of the day, to look like a canal. He was never short of funds, had modest needs, gave to other poets far more than he received himself, and left a fortune of £11,000 at his death. He was a voluminous writer, dedicated to the cause of writing, but above all he wanted to exercise power, to be heard, gain influence, be a social force. He despised scholars who took no part in the world's affairs. He wanted fame, not so much for himself but for his ideas, and for this reason he habitually wrote for print, for international editions if possible. He kept his own identity secret whenever possible, at least from the general public, by assuming pseudonyms like Isaac Bickerstaff, Martinus Scriblerus, and the Drapier, and only published one piece in his own name, and that an innocuous pamphlet on the 'correcting, ascertaining and improving of the English tongue'. And he persistently refused to accept any cash return for his literary work: on one occasion Harley sent him £50 for some political journalism, and Swift not only sent it back but demanded and exacted an apology. He must have been uniquely profitable for his publishers: some of his work sold extremely well—the pamphlet *Conduct of the Allies* (1711) reached seven editions in two months, 11,000 copies altogether, and *Gulliver's Travels* was such a success, running through its first impression in a week, that, uniquely in literary history, the booksellers increased the price of the book while it was actually on the stalls. But he would never have received a penny for any of his work if Pope had not intervened. It was Pope who arranged for the publication of *Gulliver's Travels*; the publisher 'knew not whence, or from whom, dropped at his house in the dark from a hackney coach'. And it was Pope who persuaded him to accept a fee of £200, although typically Swift had the publisher believe that the money was taken on behalf of Mr. Lemuel Gulliver 'for the use of poor seamen'.

There was none of this unprofessional nonsense from Pope. After 1715, he set about establishing his own financial security by a subscription translation of Homer, which came out in stages up to 1726. At six guineas a time, it was the success of the age.

Pope was given £200 for each of the six volumes of the *Iliad*, together with free copies for subscribers and for presentation; £100 for each of the volumes of the *Odyssey*, together with free copies. It is estimated by Johnson that he made over £5,320 on the *Iliad* (Lintot's own figures put the estimate nearer £4,000), and £4,500 on the *Odyssey*, although for this he had to pay small sums, of £100, to his two collaborators, William Browne and Elijah Fenton (and then he was sharp with Lintot for refusing Browne free copies for *his* subscribers!). Despite losses in the South Sea Bubble, Pope was established with an affluent income for life.

Thereafter, unrestrained by any kind of Renaissance humility about his own worth, Pope became the complete literary professional, publishing a collected edition of his verse in 1717, at the early age of 29, and another in 1735, collected editions of his literary correspondence in 1737 and of his other prose in 1741, editing Buckingham in 1723 and Shakespeare in 1725 (his return for this incidentally was about £217, although the edition sold only between 600 and 750 copies), a book of Italian translations in 1740, and launching with Swift in 1727 his own series of Miscellanies. His prosperity was such that it is little wonder that wild rumours circulated, such as that he was once offered £4,000 for a single couplet. Without becoming in any sense a hack, he managed to combine the roles of patron and poet, gentleman and literary professional, representing the nearest contemporary equivalent, in status and achievement, to the poets of Augustan Rome. He was the first writer who made more money than his publishers, and he was master of the trade. His handling of the pirate Curll is superb. Curll had published without authority some *Familiar Letters* by Pope in 1726; the poet therefore arranged for him to receive the manuscript of the official volume of letters, *Literary Correspondence for Thirty Years*, which Curll promptly printed, without observing that Pope had maliciously included letters by peers, the publication of which was illegal. Curll was duly arraigned at the Bar of the House of Lords, and Pope, exploiting the free publicity, immediately issued an authorized edition of the letters, less the offending items, and made good profits. This instance reveals how completely the tables have been turned since the days when the stationers held unchallenged dominion in the printed-book market. With Pope the writers themselves are established as equal beneficiaries of the success of their books. And this triumph was achieved without any loss of social status: Pope remained the literary squire, a man apart from the common herd of Grub Street.

At about the same time other writers were enjoying similar success, only the less spectacular compared with Pope's. Samuel Richardson's is the most extraordinary. Here was a prosperous and rather unadventurous London printer: freeman of the Stationers' Company and printer of the journals of the House of Commons. He had no intellectual standing, had read very little, and took no interest in political or religious controversies, holding that politics was contemptible and that it was best not to look too closely into religious matters in case enquiry raised doubts. Except for the Duke of Wharton, the aristocracy hardly noticed him as a person, and although he knew Johnson, Aaron Hill, and Edward Young, he had no friends in the profession of letters, except for 'bluestockings' like Hester Mulso and Sarah Fielding. Before he hit upon the novel, he had written nothing at all, and even after his three novels he had nothing to offer except one essay for the *Rambler*. When the first part of *Pamela* was printed, the two duodecimo volumes were priced at only 6*s*., the copyright valued at only thirty guineas, and Richardson withheld his name from print. Within a year six editions had been exhausted, and the next novel was priced at a guinea, to sell 3,000 sets in the first two and a half years. Soon this very ordinary tradesman was accorded greatness by such men of letters as Adam Smith, Blake, Voltaire, Baron Grimm, Argenson, Diderot, Prévost, Rousseau, Goldoni, and Goethe. Johnson called him 'the greatest genius that has shed its lustre on this path of literature'. Horace Walpole reported that he had stupefied the French. He stormed into every country in Europe, establishing the novel in several of them, inspiring countless imitators and consolidating Defoe's influence into a positive Anglomania. Richardson still sits uneasily in the company of more dedicated men of letters, but his career is proof enough that the English profession has at last arrived.

The profession offered a refuge for Henry Fielding when his career in the theatre had been brought to an end by Walpole's legislation. From his youth, like most gentlemen, he had dabbled in poetry, and when he was forced, by sheer lack of funds, to abandon his course at the University of Leyden, his first thought was to earn his living as a 'hackney-writer'. Nance Oldfield's introduction turned him for a while into the theatre and into the writing of twenty-eight plays. It was not until 1739 that he became a journalist, in the first instance editing the Opposition journal, *The Champion*. At a time when his work as a barrister had yet to yield fruits, and when he had lost the satisfactions of satirical drama, he adopted literature as a means to an income, and as an outlet for his ideas of social reform. In the years that followed he published many pamphlets, chiefly dealing with the amelioration of the poverty that in his view caused crime, and he edited other periodicals, including *The Jacobite's Journal* and the *Covent Garden Journal*. Soon he discovered that novels, besides providing a new medium of social satire, yielded a good income. His first attempt, *Joseph Andrews* (1742), sold at 6*s*. for two duodecimo volumes; it went through three London editions, a total impression of 6,500 copies, in thirteen months, and seven editions altogether in five years, reaching publication in Dublin, Amsterdam, and Paris, and earned Fielding precisely £183. 11*s*. The next year he ventured into subscription print with three volumes of Miscellanies, including some youthful verse, essays on good breeding and character, the satire *Journey from This World into the Next*, and a second novel, *Jonathan Wild*. Four hundred and twenty-seven subscribers—including the Prince of Wales, Walpole, Chesterfield, Marlborough, Fleetwood, Newcastle, Bedford, Lyttelton, Pitt, Garrick, and many lawyers—took a total of 556 sets, 214 at two guineas and 342 at one guinea.

Established now quite comfortably, Fielding did not publish a third novel until 1749. By then his political friends had secured for him the position of J.P. for Westminster and Middlesex, 'Bow Street Magistrate', with a salary of £400 a year. He also had sufficient energy, despite the heavy burdens he undertook in reorganizing the Metropolitan Police, to take an interest in a business jointly with his brother, Sir John. Thus, hard-working writer as he was, he had several means of income and he did not dedicate himself, like Pope, wholly to the literary profession. Nevertheless, most of his security came from books. *Tom Jones* was issued duodecimo at 16*s*. or 18*s*. a set of six volumes. The publisher bought the copyright for £600, but later was so pleased with the sales he gave the author another £100. The book ran into four London and one Dublin editions in the first year, and within eight years had been translated into French, Dutch, German, and Italian. Fielding seems to have made an ingenious attempt, apparently successful, to have the best of both worlds, to have subscription patronage and a best-seller simultaneously. Readings of the manuscript before publication were arranged with groups of friends, Lyttelton and Pitt among them, and as the earlier volumes came from the press they were circulated privately among special patrons. Lyttelton, for one, 'run up and down the town, and made visits and wrote letters' acting as a tout among the right people, with the effect that the book was the talk of the coffee-houses before it was even published. The fourth novel, *Amelia* (1751), was financially at least even more rewarding. When it appeared in four duodecimo volumes at 12*s.* the set, the whole of the first impression, of 1,000 copies, disappeared on the first day, while the second impression, of 3,000 copies, went nearly as quickly, and Fielding sold the copyright for 1,000 guineas.

Despite the many irons in his fire, Fielding treated the novel with professional respect. He saw the novel as the prose equivalent of epic verse, and used plenty of literary allusions, quoting in *Tom Jones*, for instance, from seventeen classical and fifty-two modern authors; he added as prologues and epilogues to sections of the novels learned essays about life and literature. Like the other Augustan novelists, he did not ignore the material rewards of writing, but he had no desire merely to exploit commercially a public taste. Like the others, he was a serious commentator on the social scene, highly valuing the imagination, teaching through the imagination; he insisted that his fiction was a form of truth; he wrote with his whole attention concentrated upon human nature. These Augustan novelists saw themselves as *entrepreneurs*, helping society to understand itself and to cure its sicknesses, believing as firmly as any doctor or lawyer that they had an essential part to play in securing the well-being of all. Pope in verse, and Fielding in prose, represent at its best the social purpose and achievement now possible with a literary profession established. Fielding had moved as far from the romance as Pope in his field had moved away from the leisure-hour ballad. Literature had now a high social function, and its servants were integrated in society, carrying a social status as high as any accorded the leisured amateurs, secure and independent as only the rewards of the printed-book trade could make them.

But in most of the instances I have quoted fortune had favoured the writer: he had private means, or alternative work bringing other emoluments, which enabled him to hold on to his literary integrity. Samuel Johnson's success in the profession was aided by no such advantages; his is a victory for sheer professional endeavour. This son of a bookseller left school at 16 and worked in bookshops, in Lichfield and Birmingham, for two years before he was assisted by friends through Oxford. He started life as a schoolmaster at Market Bosworth grammar school; he inherited only £20 from his father, and married a widow with the modest fortune of £800. When he had failed with a school of his own, he turned to writing as the only alternative open to him as a living. He had earned five guineas from the Birmingham publisher, Warren, for a translation of Le Grand's *A Voyage to Abyssinia*, enough to decide him to seek his fortune in London. At first he still kept one eye open for posts in schoolteaching, trying unsuccessfully, for instance, for a school in Leicestershire. But within a year or two he was totally committed to the literary profession, and there was no turning back. He was fortunate in discovering, in Edward Cave, the editor of the *Gentleman's Magazine*, a man who appreciated and helped on his youthful talents, accepting from him criticism and dissertations and employing him as a reporter of parliamentary debates (and since, in those days, journalists were not allowed in Parliament, Johnson's reports required much imaginative skill). He was fortunate, too, in finding a friendly publisher, Robert Dodsley, who was also interested in his work: their co-operation began in 1739 with the publication of the poem *London*, which earned Johnson ten guineas. Unlike the other professions, writers have never been able to exercise any measure of control over entrance into the profession: there have never been systems of examination or certification governing admission. The nearest equivalent has been the power exercised by publishers, and their readers, and the editors of the periodicals: if a writer's work appeared under the imprimatur of a reputable man, one who could be trusted for his literary taste as well as his business acumen, *ipso facto* he was a member of the profession. In the early years there were few publishers and editors who were more than commodity factors; Johnson was fortunate to fall in, so soon, with two men who stood out from their colleagues as genuine patrons of literature.

All kinds of literary work were acceptable to Johnson: short biographies, essays, prose satires, translations. In 1743–5 he compiled a catalogue of the Harleian Library, and became editor of the *Harleian Miscellany*. In 1744 he published his first important biography, the *Life of Richard Savage*. All this time he found steady employment on the *Gentleman's Magazine*. By 1749 he had made his first acquaintance with the theatre: his tragedy *Irene* ran at Drury Lane for nine nights, Johnson receiving the profits from three, amounting to £195. 17*s*.; he then sold the book of the play, which went into three editions, for another £100. In the same year his name appeared for the first time on a title-page, when his satire based on Juvenal, *The Vanity of Human Wishes*, earned him fifteen guineas. In 1750 he started his periodical, *The Rambler, ad maiorem dei gloriam* and 'to inculcate wisdom and piety': Johnson received two guineas for each essay published in the paper, which appeared twice a week price 2*d*. with a circulation of up to 500 copies. More profitable perhaps than the periodical were the collected editions of *Rambler* essays, ten of which appeared in his lifetime, excluding Scottish and Irish editions.

In the background in these years, from 1747, as in Pope's career, there was a special work, with the promise of more substantial returns: in Johnson's case not an epic translation but his great *Dictionary*, finally published in 1755. A group of publishers had joined together to make the project viable: among them Robert Dodsley, Andrew Millar, and the first Thomas Longman. These men, he often said, were his equivalent of Maecenas. He had hoped for substantial patronage, too, from Lord Chesterfield, to whom the work was dedicated, but his sole return seems to have been £10. Johnson's opinion of the old style of patronage is well known but worth repeating here:

> Such treatment I did not expect for I never had a Patron before. . . . Is not a Patron, my Lord, one who looks with unconcern on a man struggling for life in the water, and, when he has reached ground, encumbers him with help? The notice which you have been

> pleased to take of my labours, had it been early, had been kind; but it has been delayed till I am indifferent, and cannot enjoy it; till I am solitary, and cannot impart it; till I am known, and do not want it.[1]

These are bitter words, understandable after the death of his wife, and true in the sense that Johnson had struggled through to his present reputation (symbolized in 1755 by the granting of a M.A. degree) without assistance at all from aristocratic patrons of the traditional kind. But Johnson was still far from being prosperous.

The original plan for the *Dictionary* was that it should take him three years, for which he would receive the handsome return of £1,575. In fact, the project took him eight years for a return of £1,675, out of which he had to pay his copyists, a much less substantial reward. There is evidence that he was in financial difficulties: in early 1756 he was arrested for a debt of £5. 18*s*., and was relieved by Richardson; in 1759 he borrowed six guineas to send to his dying mother. He estimated himself he needed £30 a year as minimum subsistence expenses, before taking into account the cost of books, the expenses of club and other social life, and the other inevitable costs of a literary life. His total income, in his first twenty years in London, seems to have been less than £100 a year, and this was not enough. He collected fees from any opportunity which appeared: a guinea for a newspaper prospectus, £10 for correcting for the press a volume of poetry, as well as steady returns for essays and reviews, in Christopher Smart's *Universal Visiter*, in the *Literary Magazine*, and as 'The Idler' once a week in the *Universal Chronicle*. To pay for his mother's funeral expenses, he wrote his novel *Rasselas* in a week, earning £100. For all his industry and success, it was a hard life.

Real security did not come until he was 53 until in 1762 Lord Bute, the Prime Minister, granted him a State pension of £300 a year. Johnson had been too proud to seek a pension, just as he had been too proud to curry favour with aristocratic patrons. He regarded a pension as 'pay given to a state hireling for treason to his country',[2] and insisted that he was 'a man who has neither alliance nor interest'; as for favours, he 'has not merited them by

[1] Letter to Lord Chesterfield, February 1755.
[2] A definition in his *Dictionary!*

service, nor courted them by officiousness'. All the same, the State recognized the value of his single-minded devotion to the literary profession, in so many different fields, and there was an immediate relaxing of Johnson's industry. He spent more time in talk at the Turk's Head and with his friends. His subscription edition of Shakespeare, projected in 1757, was not completed until 1765. Charles Churchill indeed taunted him:

> He for subscribers baits his hook,
> And takes your cash; but where's the book?

Johnson gave two 'good reasons' for not printing his list of subscribers: he had lost their names and spent their money! His relaxed attitude as a pensioner only serves to emphasize the pressure which drove him to such prodigious efforts in the hard years, the years, as he once suggested himself, of 'toil, envy, want, the patron and the gaol'. Johnson himself avoided the worst perils of the struggling literary professional; but there can have been little safety margin.

Unlike Pope, Johnson does not seem to have been able to strike hard bargains with his publishers. The most important work of his last years, his *Lives of the Poets* (1779–81), involving fifty-two biographies, earned him only a total of 400 guineas. He asked for only 200, and we have Malone's testimony that he could very easily have secured 1,000 or 1,500. There are some contradictions to his character: though he wrote for money, being no blockhead, he seems to have had little concern to exploit his talents for the best possible return, to have been in a sense unable to look after himself. In much the same way, though he was a fierce Tory with entirely decided views about politics, apart from an occasional pamphlet, he stood aside from all the political controversies and opportunities of his age. Johnson seems to have dedicated himself exclusively to a literary ideal, difficult though it must have been to express that ideal in a commercial world where he had to write for his bread and butter. In harder circumstances than Dryden or Pope, he achieves the same dignity and status. It might be rash to seek to identify, in a few words, the ideal, the driving force, behind his life-work: in different places in his work one can find Johnson expressing almost every conceivable literary ambition. He thought highly, like every Augustan, of fame and immortality: 'Not only the writer of books, but the commander of armies, and the deliverer of nations, will easily outlive all noisy and popular reputation.' It is significant to find him thus coupling writers with the commanders of armies and deliverers of nations, indicative of the high place he accorded literature in his scale of values. But perhaps a more modest statement is more revealing and more central: 'The only end of writing is to enable the reader better to enjoy life or better to endure it.'[1] His own writing seems to have enabled Johnson better to enjoy life, or better to endure it. He needed the imaginative outlet. And it is fitting that this master of all the Augustan prose arts—biographer, journalist, translator, editor, dictionary-maker, novelist, satirist, essayist, letter-writer—should achieve his ambition in this age when prose gave the profession of letters the opportunity to establish itself. He was a good poet himself, and not unacquainted with the theatre, but he believed that, 'except for the music of poetry, every other power by which the understanding is enlightened, or the imagination enchanted, may be exercised in prose'.[2]

The literary profession, with every appropriateness, establishes itself finally, after Dryden and Pope, in the career of Samuel Johnson. Here at last security is achieved without loss of independence, high status without the stigma of commercialism, dignity without the slackening of full-time industry and devotion. Like any leisured amateur, Johnson spent his life doing what he wanted to do; like the true professional he was, he made enough money to be true to himself.

[1] *Works*, ed. Hawkins (1787), X. 245.
[2] *Rambler*, p. 86.

# VIII

## The Romantic Dilemma

*One impulse from a vernal wood*
*May teach you more of man,*
*Of moral evil and of good,*
*Than all the sages can.*

WORDSWORTH, 1798

THE literary profession in the eighteenth century seems to possess all the characteristics one expects of a true profession. Writers devoted their lives to literature, provided a skilled service which was highly valued, and achieved in different ways reasonable measures of security and independence with adequate rewards, now almost wholly in cash terms, and a commensurate social status. The whole fabric of a profession had been established: a sound book market, a wide variety of periodicals and magazines, publishers and editors who served as responsible entrepreneurs, a system of copyright, a proper scale of rewards, and a public organized in an appropriate system of communication. Literature had arrived as a 'fourth estate'. And yet the balance was precarious: a profession is inevitably valued for and by its own standards, standards alone differentiate the true practitioner from the quack, and the literary profession has always had to keep under control its own particular, and insidious, form of quackery. At the beginning of this history I insisted that literature was an art intimately connected in its very nature with the things of the imagination and the spirit which make men human, that the audience's prime motive is curiosity and the profession's prime service enlightenment, and that good literature occurs where men are enlightened by writing. The temptation which writers have most had to overcome, the temptation which most undermines their standards, has been the ease with which the public may be served with matter which does not nourish their imaginative curiosity. All too readily, 'what the public wants', frequently a very different thing from what the public needs, may be defined in a selling formula which yields handsome returns to the publishers, who in their nature are salesmen rather than intermediaries for writers, and to authors who are willing to value rewards above standards. The decline of drama in the eighteenth century may be attributed, directly, to the growth of an entertainment industry which thought of plays, exclusively, as a commodity to be sold. The novel was equally vulnerable: instead of providing *what's new*, the novelist may readily entertain by catering for a predictable response, by serving up, in fact, what is old and familiar in a superficial guise of novelty. The poem, too, is not invulnerable: its music and imagery are too apt for exploitation by those who have learned the techniques of manipulation.

I am suggesting that unless a writer genuinely and devotedly concerns himself with expressing what he uniquely knows about human nature, with applying himself to an honestly imaginative enquiry about the nature of man, then he will cross the line between good literature and bad, between professional service and quackery. All kinds of compromises and adjustments are possible and indeed necessary: the writer has to deal with, and live in, a real and not an ideal social context. But there should be no doubt about his fundamental standards and integrity. The dividing line between Pope and Johnson, on the one hand, and Grub Street on the other, is not a social distinction, one of degree and class: it is a difference which only becomes clear when one considers the quality of what each side has to say about human nature. An honest observer may live in a garret, while the literary prostitute (the term is exact and far from melodramatic) may live in a palace. One can only tell the difference between the true professional and the fake, in all his manifold varieties, by the quality of the work done. To maintain standards, a writer had to fight temptations in himself, in particular the desire to please and entertain by the exploitation of his skill and technique, and temptations from his public, whenever his readers' claim to know what they wanted differed from his knowledge of what he and they needed to undertake together. Scylla and Charybdis indeed: a little too far one way and the writer was drawn into a whirlpool of false standards; a little too far the other and he found himself rejected by the public and wrecked on a particularly barren rock where he could talk only to himself. In the early and middle eighteenth century a considerable number of writers achieved balance and stability; but in these times the social context of literature was particularly encouraging and favourable. A time was rapidly approaching when the social context had many features which can only be called anti-literary; as we shall see, literary professionals had to face their own kind of Romantic dilemma. The temptations in store may be best anticipated by noting them, latent, potential and as yet undeveloped, in the careers of four latter-day Augustans, two novelists and two poets.

In the novels of Sterne and Smollett there is implicit, besides so much that is good, an overriding satisfaction in playing up to the part of a public entertainer. In itself, this is a venial vice perhaps; but, emphasized to the exclusion of the proper consideration of other factors, this is a weakness which, as time goes on, undermines much of the integrity of the literary professionals who concentrate upon novels. Like his predecessors, Sterne came upon the novel almost by accident. By the time he was forty he had established himself comfortably enough in his chosen profession of the Church. He was a country rector and a prebendary of York Minster, he had made a prudent marriage with a lady who had a private income, and he was worth rather more than £200 a year. Like so many of his colleagues, he had the tastes of a squire as much as a parson; indeed, he came from a landed family with roots in Suffolk, Nottinghamshire, and Yorkshire, and his grandfather had been a squire in the Halifax district. He rebuilt his parsonage, planted orchards and elms, built an arbour and designed walks in the garden. At one time, somewhat misguidedly, he tried to become a farmer as well, adding the thrill of the market to his other parish enthusiasms: he bought seven cows and some geese, and planted barley and oats, but neither he nor his wife had any business acumen and the venture failed. But, like the true squire, he bought his daughter a pony and trap, and entertained the villagers with his bounty, on one occasion roasting a whole ox at a village feast. He was friendly with landed gentlemen, in particular with Squire Croft of Stillington Hall, and with John Hall-Stevenson, whose 'Crazy Castle' at Skelton housed a collection of Rabelais.

Like most of the gentry, his experience of the arts had been that of a dilettante, painting an occasional picture and writing an occasional poem. He appeared to be proceeding placidly along the road of an ecclesiastical career; perhaps he was not good enough to emulate his great-grandfather, who had become Archbishop of York, but a bishopric was not beyond him. Unfortunately, his road became blocked after he had become involved, against his better judgment, in the game of party politics he himself abhorred, but which his relatives played. In disgust he wrote for a friend, Dean Fountaine, an allegorical pamphlet, of a bitter kind, on the subject of pluralities. The intention had been to seek print locally for this *Political Romance*, but the pamphlet was so good that the Dean advised caution, timid of inflaming a war of words. Nothing therefore came of it; but through this means Sterne discovered that he enjoyed writing very much, that he was a good writer, and that in this new pastime he might be able to compensate himself for his lack of preferment. 'I wrote not to be fed, but to be famous,' he once said. And he began to write *Tristram Shandy*.

He intended at first only a private audience. No publisher would accept the first two volumes as a commercial proposition, and with the aid of a loan of £100, Sterne arranged for private printing at York in 1759. Only 200 copies were printed, but a few found their way to London, and one was sent to David Garrick through the agency of a friend. Garrick was so impressed by the book that he spread the news among his friends, and virtually single-handed created a demand among the fashionable set. Robert Dodsley, taking the new writer under his wing, covenanted for a new edition, paying Sterne £250 for it, together with £300, increased later to £500, for the next two volumes. All told, four editions appeared in a year. The rest of the novel followed in instalments, a kind of serial story that never seems to have palled, the impressions increasing to 5,000 a time. Only Sterne's eventual death cut short the stream of instalments, with Tristram still only 5 years old.

Sterne won his fame: he was lionized by the nobility, invited to Windsor, had frontispieces drawn by Hogarth, had his portrait painted by Reynolds, and his bust sculptured by Nollekens. What sold the book was the humour, a *risqué* suggestiveness, a skating about the thin ice of obscenity. Some readers, among them Johnson, Goldsmith, and Smollett, condemned in angry pamphlets the antics of this most unclerical clergyman, but Sterne, unperturbed, found satisfaction in the role of 'Yorick, the court jester'. He profited from his popularity by publishing in 1760 a subscription edition, with 600 subscribers, of the *Sermons of Mr. Yorick.* Later, in 1768, he published more *Sermons*, with 693 subscribers paying 5*s.* each, and in 1768, a third subscription edition with 300 subscribers, *A Sentimental Journey*, an account of his travels in France and Italy. Sterne loved contemplating his list of subscribers: 'a prancing list', he called it, '*de toute la noblesse*'. From his literary work came such prosperity that he was able to live abroad, from 1762, looking after sickly lungs and, except for one sermon delivered before the British Ambassador in Paris, taking no further interest in ecclesiastical duties.

Like his predecessors, and other 'sentimentalists', Sterne was critical of society, and had reformist ideas about the commercialism that had produced the slave trade, about cruelty to children and animals, and about other social evils like quack medicine. It was this, as much as his unique humour, that endeared him to Voltaire, Diderot, Goethe, and Heine, who once said that he was 'the born equal of William Shakespeare'. And his humour for all its salaciousness was based upon incongruities of human nature apparent to a sensitive and charitable man, and was therefore in keeping with his literary aim of helping his readers 'love the world and our fellow creatures better than we do'. Sterne would doubtless have gone on writing, even in a less successful social context, out of the sheer joy of expressing himself and what he understood about human nature; and it is this devotion which makes him, relatively late in life, a true professional of letters. But it must be admitted that he relished playing the jester for its own sake, and unlike Swift with the primary motive of drawing attention to his ideas. He delighted in the role of public entertainer, in the salon if not in the street, and there are times when he appears to be playing to the gallery, full of self-esteem, doing what was expected of him (a vice particularly open to the author of a serial story) rather than taking his audience through fresh imaginative experience. The very surrealism of the novel—its typographical oddities, irregular pagination, unorthodox punctuation and syntax, and general disjointedness—was itself a sophistication, indeed a delightful gimmick, which Sterne played with and exploited.

If the entertainer waylays the novelist in Sterne, it sometimes swamps the novelist in Smollett. This son of a Scottish landed family had all the extravagant instincts of the would-be squire, and needed all the money he could earn from writing, together with the income his wife derived from West Indian investments and inheritances, to support a high standard of living. He estimated that, altogether, with clothes of proper quality, good furniture, servants and hospitality, it cost him about £800 a year to live at Monmouth House in Chelsea. He had his portrait painted five times, once by Gainsborough, was a subscriber to many subscription editions, was a contributor, nearly always unostentatiously, to many charities, and a citizen of high standing for whom the bells of Old Chelsea Church were rung on several occasions. Yet from the beginning he had had no private means; he made his own way in the world. Until he was 32 his ambitions lay in a medical career: he was a surgeon at different addresses in Downing Street, May Fair, Beaufort Street, and Chelsea. He reviewed medical works and wrote one learned paper. But he was too quick-tempered and forthright for this profession; as contemporaries reveal, 'he could never render himself agreeable to the ladies', and 'he could never stoop to impose on credulity nor humour caprice'.[1] In the end, he preferred to change to writing. Like most young men of his degree, he had toyed with poetry and drama from his youth, and by his middle twenties had appeared in print as the author of some not very distinguished satire modelled on Pope. His youthful neoclassical play, *The Regicide*, he hawked about for years without success, very much like Melopoyn in *Roderick Random*, seeking to interest Chesterfield, Garrick, Rich, Quin and others. He wrote an *Alceste*, a mixture of opera, tragedy and masque, to Handel's music, and was paid £300 for it, but it was never

[1] John Moore, the first editor, in his memoir (1772).

staged. He met a similar failure with a comedy, *The Absent Man*; the truth is that, like so many literary gentlemen of the period, he had no sense of theatre, and what he had to say in drama was no longer a commercial proposition. He satisfied himself by publishing *The Regicide* in 1749 in a subscription edition. It was not until 1757 that he had a play staged at Drury Lane (by which time he was 38), and then only because he lowered his standards to those of the theatre in a farce entitled *The Reprisal, or the Tars of Old England*. Smollett was prepared to compromise principles for the sake of his career.

His career is very like Johnson's in other respects. From 1748 onwards he engaged in translations. One of the first was an anonymous translation of Le Sage's *Gil Blas*, 3,000 copies issued in four volumes with thirty-three cuts, new letterpress and superfine paper. After more Le Sage and some Voltaire, he issued his *Don Quixote* in 1755, a subscription edition, two quarto volumes at two guineas. He became joint editor of a complete edition of Voltaire in thirty-five volumes. He wrote book reviews for the *Monthly Review*, and then in 1756 launched his own periodical, *The Critical Review, or the Progress or Annals of Literature and the Liberal Arts*, prepared, so it was said, by a 'Society of Gentlemen' (in actual fact, a professor, a doctor, a printer and himself), aimed specially at 'the gentlemen of the two Universities'. He also launched in 1760 a sixpenny monthly, *The British Magazine, or Monthly Repository for Gentlemen and Ladies*. He was concerned in a seven-volume anthology of travel essays, for which he contracted to write 100 sheets in fifteen months at one and a half guineas a sheet. He prepared for the press a travel book by Alexander Drummond, earning 100 guineas. He edited a collection of scientific essays. He contributed to *A Compendium of Voyages*, at one and a half guineas a sheet, and to the *Universal History*. He was concerned in a *Complete History of England*, published between 1755 and 1758, and accomplished the Herculean task of writing 2,600 quarto pages in fourteen months for £2,000. His industry is comparable with Defoe's and Johnson's.

Smollett saw himself as the potential leader of a new *Academy of Belles Lettres*. He called Johnson the 'Grand Cham of Literature', and clearly aspired to succeed him. But it must be said that behind this Augustan, squirely front, there was also an astute business mind, exploring all the possibilities of promoting greater and still greater book sales. The *History*, for instance, was issued in later editions in a cheaper octavo form, and then, more startlingly, in sixpenny weekly numbers. Further, it was advertised by methods well in advance of the age. A packet of advertisements was sent to every parish clerk in the kingdom, with half a crown included and the request that they be placed in the pews of the church. This project must have cost something like £1,250, excluding the cost of postage, and represents a form of salesmanship at which even the modern promoters of detergents might raise an eyebrow. The work made a profit of £10,000, the largest ever made up to this time on any one book. It was in the same spirit that Smollett turned to the novel, as a means to an income rather than as a means of expressing himself about society. He was a true literary professional in that he found no vocation so satisfactory as that of putting pen to paper; nothing else kept him at peace within himself. But the salesman at times pushes to one side the artist.

*Roderick Random* was probably the first novel ever written with the deliberate intention of giving the public what it wanted. Superficially, it is a 'satire upon mankind', but in fact it is the prose equivalent of plays like *The London Merchant*, a story designed to appeal directly to the prejudices of the audience. Roderick is the poor boy who makes good. He is inflicted with tribulation after tribulation in breathless succession—no sooner is one disaster resolved than he is plunged into the next. The dice are loaded against him even more outrageously than they are loaded against Oliver Twist, but after much adversity there is a happy ending, the hero vindicated and triumphant. Only Smollett's personal commitment of sympathy to the underdog, and a strong streak of autobiography, save the novel from being entirely a commercial contrivance. The book sold 6,500 copies in two years, and the hero's name became a household word, the name adopted for a contemporary spy, a racehorse, a jestbook and a comic opera. Smollett's next three novels were also experiments in catering for different aspects of public taste: a political satire, a Gothic extravaganza, and an imitation of Cervantes. The last of them, *Sir Lancelot Greaves* (1760–1), was first printed in instalments in the *British Magazine*, the first novel ever to be so serialized, Smollett's business instincts once more pioneering a formula to become familiar in the nineteenth century. Perhaps Smollett's only genuine novel was his last. *Humphrey Clinker* (1771), though written in a time of sickness, is free from the exhibitionism of the earlier books: it is his most generous and compassionate work. Half the book is fact rather than fiction, providing social, political and topographical information. The novel was just as successful, commercially, as its predecessors: it was widely reprinted, and yielded Smollett £210 on the sale of the copyright.

For all his success, Smollett seems to have been fundamentally a man with a permanent sense of grievance. He was too quick-tempered, too hypercritical, to win the affection and esteem enjoyed by his predecessors. His outspoken criticism of the French and the Italians made him the first major British writer since Defoe to be unpopular on the Continent. He made too many enemies in his own country: indeed, his biting tongue, and readiness to support words with blows, had put him in prison more than once. Angry young man, bitter old man, everything was often reduced for him to terms of personal gain and loss. One moment he was playing, extravagantly and irresponsibly, to the gallery; the next, he was slapping down everyone, and everything, in sight, so that his public tired of his destructive misanthropy. He is a strange mixture altogether. For some reason he was temperamentally unable to find satisfaction in the balances and compromises of the times; for some reason his literary work becomes an exhibition of temperamental individualism and self-centredness. He is the literary equivalent of the actor-manager of his day, seeing in his art, too exclusively, the exploitation of personality. He was naturally full of idiosyncrasies, but one feels that he was determined to play the role of a public eccentric. In short, Smollett in one way, like Sterne in another, provides a first example of an aberration which waylaid the literary profession in later years: a 'personality cult' interferes with his true professional integrity.

Much the same aberration affected some of the poets. There is no doubt that Thomas Gray, for instance, was a highly talented poet: his *Elegy in a Country Churchyard* is probably the most widely read poem in the English language, and his *Impromptu on Lord Holland's Seat* is in many opinions the finest short satirical poem in this age of great satire. But he wrote only a few dozen poems all told. His attitude puzzled and infuriated Johnson: 'He had a notion not very peculiar, that he could not write but at certain times or in happy moments; a fantastic foppery, to which my kindness for a man of learning and virtue wishes him to have been superior.'[1] Instead of thriving as a writer, Gray deliberately cultivated an attitude of melancholy detachment from the world, and this attitude, which became a familiar, even an expected, characteristic of writers in the nineteenth century, requires serious explanation.

In his youth Gray had grand ambitions. His father was comfortably off as a scrivener, and there was enough money in the family to send him to Eton and to Cambridge; he did the fashionable Grand Tour of Europe, and then entered the Inner Temple to read for the law. He was at home in high society, making friends of Richard West, son of the Lord Chancellor of Ireland, and Horace Walpole, son of the Prime Minister. He seemed set for an important political career. Then in the early 1740's Gray's life seems to have tumbled to pieces. His father died in 1741, leaving very little money and none for the kind of social life Gray had been living. Immediately afterwards, Gray quarrelled with young Walpole, and the estrangement covered the critical years to 1745. In 1742 West suddenly died. Gray seems to have been unable to ride these adversities: quite suddenly he seems to have decided to retreat from the world and to devote his life to lecturing in Cambridge and to his mother at Stoke Poges. He became in 1766 Professor of Modern History, and specialized as well in the Germanic languages, particularly Icelandic and Norse. Nothing seems to have budged him from his self-imposed hermitage. At one time he had the chance of marrying a rich heiress, Henrietta Speed, but he never really made the effort, and was only slightly piqued to discover that she ultimately married a Sardinian baron ten years younger than herself. Indeed, he was rather consoled to discover in 1766 that she had become 'a prodigious fine lady, and a Catholick, and fatter than she was: she had a cage of foreign birds and a piping bullfinch at her elbow, two little dogs on a cushion in her lap, a cockatoo on her shoulder, and a suspicion of rouge on her cheeks'. Gray is not the first Augustan poet to have the instincts of the perpetual

[1] *Life of Gray*, G. B. Hill, ed., *Lives of the English Poets* (Oxford, 1905), III 433.

bachelor; but his refusal to make a prudent marriage, when the opportunity was presented, puts him apart from many of his colleagues.

It was the same with his poetry. Gray had good connexions: aristocratic patrons like the Duke of Chandos and Lady Cobham, a good publisher in Robert Dodsley, and a friend in Horace Walpole, who was willing to act as entrepreneur and anxious to help him into the profession. He made nothing of his opportunities and refused the Laureateship when it was offered him, after Cibber, in 1757. Once or twice he wrote by command, for instance the *Ode to Music*, for the inauguration of a Cambridge Chancellor, but badly. With Dodsley he published the *Ode on Eton College* (1747), in an eight-page folio priced at *6d.*, *Six Poems* (1753), and *The Bard* and the *Progress of Poetry* (1757), earning on this last occasion forty guineas. But his publications were scanty and infrequent, and he refused to take a penny for his greatest success, the *Elegy*. This poem had been intended only for private circulation in manuscript and Gray had refused all Walpole's pleas for publication. In the end, Gray only consented to have Dodsley publish it anonymously, to anticipate by one day unauthorized publication in the *Magazine of Magazines*. The poem ran into four authorized editions in two months, and then quickly into another seven. Dodsley is reported to have made a profit of nearly £1,000 from Gray's poetry, chiefly from the 1768 collected edition and the *Elegy*. But the poet insisted, with an almost Elizabethan compunction, on profiting as little as possible.

In Gray, and in other contemporaries like William Collins, there are the beginnings of a new attitude towards poetry, an attitude to be made familiar by the Romantics. He was not interested in poetry which merely flattered the prejudices of the squirearchy. He accepted the high claims made for poetry by neo-classical critics, and went beyond them to the belief that a poet had a special kind of inspiration and insight, was a seer rather than a social commentator, writing in a poetic diction of his own rather than the language of the day. As far as the literary profession is concerned, this claim became in a real sense *anti-literary*, and hence Johnson's disgust. When the poet accepted the status and esteem won for the profession by Dryden and Pope, it was hard to see how he could find the necessary security and independence through his writing, if he also held, as Gray did, to statements like this: 'I by no means pretend to inspiration, but yet I affirm, that the faculty in question is by no means voluntary. It is the result (I suppose) of a certain disposition of mind, which does not depend on oneself, and which I have not felt this long time.'[1]

Collins, too, seems to have been disheartened and turned away from the profession. He started well: straight from Winchester and Oxford, he became a professional poet, selling a thousand copies of the subscription edition of his *Odes* in 1746. He concerned himself, too, with prose: a history, notes for the *Biographia Britannica*, a translation of Aristotle's *Poetics*, and so on. But gradually the flame petered out. Thanks to successive strokes of good fortune like a patrimony, the sale of his father's house, and an inheritance, he was never forced to earn his living from print. There were also difficulties with his health: he finally went mad and died at the early age of 39. He seems to have had plenty of good intentions, but never the aptitude or the devotedness to play his proper and serious role in the community. Johnson suspected he made use of poetry as a means of escape from life: he seemed to want to write of fairies and genii, 'of giants and monsters; he delighted to rove through the meanders of inchantment, to gaze on the magnificence of golden palaces, to repose by the water-falls of Elysian gardens'. This ambition must have been ill at ease in an age which believed, as Imlac remarks in Johnson's *Rasselas*, that 'the business of the poet is to examine, not the individual, but the species; to remark general properties and large appearances; he does not number the strokes of the tulip, or describe the different shades in the verdure of the forest'.[2] An age was soon to come in which poets *would* number the strokes of the tulips, but not yet. In the meantime, Collins appears lost and out of his element.

After the perfection of Pope, poetry was bound to have its special problems. Johnson recognizes this in his eulogy: 'New sentiments and new images others may produce; but to attempt any further improvement of versification will be dangerous. Art and diligence have now done their best, and what will be added will be the effect of tedious toil and needless curiosity.'[3] What is

[1] Letter to Wharton, June 1758, *Correspondence* (1935), II. 571.

[2] *Rasselas*, X, *Works*, ed. Hawkins, XI. 31.

[3] *Life of Pope*, ed. Hill, III. 251.

striking about the careers of Gray and Collins is an anti-literariness of attitude, an anti-professionalism which contrasts sharply with the dedication of Dryden and Pope, Defoe and Johnson. The same malaise can be found in the career of relatively successful literary professionals of the same time like Oliver Goldsmith. This writer entered the profession the hard way, as a publisher's reader, reviewer and hack, before attracting public attention with his *Enquiry into the Polite State of Learning in Europe* (1759). He then started a short-lived periodical, *The Bee,* and wrote essays for other periodicals, before making his reputation with the novel, *Vicar of Wakefield,* in 1766 (although it earned him only sixty guineas). Thereafter he entered a short period of prosperity, earning at best £2,000 in one year, but being impractical and improvident he was in debt to the scale of £2,000 at his death. Yet for all his success, Goldsmith's heart was not in professional writing: he disliked successful professionals like Charles Churchill, and was always trying to disengage himself. Goldsmith, who 'wrote like an angel but talked like poor Poll',[1] was another misfit in the Augustan world of letters and conversation. He wrote two good plays for the theatre, but found that the playhouse afforded no true outlet; he tried to interest the *élite* in subscription pieces of poetry, but in the end was forced to sell direct to a publisher, *The Deserted Village* for a hundred guineas and the *Traveller* for twenty guineas; for some reason he never followed up his successful novel with any other work in the same medium, and equally his successful biography, the *Life of Richard Nash of Bath,* had no successors. Goldsmith, *mutatis mutandis,* displays the bitter melancholy, disgruntledness and detachment of Smollett, Gray, and Collins.

One insistent claim made by the Romantics was that writers, especially poets, had a special vision of truth which ought not to be socially corrupted or circumscribed: they should be free to write as their inspiration took them; it was enough for society to protect their special gifts and profit from their prophecies and insight. The Romantic dilemma, as far as the literary profession was concerned, was how to adapt the social context of literature to make room for this new claim. The dilemma became sharper when the reading public demanded an immediate and practical

[1] G. B. Hill, ed., *Boswell's Life of Johnson* (Oxford, 1887), II. 235–6.

use for writers' dreams and visions, not as a means to truth and an understanding of life, but as a kind of anodyne, a means of escape from life. Wide schisms were to open between what the public expected of literature and what the writers wanted to do: after an age of balance, an age of most extraordinary unbalance, producing in extreme instances literary schizophrenia. Writers who were unable to attain the recognition and freedom they desired were apt to take refuge as 'unacknowledged legislators' in ivory castles of their own making, or to explode into various kinds of anti-social and eccentric activity.

The major catalyst of change was the gradual transformation of society known as the Industrial Revolution. As industrialization proceeded, the writers became more strident in their claims of special vision and the readers more strident in their demands for an anodyne. This is not the place to discuss the general social history of the times, the vastly increasing population, the growth of the large cities, the development of new towns particularly in the north, the transition from craftsmen to machine-tenders, the failure of humane amenities to keep pace with the growing population in the towns, the setbacks to education and literacy, the poverty, hardship and brutality of the age. One consequence of industrialization was that, socially, the nation took a massive step backwards in the early nineteenth century from the relative humanitarianism of Augustan times. Reform measures, of education, health, labour and welfare, inevitably lagged behind the march of industry. In the industrial towns the first choral society did not appear until Birmingham launched one in 1841, the first public park was opened in Manchester in 1846, and the first public libraries, as distinct from the more expensive circulating libraries, did not appear until the 1850's.

This is not to belittle the work of the educational reformers in the late eighteenth and early nineteenth centuries, the efforts, for instance, of Raikes and his friends in the Society for Promoting Sunday Schools, from 1785, or of the Religious Tract Society from 1799, and events like the opening of 'evening schools for those who cannot attend in the daytime'.[1] It was just a plain fact that industrialization proceeded at a far faster pace than the reformers could conceivably maintain. The situation could only be properly met by massive and revolutionary measures of

[1] Sarah Trimmer, 1801, quoted in J. W. Adamson, *History of Education*, p. 231.

compulsory education for all, and these were delayed until the last decades of the nineteenth century. In the meantime, children were to be found working in mills for sixteen hours at a stretch, with only hour or half-hour meal breaks; in Bristol in 1830, 2,500 out of 6,000 children had no schools at all; in Liverpool in 1830 one in five labouring families lived in cellars, and in the Ancoats district of Manchester only four out of every ten children lived to be 5 years old.

The printed-book market reflected the times. On the one hand, it continued to expand. Between 1792 and 1802 the yearly average of new books reached 372, nearly four times its Augustan norm. In the next twenty-five years the figure increased to 580. And there were indications of a widening public: publishers like Harrison, Bell and Cooke producing penny chapbooks, cheap editions and reprints, and novels in sixpenny weekly numbers with sales of 10,000 and more. But the chief audience remained an *élite*, if a larger one. First editions tended if anything to be priced even more highly, *Jane Eyre*, as a typical instance, being published in three volumes at one and a half guineas. Popular digests like *Half-Hours with the Best Authors* cost *5s.*, and weekly periodicals like *The Spectator* 1*s.* The best reviews, like the *Quarterly* or the *Edinburgh Review*, which Sir Walter Scott declared 'no genteel family could afford to be without', cost 6*s.* a copy. In the theatres the cheapest seat in London was 1*s.* Thanks to stamp and advertisement duties, newspapers were increasingly expensive: after 1855 new legislation made the penny daily a practical possibility, but before then the *Times* cost 7*d.* and the *Daily News* 2½*d.* Such prices were clearly beyond the means of the vast majority of the population. But the expansion of the trade, towards the ultimate goal of a mass market, was steady and massive, and with it writers felt the sharp edge of the romantic dilemma.

Briefly the problem might be posed thus. In the air, like so many other radical notions in this age of the French Revolution, was the hope that very soon writers might be able to write directly for the masses. Disturbed and indeed anguished by social developments, by the impoverishment and brutalization of life for working men and women, most writers wanted to comfort the masses: there was hardly a single writer in the entire nineteenth century who was not in some sense a radical and a rebel.

Most writers also felt that the things they wanted to do would be better appreciated by the wider audience. But, in fact, the real audience, the people who provided a livelihood in the printed-book market, consisted of a comfortably-off minority; there was a new collective patronage exercised by the urban industrial plutocracy and its satellites, an educated *élite* enlarged as the result of the accession of all those whose standard of living had been enhanced by industrial wealth.

The new plutocracy made its mark in culture. On the one hand, the new patrons, like all men with roots in commerce, insisted, more keenly than ever before, that art should be useful and didactic: an emphasis which encouraged, to give only one instance, portrait-painters to become more and more 'photographic', even more so when, ultimately, the camera had been invented. On the other hand, they liked a good deal of sentimental ornament to express their opulence and to disguise their utilitarianism. They liked in architecture, for instance, what Professor Pevsner has described, *pace* Betjeman, as 'a blend of coarse opulence and old-maidenly fussiness, bloated bulgings, sentimental quirks, a marked tendency to top heaviness, and an epidemic concealment of straight lines under pot-bellied curves'. In music they encouraged a movement simultaneously towards sweet sentimentality and programme didacticism, towards melodies that also told stories. In literature there was constant pressure upon writers for works of consolation and escape, books which would take industrial audiences away from the drab life of routine into dreams of romance and peril. And, as might have been expected, when the poorer sections of society were at last able to express a preference and take an interest in art, they developed similar tastes. It is worth remembering that the most popular book in the first public libraries was the *Arabian Nights*, and that in a great age of poetry the best writers of the century, except for their exotic romances, earned less for their poetry than Tom Moore for his *Lalla Rookh*, Martin Tupper for his *Proverbial Philosophy*, Sir Lewis Morris for his *Epic of Hades*, and Sir Edwin Arnold for his *Light of Asia*, third-rate works all of them. In the real market poetry faced the dangers of the slippery road which led to Patience Strong and the Christmas-card industry, the novel the road down to the pulp thriller-magazines, and drama the decline towards the nadir of *East Lynne*.

All kinds of writers, whatever their personal means, were involved in the dilemma. The poorer writers had to come to terms with the public which paid the piper and demanded the right to call the tune. Their more fortunate colleagues, who were themselves insulated by comfortable means from the poverty and distress of the day, were subjected to many kinds of conscientious scruple and feelings of guilt. All looked forward to a happier time, but mass literacy had not yet been achieved, and the dreams in every case, from Blake to Tennyson, were frustrated, and writers had to come to terms with the real public which could afford to buy books. It is little wonder that the heavy pressures of their own contradictions, the conflict of a social urge impelling them to comfort society and a personal isolation driving them within themselves and their own feelings and visions, produced some eccentric writers: instead of typical members of their society, as in Augustan times, writers tend to be, or become, social exiles and outcasts. This is the age of the misfits, of Coleridge and De Quincey taking opium, Byron the sexual rebel, Shelley the potential suicide, Leigh Hunt the first 'Bohemian'. In time it came to appear the natural thing that writers should be at least a little odd and idiosyncratic. Publishers exploited the expectation of eccentricity: there is, for instance, the appearance in London in 1871 of a character from the United States called Joaquin Miller. He had been a cook, a miner, a lawyer, a pony express rider, an editor and a judge, and he came to town wearing a beard, long hair, a sombrero, quirt, chaps and high-heeled boots, and smoking two cigars at once. He was made a member of the select Savage Club and his *Songs of the Sierras* sold 11,000 copies, and critics rated him equal to Poe and Whitman. It was a time when at the age of 47 a down-and-out weaver called William McGonagall alleged that a voice had called to him in a vision 'Write! write!' so forcibly that he danced with happiness and turned out a collection of the most extraordinary but memorable bad doggerel in the language. Personal eccentricity was both the penalty imposed by an unhappy social context and an extremely useful stock in trade.

In the period between 1780 and 1870 the poets had the keenest difficulties with the market. Their struggle for recognition seems to have been hard at all times in this period. In the beginning some poets profited from Augustan-type subscription editions:

Robert Burns surprised himself by earning between £500 and £600 for the 1787 edition of his poems, and William Cowper was offered £1,000, with copyright intact, for the subscription edition of his translation of Homer, which sold to 700 subscribers at three guineas each. But the 1790's were also the period when Blake failed to find any success at all for his ventures in public print, and Coleridge and Wordsworth had their *Lyrical Ballads* remaindered. It is of this time that the bookseller, James Lackington, reported in disgust when he had made a tour of the provincial bookshops between London and Edinburgh: he found 'very few of the works of the most esteemed authors. . . . It is true, at York and Leeds there were a few (and but very few) good books; but in all the other towns between London and Edinburgh nothing but trash was to be found.'[1]

In the period between 1810 and 1840 conditions improved a little for the poets. Under the leadership of some good literary publishers, some poets achieved good sales: notably, Walter Scott and Tom Moore with the third Thomas Longman, and Byron with the second John Murray. It was Murray who gave George Crabbe £3,000 for the *Tales of the Hall* and the copyright of his earlier poems. But significantly, it was only the romantic ballad, the tale of far away and long ago, which really caught the public fancy, and before the end of his career Murray sold out all his rights to the poets, except for Crabbe, on whom he had made a loss, but whom he personally liked. In this period, too, Keats was rejected by the public, and Wordsworth confessed to Tom Moore that all his writings before 1835 had not earned him above £1,000. It was a highly competitive time and publishers seldom saw any reason to give the poets preferential treatment: Thomas Campbell lost his temper with them, calling them 'ravens, croakers, suckers of innocent blood, and living men's brains'. Walter Scott, with more personal experience of the trade, more kindly suggested that it was 'the most ticklish and unsafe and hazardous of all professions, scarcely with the exception of horse-jockeyship'.

There were various attempts between 1840 and 1870 to make poetry more saleable: sixpenny weekly part editions and cheap library reprints. It was in the 1840's that Charles Tilt

[1] Lackington's views are recorded in his *Memoirs* (1791), p. 286, and *Confessions* (1804).

established his *Miniature Library*, David Bogue his *European Library*, and George Bohn his succession of standard libraries—forerunners of the cheap editions for the mass market of the last years of the century. But by this time contemporary poetry seems to have slipped out of the reckoning in book sales. The fourth Thomas Longman advised Eliza Acton, 'My dear madam, it is no good bringing me poetry; nobody wants poetry now. Bring me a cookery book, and we might come to terms.'[1] At a period when novelists and historians and other writers were earning rewards beyond the dreams of the Augustans, Browning was driven to publish in pamphlet form at his own expense and without profit, and Tennyson waited decades for any kind of security. Yet in 1838 and the years following Martin Tupper earned over £10,000 for the *Proverbial Philosophy*, the first of the four series of which ran into the extraordinary number of sixty editions. It is little wonder that the Romantic poets, almost without exception, are distinguishable by their uncertainty and unhappiness about their social context and function. The story of the decline and fall, in the printed-book market, of this major art is best understood in an account of the distress and conflict suffered by individual poets.

It was fortunate for William Blake that he was apprenticed early in life to an engraver and became a professional engraver. Fortunately, too, from one viewpoint at any rate, his marriage was childless; he had only his wife to support, and she trained herself to help her husband as a colourist and bookbinder. Certainly, there was no living for him as a writer. He made two ventures into public print as a poet: in 1783 his *Poetical Sketches* were published, at the expense of two friends, the sculptor Flaxman and the Rev. Henry Mathew, and in 1791 one of the more discriminating publishers, James Johnson, accepted *The French Revolution*; both books were complete failures. Nearly all his other works were printed by himself, with his own engravings and illustrations. In this way he was able to supply luxury books to a handful of rich patrons, like William Hayley, and supplement the earnings from his pictures. For instance, after printing the *Songs of Innocence* and *Songs of Experience* separately, he bound them together in one volume and released copies varying in price, according to the customer, from 30*s*. to

[1] Quoted in F. A. Mumby, *Publishing and Bookselling* (1930), pp. 283–4.

over five guineas. His main income, never very comfortable, came from the sale of pictures (he exhibited at the Royal Academy) and from engraving work for the publishers: he earned a guinea a plate for illustrations to Young's *Night Thoughts* and twenty guineas for his work with Blair's *The Grave*. As far as poetry is concerned, Blake was happy merely to be paid for his time: having spent twenty guineas' worth of time on a copy of *Jerusalem*, it distressed him not to find a customer for it. Much of his work lay about in sales-rooms for years waiting for the single customer to have his curiosity titillated. All this was the cause of deep, irremoveable distress for Blake. He had no respect for his patrons at all: Cromek was 'a petty sneaking knave', Flaxman a blockhead, Stothard a 'golden fool'; as for Hayley the 'pickthank', the 'rascal'—his 'mother on his father him begot'. He was best pleased when they attacked his work:

> My title as a genius thus is prov'd:
> Not prais'd by Hayley, nor by Flaxman loved. . . .
>
> When Hayley finds out what you cannot do,
> That is the very thing he'll set you to. . . .
>
> Thy friendship oft has made my heart to ache:
> Do be my enemy—for friendship's sake. . . .

It is not enough to trace the 'madness', with which Blake was charged by his contemporaries, to unkind treatment by his parents in childhood, favouritism for his brother, and so on. In fact, Blake led a sane life and held his own in a commercial world, and his marriage was an uncommonly happy one. His great difficulty was the incompatibility of his 'vision' and his social context. It was in his art that Blake revealed, fiercely and unrepentantly, the 'madman'. He was happiest in the years before 1792, when he had a real and sympathetic audience in the group which met in James Johnson's house: William Godwin, Mary Wollstonecraft, Joseph Priestley, and Tom Paine. But when Paine fled the country and the publisher of the *Rights of Man* was imprisoned for eighteen months, the group broke up, and Blake spent most of the rest of his life talking to himself and his wife Catherine.

The loss of a public audience was disastrous to Blake, because he saw himself as

> . . . the Bard!
> Who present, past, and future, sees.

He was 'in God's presence night and day'. He did not dare to pretend to be the author of his poetry, only the secretary: 'the authors are in eternity'. As far as *Milton* was concerned:

> I have written this Poem from immediate Dictation, twelve or sometimes twenty or thirty lines at a time, without Premeditation, and even against my Will; the Time it has taken in writing was thus render'd Non-Existent, and an immense Poem Exists which seems to be the Labour of a long Life, all produc'd without Labour or Study.[1]

This 'grandest poem that the world contains' prophesied the glory that would come again to 'England's green and pleasant land', if society would only espouse the anarchism of his views on education, sex, religion, war and morality. The tragedy was that nobody would listen. Blake alternately was defiant about the 'weak men' who could not elucidate his ideas and insistent that there was nothing to prevent such understanding except folly (children had no difficulty, he argued). The gradual assumption of mysticism, deep and dark, the gradual descent into symbolism and obscurity 'altogether hidden from the corporeal understanding', the gradual gathering together of the voice and tone of the Old Testament prophets, these were the inevitable defence of a visionary poet who had no alternative but to retire into himself and write for posterity. Blake's doctrine is so strange that he would have remained a strange poet even if he had found a fit audience. With nobody to listen to him except a gentle and loving but at times utterly bewildered wife, and a small circle of fellow artists, publishers and rich patrons who had no interest whatever in his message and who valued him therefore for all the things he himself considered inessential and peripheral, Blake became an extreme instance of the unbalanced artist familiar in the history of the poetry of the early nineteenth century.

He was by no means unique. Samuel Taylor Coleridge as a child was another dreamer and visionary. He, too, had an unsettled childhood, losing when only 9 the parents who spoiled him. Unlike Blake, he had a sickly constitution, suffering from rheumatic fever, dysentery, boils, gout, dropsy and erysipelas, disorders that brought on his opium habit and reduced him in his forties to mental and physical degeneration. But his most decisive

[1] Letter to Thomas Butts, 25 April 1803, *Letters* (1956), p. 85.

disadvantage was his sheer ineptitude, an inability for all his brilliance and talent to find a social context in which he could move freely and happily. He was so inept at Cambridge that he ran into debt in a matter of days and ran away to join the Light Dragoons under the name of Silas Tomkyn Comberbacke, whence after four months inefficient service he was bought out by his brothers. He could have been a fellow of his college, but at the crucial moment he alienated the authorities by his pacifism and republicanism. He was one of the leaders of Southey's scheme to emigrate, twelve men and twelve women, to establish an ideal pantisocracy on the Susquehanna, always the grand planner whose schemes came to nothing. Fatally attracted to maternal, managing women, he married a woman described by Dorothy Wordsworth as a 'sad fiddle-faddler . . . much to be pitied. . . . Her radical fault is want of sensibility'; and then, falling in love on at least two later occasions, his moral convictions denied to him what might have been relief and security.

He managed his career with the same ineptitude. At the university, he had a scheme for a subscription edition: he collected 450 names, and then failed to write the book. He edited *The Watchman*, a fourpenny paper, for two and a half months, and then tired of it. He made a piecemeal living writing for the *Critical Review* and the *Monthly Magazine*, and earning a guinea a week for verses in the *Morning Post*, together with part-time tutoring. He became Unitarian minister in Shrewsbury, at £150 a year, but hated hired preaching and after a few months gave it up. He was successful as a leader-writer for the *Morning Post* at four guineas a week, and the Editor was so pleased with him he offered a share in the paper and the prospect of £2,000 a year: Coleridge refused, saying, 'I would not give up the country and the lazy reading of old folios for two thousand times two thousand pounds. . . . Beyond £250 a year, I consider money as a real evil.'[1] The truth is he could never have supported himself on anything like £250 a year if he had not had good friends to give him hospitality in emergencies, the Wordsworths, Tom Poole, Gillman.

And so his strange career continued. He went to Malta for his health in 1804, and found himself a successful under-secretary in Government service at the high salary of £50 a month. He

[1] Letter to Poole, 1800. *Essays on his Own Times* (1850), XC.

could have made a diplomatic career in the Mediterranean, but did not. He lectured at the Royal Institution for £100, but was dismissed after giving bad lectures or sometimes failing to put in an appearance at all. He ran *The Friend* for six months, and lost £200 thereby, after failing to adapt himself to his environment: some of his essays broke off in the middle of a paragraph, even in the middle of a sentence. The printed-book market was open to him, and unlike Blake, he earned solid if unspectacular rewards: £20 for *Kubla Khan*, £80 for *Christabel*, £150 and half the profits for *Biographia Literaria*. And unlike many of his poetic contemporaries, he wrote a play which was actually staged: *Remorse*, which ran for twenty performances at Drury Lane in 1813 and earned him £400. But always he needed friends to help him out. Byron gave him £100, De Quincey £500, and in the end there was State recognition: a pension of a hundred guineas a year from the privy purse in 1824, cancelled on the death of the King, but immediately made up by an annuity from his friend Frere. When he died he left nothing but an insurance policy and his literary rights.

If the fault of Blake's failure rested at least as much in his audience, or lack of it, as in the poet himself, it can be said of Coleridge that the fault was almost entirely his own. Quite apart from difficulties of health and temperament, he was quite unable to take seriously any of the social functions that came his way. He seems to carry Gray's dilettanteism to its logical and demoralizing extreme. For some reason he was unable to take himself seriously. He admired the successful Laureate, Southey, with an extraordinarily naïve adulation, embarrassing his friend by calling him 'Honoured Sir' in public. He thought highly of Wordsworth, too: 'Wordsworth is a great, a true Poet—I am only a kind of Metaphysician'.[1] He was the greatest critic of his time, recognized as such by the contemporaries who made him an Associate of the Royal Society of Literature, but he reserved most of his best and most characteristic brilliance for table-talk. He had no confidence in the good opinion held of him by others, even of highly qualified verdicts. He preferred a lazy, obscure life, happiest in the small domestic circle with congenial company. He refused to dedicate himself to the profession of letters.

Different historians have produced many explanations of a

[1] Letter to Wrangham, 19 December 1800, *Unpublished Letters* (1932), I. 165.

psychological kind to explain why this was so. There may be sufficient reason in his bad health and drug habit. Catherine Poole thought he was a man entirely led away by the feelings of the moment. He called himself a 'tomorrower . . . sloth jaundic'd all'; he lacked the talent 'to become a popular writer'.[1] He was fundamentally a visionary, rapt in his own theories of the power and functions of the imagination, who above all wanted peace to think and talk and write, poetically and critically, about this one theme. He needed if not a pedestal at least a secure hermitage from which his utterances might be properly received. Unfortunately, the openings offered him by his friends, patrons and publishers were mundane: responsibilities requiring systematic work, and therefore distractions from his own inner purpose. He made claims like Blake's: 'There is in genius an unconscious activity; nay, that is the genius in a man of genius.' He was equally an egotist, believing that the egotism in a great writer was a 'revelation of spirit'.[2] He believed that the imagination of the poet was an echo 'in the finite mind of the eternal act of creation in the infinite I am', the heart of all the processes that make us civilized. 'Deep thinking is attainable only by a man of deep feeling . . . all truth is a species of revelation.' Perhaps Coleridge expected too much of life, and then in natural reaction took too little. Certainly, he was never able to live for long the life of contemplation which he most loved; and in being forced, again and again, back into the real world in which he had no confidence in his own abilities and no staying power, his life became one of despair and disappointment.

His friend Wordsworth fared no better in the end, although he started with many advantages, robust health, a balanced and sensible attitude to his social environment, and above all, private means. Wordsworth's father, a lawyer and land agent, was not rich, but the son was left a small annuity, and this was augmented by a wealthy grandfather and a later legacy of £1,000. Wordsworth never had to work for a living, but was able to spend his time travelling, writing and studying, the kind of life Coleridge wanted for himself. He could afford to wait for the slow recognition of the public, receiving the sinecure of stamp distributor for Westmorland in 1813, a pension of £300 a year from the

[1] *Biographia Literaria*, p. 94.
[2] *Table Talk* (1835), II. 87.

Civil List in 1842, and the public position of Poet Laureate in 1843. Recognition was indeed slow. His first venture into public print, the *Lyrical Ballads* (1798), was a failure: the book was remaindered in the end, and the publisher, Joseph Cottle, thought so little of the prospects of future profit that he handed back the copyright to the authors. He was able to find publishers to produce successive collected editions, in 1807, 1815, 1820, 1827, 1832, 1837, 1838, 1845 and 1849, but his total earnings from print up to 1835 were not above £1,000. It took four years, for instance, to sell the 500 copies Longman printed of the collected edition of 1820. After 1835 returns were a little better. Edward Moxon, a literary publisher who also helped Southey, Lamb and other major writers, gave him £1,000 for the six-volume edition of 1837: but significantly, Moxon lost by his generosity. It was not until his last years that Wordsworth's poems became a profitable proposition in the trade. Like many of his colleagues, Wordsworth decided, in the end, that 'time is the only judge in literature that can be absolutely depended'. He, too, put his trust in posterity.

In fact, this is a story of disappointment for the poet, however sensibly he rationalized his loss. Wordsworth had consciously thought of himself as a new Milton, attaining a national audience with new poetry, including epic poetry, which would alleviate the distress of mankind. He particularly hoped in his youth to reach the lower classes, who needed his help most. Hence his attempts at chapbook circulation among the masses with ballad-poems like *We are Seven*; hence, too, his early insistence on a poetic language which should be as near as possible to the normal speech of working people. It would have galled him to hear the verdict of the garden-boy at Rydal Mount: 'Well, you see . . . there's pomes and pomes, and Wudsworth's was not for sich as us.'[1] It was the function of poetry 'to console the afflicted; to add sunshine to daylight by making the happy happier. To teach the young and the gracious of every age to see, to think and to feel, and therefore to become more actively and securely virtuous.'[2] Concerned, as he was at first, with ideas of liberty, equality and fraternity, the greatest happiness of the greatest number, and with God omnipresent in everyone and

[1] H. D. Rawnsley, *Trans. Wordsworth Soc.* (1884), p. vi.
[2] *Letter to Lady Beaumont*, 21 May 1807.

everything, he saw himself as the bard who would turn the key to universal happiness with his visions of the beauty and dignity of nature. He was always a lonely man: Coleridge found him 'silent and self-centred', and whether as a solitary youth walking the hills, or a man who remained solitary even when surrounded by his wife and children, or a cantankerous and unsociable old man, he was always aloof and unapproachable, a poet in sympathy with the solitaries he describes, the solitary reaper, the leech-gatherer, Toussaint l'Ouverture alone in his cell, Lucy whom there was none to love. His whole life is a story of inevitable isolation, events contributing to keep him different and aloof: the separation from his young mistress Annette, his social position as the son of a landlord who could never be accepted as an equal by the countryfolk he loved, public suspicion of his eccentricity. In all this the failure to reach with his poetry an audience proper to his own conception of the social function of the poet, his failure to communicate, was central and focal.

When at last he won public esteem he was nearly 70. His concern for the poor had reduced itself to querulous discussion of poor-law reform and workhouses, as in the 1838 preface. His vision of nature had become a mere description of places seen on walking tours. His philosophy had become staid, conservative and conventional. His revolutionary preface to the *Lyrical Ballads* had been amended and then hidden away in small print in the appendices of collected editions, because he regarded it as interesting only as a museum piece, irrelevant in the main to his life's work. Shelley's comment marks the stages of his decline and fall: 'He was at first sublime, pathetic, impressive, profound; then dull; then prosy and dull; and now dull—O, so very dull! it is an ultra-legitimate dulness.'[1] And cynically, the page at Rydal Mount testified: 'There's no doubt but what he was fond of quality, and quality was very fond o' him.'

In Keats's twenty-five years there was no time to suffer this kind of development. Here was another visionary, a poet with another vision of the truth of beauty, who wanted the opportunity to express himself as a professional writer. He had been apprenticed early to a surgeon, and for a short while was a dresser at Guy's Hospital, but by the time he was 20 he had abandoned the study of medicine for poetry. Since his own

[1] *Peter Bell the Third* (October 1819), dedication.

private means were very tiny, he was dependent upon the hospitality of his friends: Leigh Hunt, Hazlitt, Shelley, the painter Severn. He managed to interest publishers: Charles and James Ollier published his first volume in 1817, and Taylor and Hessey *Endymion* in 1818, but the latter firm failed, and Keats was drubbed particularly by the reviewers of Edinburgh, whose *Edinburgh Review* and *Edinburgh Magazine* were major leaders of opinion at this time. There was never any public audience for Keats until twenty years and more after his death. Yet, Keats had all the makings of a dedicated professional writer. He had a wide range, interesting himself in satire and light verse, as few Romantics were capable of interesting themselves. He deliberately set himself chores and experiments. It was no dilettante who said: 'A long Poem is a test of Invention, which I take to be the Polar Star of Poetry, as Fancy is the Sails, and Imagination the Rudder. Did our great Poets ever write short Pieces? I mean, in the shape of Tales—This same invention seems indeed of late Years to have been forgotten as a Poetical excellence.'[1] He was willing, too, to learn from experience. He took to heart his publisher's complaint that he was 'such a man of fits and starts', recognized that his mind was 'like a pack of scattered cards' (so he told Shelley), and systematically set to work to improve himself, as the *Fall of Hyperion* reveals. He was able to say later: 'In *Endymion*, I leaped headlong into the Sea, and thereby have become better acquainted with the Soundings, the quicksands, and the rocks, than if I had stayed upon the green shore, and piped a silly pipe and took tea and comfortable advice —I was never afraid of failure, for I would sooner fail than not be among the greatest.'[2] In the end he was able to lecture his friend Shelley on the subject: 'The thought of such discipline must fall like cold chains upon you, who perhaps never sat with your wings furled for six months together.'[3]

The pathos of Keats's life-story has obscured much of his determination. 'The roaring of the wind is my wife and the Stars through the window pane are my Children':[4] such a statement leads to sad thoughts about his relations with Fanny Brawne and

[1] Letter to Bailey, 8 October 1817, M. B. Forman, ed., *Letters of John Keats* (Oxford, 1931), I. 55–56.

[2] Letter to Hessey, 9 October 1818, Forman, I. 243.

[3] Letter to Shelley, August 1820, Forman, II. 553.

[4] Letter to George Keats, October 1818, Forman, I. 261.

Isabella Jones, but it also reveals his single-minded dedication to the vision that might ultimately be

> . . . a friend
> To soothe the cares and lift the thoughts of man.

He had no envy of the most successful poet of his day, Lord Byron: on the contrary, he quietly insisted: 'There is this great difference between us. He describes what he sees—I describe what I imagine. Mine is the hardest task.'[1] He was bruised by the critics, but affirmed: 'I feel assured I should write from the mere yearning and fondness I have for the Beautiful even if my night's labours should be burnt every morning, and no eye ever shine upon them.'[2] This statement is an extravagant declaration of independence, but it is also testimony of devotion in the face of difficulties. Keats is not defeated as Gray was defeated.

But the poets of his day required such determination. Poetry no longer occupied the special place it had held in Augustan esteem. It was now fighting for survival, the first of the literary arts, but not the last, to fall foul of the Romantic dilemma. Each poet, and each writer, of the nineteenth century had to come to terms, in his individual way, with the competition of the printed-book market. The age is full of visionaries who disdain, or pretend to disdain, the earth, of salesmen who compromise or falsify their credentials. The literary profession of the time includes, side by side, idealists of burning faith and frauds of bare-faced cynicism, professionals dedicated to their trade and amateurs playing the market, aristocrats and revolutionaries, heroes and rogues, men of unquestionable genius and men of most questionable ingenuity. The mixture becomes more and more explosive as society approaches the ultimate of the mass market.

[1] Letter to George Keats, 17–27 September 1819, Forman, II. 452.
[2] Letter to Woodhouse, 27 October 1818, Forman, I. 246.

# IX

## Artists and Salesmen

*'No, sir, you need not live, if your body cannot be kept together without selling your soul.'*

CARLYLE, to a hack, 1831

EVERY good artist to an important degree is devoted to art for its own sake: ready, for instance, to discipline himself by experiment, exercise and sheer hard work and thus to master his chosen material and freely express himself within its laws. But professional devotion implies something more, something over and above this loving commitment. The very word *profession* connotes a willingness to serve the community; more than that, a conviction that the service is good and important and above all necessary. This conviction is more difficult for the artist than the doctor or the lawyer, whose social justification is usually, although not always, self-evident. There have been many occasions in the history of medicine when doctors have had to overcome popular resistance to new methods and new principles; all professions, indeed, have crises when professional integrity alone carries the day against hostile prejudice, when what the public wants and what the public needs are two different and contradictory things. But the artist seems to have been faced with crises of public relations throughout his history; by its very nature art continually invites its audience to look at life with fresh eyes, continually comes into conflict with all the human being's resistance to change. To overcome opposition, and thus to realize his service in actuality, the professional artist has to have faith in himself, whatever the short-term reactions of his public. This is a difficult faith, since it must override the natural diffidence and undemonstrativeness of a sensitive man, to whom, often, his own successful creations are sincerely a source of surprise and wonder. The professional artist needs therefore an ambivalence, a modesty towards his own work which is inevitable if he is to remain free to make discoveries with it, and at the same time a pride and arrogance and toughness in holding true to his own ideas in the face of public criticism which he cannot accept. Something of this ambivalence must lie behind the persistent yearning of the artist for immortality: posterity will recognize the value of the work even if contemporary society is hostile, and the audience of posterity is naturally addressed with both humility and pride.

The balance, delicate and fragile, was particularly difficult to maintain in the nineteenth century, when artistry and salesmanship so often pulled the man in contrary directions. It was an age when the possession of private means, apart from professional earnings, was an almost indispensable asset in the preservation of integrity. Few writers achieving important art were dependent upon professional income; most had a job, in another profession, in business or in Government service, to supply them with a livelihood. One of the few advantages the woman writer possessed was the independence which came from being supported by a husband or father: from Jane Austen to George Eliot, from women of high talent like the Brontës and Christina Rossetti to the lesser-talented Elizabeth Gaskells and Susan Ferriers, women were insulated from the corruptions of trade. As for the men, many were clergymen, like Charles Kingsley, John Newman, Sydney Smith, John Keble, and Gerard Manley Hopkins; so, too, were lesser talents, like William Bowles, William Barnes, Reginald Heber, and Arthur Stanley. Many were dons: John Ruskin, Mark Pattison, C. L. Dodgson (Lewis Carroll), Charles Reade (who was also a barrister), and others. Others were involved in other kinds of educational work, like the two fellows of Oriel College, Arthur Clough, who entered the Education Office, and Matthew Arnold, who was an Inspector of Schools before becoming Oxford's Professor of Poetry. Some were barristers like Francis Jeffrey, the first editor of the *Edinburgh Review*, Wilkie Collins, and Jeremy Bentham. Many were in business of one kind or another: William Ainsworth as a publisher, Walter Bagehot as a banker, John Galt in the Canada Company. Many were involved in political or governmental service: Lord Macaulay, Lord Lytton, Anthony Trollope, W. M. Praed, Charles Lever, John Frere, and others. John Stuart Mill and Thomas Love Peacock were at the India Office. Coventry Patmore was a librarian at the British Museum. Robert Burns, John Clare, Robert Bloomfield, and James Hogg were in farming. Besides the writers who had other jobs, there were many who were independent with private means: Edward Fitzgerald, Samuel Rogers, Alexander Kinglake, Edward Lear, Thomas de Quincey (who squandered his inheritance), and Thomas Love Beddoes.

The blessings of an alternative means of livelihood, and the dangers which had to be met when alternative means were unavailable or inadequate, are best exemplified in the careers of individual writers. The story of Sir Walter Scott is particularly significant. Here was a highly talented writer of great industry whose professional integrity frequently played second fiddle to his ambitions. From youth, indeed, writing appears to have been a means to an end, providing the money by which he could live the life of an important landed gentleman. He always insisted he had descended from old families of landed gentry, although his own parents were connected with the professions: his father was a solicitor (a Writer to the Signet, in Scottish terms), and his mother the daughter of a professor of medicine. His father provided him with a private income, and accepted him as apprentice. He was called to the Bar at the age of 21, and ultimately became Sheriff of Selkirk, at £300 a year, and an advocate in the Court of Session, a place worth £1,300 a year. Throughout life he was always prouder of the fact that he was an advocate than that he was a writer. He took up writing as a means of extra income. When he was 25 he published a small volume of translations from German poetry, and discovered from Schiller and Goethe how to write romantic ballads and thus capitalize his literary wit. In 1802 he edited a profitable anthology, including some of his own poems, *Minstrelsy of the Scottish Border*, and then in 1805 became a best-seller with *The Lay of the Last Minstrel*, which sold 27,300 copies in the next eight years. This was followed by other popular successes, *Marmion* (1808), *Lady of the Lake* (1810, selling 17,000 copies in three years), *Rokeby* (1813, five editions in one year), and the *Lord of the Isles*, which he sold for £4,200.

Byron exploited the vogue for the romantic thriller created by Scott. But Byron never quite reconciled himself to the popularity and enormous rewards this kind of writing brought. He could strike hard bargains, insisting with John Murray, for instance, that 'If Mr Moore is to have three thousand for *Lallah*, etc.; if Mr Campbell is to have three thousand for his prose on Poetry . . . I ask the aforesaid price for mine.'[1] But he never forgave the Press for the savage attacks made in the *Edinburgh Review* on *Hours of Idleness* (1807), a volume of poems about which he cared far more than his later successes. He despised the trade, writers with 'pen peeping from behind the ear, and the thumbs a little inky': 'Who would write,' he once protested, 'who had anything better to do?' So he kept from print his short lyrics about love and life. With the exception of the satire, which appears to have been important to him—'I cannot give up my Don Juan. I do not know what I should do without my Don Juan'—his published work seems to have been written with his tongue in his cheek, and its success was embarrassing. He earned £2,700 for the copyright of *Childe Harold I* and *II*, and *The Corsair*, and then gave it away. He wanted to give the publisher the copyright to *The Siege of Corinth* and *Parisina*, and had to be forced to accept 1,000 guineas. Altogether, he earned £23,540 from the sale of poetic copyrights alone, and yet insisted on maintaining the pose of a dilettante. Hence perhaps in favourite poems, *Don Juan*, for instance, his deliberate horseplay, throw-away lines, and a refusal to remain dignified for long:

> . . . as my Muse is a capricious elf,
> We'll put about, and try another tack,
> With Juan, left half-kill'd some stanzas back.
> (IV, 74)

In the end, the music and the romantic diction of the ballads sickened him: he preferred to

> . . . rattle on exactly as I'd talk,
> With any body in a ride or walk.
> (XV, 19)

[1] R. V. Prothero, ed., *Letters and Journals* (1904), IV. 165.

Sir Walter Scott had no such qualms. From Scott's viewpoint the main thing wrong with the ballads was that poetry did not earn enough. By the time he was 40, Scott was worth £2,800 a year, excluding about £1,000 a year from his pen. But he was not content. By this time he was married and had two sons and two daughters, and had started building an appropriate home, a huge elaborate Gothic country house at Abbotsford. He was a bad businessman in land-buying and had paid far more than he needed; and he was extravagant, too, with rebuilding plans and with the purchase of furniture and an armoury. He entertained on a lavish scale, liked to travel a good deal, and kept his family in style (a son's captaincy was to cost him £3,000 and his marriage £10,000). To increase his income, he became a partner in the printing firm of James Ballantyne and Company, and later in the publishing firm of John Ballantyne. He had ambitious schemes for making money by editions of sixteenth-century poets, Jacobean dramatists and the great Augustans, but in truth the firms with which he associated himself were not efficient and their ventures seldom profitable. The answer to his problem was found when he took up the novel in 1814 with *Waverley*. He discovered that the historical novel was a better seller than the romantic ballad. He engaged in other writing, with immense fertility, other books like a life of Napoleon, periodical articles (he had an interest in the *Edinburgh Review*), papers for the *Encyclopaedia Britannica*, and so on, but his main income came from the novels, twenty-five of them in eighteen years.

He entered into complicated arrangements with his publishers. The usual pattern was to sell to Archibald Constable the right to print two-thirds of an impression of between 10,000 and 12,000 copies for £2,500 to £3,000; then to give the remaining third to the printing firm, James Ballantyne, in which he had a personal interest, on the undertaking that Constable would buy them at trade rates. If there were need, he could also sell the copyright for another £1,500–£2,000. By these means he was able, in good years when three novels appeared, to make £15,000 or even more, rewards on a scale unattained hitherto in the profession. Abbotsford grew and flourished. He accepted a baronetcy. He married his eldest son to an heiress. He entertained the Crown Prince of Sweden and was master of ceremonies when George IV visited Edinburgh in 1822. He became familiar with the Duke of Buccleuch and other members of the aristocracy. He had his portrait painted by Lawrence and his bust sculptured by Chantrey. Unfortunately, his printing and publishing businesses were unable to survive the general trade slump of 1825, and Scott found himself in debt to the sum of £130,000, more than £40,000 of which was attributable to debts incurred by Constable and the Ballantynes. Scott had always lived beyond his means, accepting advances and bills for books not even written, and he had always spent profits rather than investing them as capital in the business. Undismayed, however, he refused bankruptcy and set out to pay off his creditors with more novels. It was an impossible task, since he refused to alter his standard of living, and the effort broke his health; when he died the debt was barely reduced. His creditors ultimately made their fortunes on his posthumous book sales.

In this context the novels were very much a means to an end. He treated them with scant respect. Unlike the poems, he published them anonymously, at least until 1827, as 'Tales of My Landlord' by Jebediah Cleishbotham, or as by 'the author of *Waverley*'. He wrote them late at night or early in the morning or whenever they would not interrupt his lairdly activities. He wrote with great speed, spending little or no time on revision or re-reading, finishing off *Guy Mannering*, for instance, in six weeks. He always had the next book in his mind before the last one was in proof. He thought all the time in terms of material sufficient to fill three volumes. When Constable wanted a novel in four volumes, which he could sell, greedily, at 32*s*. instead of the usual guinea, Scott refused the suggestion that two novels should be written in two volumes each, and blandly padded out *The Heart of Midlothian* to fill up the extra volume. Books were a commodity to be sold by bulk.

Scott's stories were deeply influential, Newman for instance suggesting they lay behind the Oxford Movement. The novelist himself was no pot-boiler, but a creative writer full of ideas. He refused to call his novels 'Tales of Other Days' or 'Sentimental Tales', and saw in them 'more a description of men than manners'. He believed in throwing the force of his narrative 'upon the characters and passions of the actors—those passions common to men in all stages of society, and which have alike agitated the human heart';[1] in this way he refused to accept the novel as a form of romance escaping from life. Indeed, he was anti-romantic in many ways, a humorist, an Augustan about the more romantic passions: even his wildest glens are inhabited by credible people and he eschewed the supernatural. He agreed with Wordsworth's theories about the 'strongest and most powerful language' used by the lower classes, when moved by the 'higher and more violent passions'. He was an excellent story-teller, with qualities of manliness and courtesy and good sense, and as Walter Allen has suggested, he 'grasped, as no other English novelist has done, the organic relationships between man and man, man and place, man and society, and man and his past'.[2] There is so much to commend in Scott and yet there is no critic who has not regretted the way his work is all too often botched to fit in with his publishing schedules. The printed-book trade had brought out the best in Johnson; it now brings out the worst in Scott. In all his fertility he has left no single novel which fairly does justice to the wide range of his talents and ideas. Besides long chapters of sheer padding, there is much else of the unorganic in his novels: plots hastily resolved, sub-plots that dwarf the main action, a tendency to settle for conventional judgments on characters and epochs, a level temperateness of tone which ill matches the speed and passion of the narrative, surprises which appear as engineered rather than inevitable. All his faults have life and energy: he believed himself that they were virtues in 'a hurried frankness of composition'. But they are nevertheless faults, symptomatic of something unserious in his approach to the work. Besides his temperament and non-literary ambitions, his essentially commercial connexion with his audience must share the blame. 'I thank God' he said in 1809, 'I can write ill enough for the present taste', a statement that reveals corruption in the writer.

The novelist with whom Scott is most usually connected chronologically for the purposes of examinations and literary histories provides indeed an interesting contrast. Jane Austen's social context was much more modest, though no less genteel. This daughter of a Hampshire parson lived all her life, apart from interludes in Bath and Southampton, in country towns and

[1] *Waverley* (1814), chapter i.
[2] *The English Novel* (1954), p. 120.

villages. True, the friends with whom she danced as a girl at country balls went on to become squires and Members of Parliament, and one the Lord Chief Justice of Ireland, but her world was the country gentlewoman's world of the time, lacking Scott's aristocratic splendours. Her father had comfortable livings and her mother a private income of £140 a year, and Jane had no kind of financial incentive in writing. From the age of 14 she wrote plays and burlesques for her family, and novels were merely an extension of this activity. She used to read chapters aloud to her sister Cassandra and then release them in manuscript for other members of the family. As her nephew the Rev. J. E. Austen Leigh reported in his *Memoir* (1870): 'She had no separate study to retire to, and most of her work must have been done in the general sitting-room, subject to all kinds of casual interruptions. She was careful that her occupation should not be suspected by servants, or visitors, or any person beyond her own family party. She wrote upon small pieces of paper which could easily be put away or covered with a piece of blotting-paper. There was between the front door and the offices, a swing door which creaked when it was opened, but she objected to having this little inconvenience remedied, because it gave her notice when anyone was coming.' These are hardly ideal conditions for literary creation, but Jane Austen was never impatient or irritable when interrupted, and she had plenty of time to work slowly on, in a life in which she was not expected to cook or do any of the household chores except superintend the 'housekeeping'. Certainly, it was better for novels to be written in this way than in the dark hours and odd moments of Scott's crowded life. In comparison, her quickest novel, *Pride and Prejudice*, took ten months to write.

When she had written three novels, a proud father attempted to get them published. *Pride and Prejudice* was offered to a publisher 'at the author's risk', but was turned down. *Northanger Abbey* was actually sold to a Bath publisher for £10, but he never printed the book and was glad later to get his money back from the family. Seven or eight years after the Bath episode her brother Henry, a banker, succeeded in having *Sense and Sensibility* published by Egerton at the author's expense, and everyone was delighted when the book sold well enough to make a profit of £150. By this time Jane Austen had need of the money;

her father had died, leaving his wife very little besides her own income, and she was anxious to augment the family income if she could. Egerton accepted *Pride and Prejudice* as a commercial proposition, and Jane resumed the writing of novels, selling *Mansfield Park* to Egerton and *Emma* to John Murray. She had none of Scott's sweeping success. The publishers were able to edge up the price of her three-volume sets, from 15*s*. to 18*s*. to 21*s*., but in fact the total profits on her first four books did not exceed £700. The other two were not published in her lifetime. Jane was delighted to learn that the Prince Regent was one of her readers and loved to assume a commercial air: her comment on the publication of *Waverley* was: 'Walter Scott has no business to write novels, especially good ones. It is not fair. He has fame and profit enough as a poet and should not be taking the bread out of other people's mouths.'[1] But she was not a commercial novelist.

In other ways she was much more truly professional than Scott. Giving herself plenty of time, she took immense pains over revision, scrupulous and meticulous pains. Her chief fear was that the later work should fall below the standard of the first, and she would have been relieved by the modern verdict that *Emma* is probably the best. She limited her material to the localities and family situations she knew from personal experience. In her integrity she ignored London high society, the lower classes, the Industrial and French Revolutions, Waterloo and all politics. There are no melodramatic terrors, abductions and wicked lords. Scott was one of the first to recognize the value of her concentration: 'That young lady has a talent for describing the involvements and feelings and characters of ordinary life, which is to me the most wonderful I ever met with. The Big Bow-wow strain I can do myself like any now going; but the exquisite touch which renders ordinary commonplace things and characters interesting, from the truth of the description and the sentiment, is denied to me.'[2] Between Scott's 'bow-wow strain' and Jane Austen's meticulousness there is a professional gulf. Far from representing the amateur against Scott's professional outlook, Jane commits herself more seriously to the work, and makes a more open avowal of principle and

[1] Letter to Anna Austen, September 1814.

[2] *Journal* (1890), I. 155.

belief thereby. This indeed is what we should expect of a novelist who in her books makes so much of the moral prestige and obligations of professional commitment. Comparing Scott and Austen, from some points of view perhaps, it was better that the nineteenth-century artist should be born a woman.

Charles Lamb was protected from commercial vanity by quite other means. He was in his forties before he found himself in professional letters. His trade was really that of the clerk, chiefly with the East India Company for thirty-three years. His salary increased steadily year by year. In 1800, when he was 25, he was earning £90 a year, with various increments, a bi-annual £10 increment, an annual gratuity of £30, and holiday pay of £10. This supplemented a small inheritance from his father. By 1805 his salary, including overtime and increments, amounted to about £200 a year. In 1815 his basic pay alone reached £480 a year, by 1821 £700 and by 1825 £730. It was a good organization to work for: when he was 50 he applied for early retirement on the grounds of ill health and was given a pension for life of £450 a year. It is true that Lamb only left £2,000 at death, and this chiefly due to an insurance policy, but he was comfortable all life through. His were the extravagances of the confirmed bachelor: wine, tobacco, good food and hospitality. He was never worried about money; what irked him was the way he felt he was wasting his life. He liked the security of his job, but always resented the inflexible business hours, of nine to three, or ten to four, and often spoke about beginning his day at four. This is the *cri-de-coeur* of the clerk whose mind races ahead of his work, a figure more and more familiar in industrial society. In addition, he had problems of health: both he and his sister Mary suffered from nervous breakdowns and fits of insanity, and it was safest that they should remain looking after each other, a ménage undisturbed by any serious prospects of marriage on either side (indeed, they adopted a daughter in 1823).

His writing appears to have begun as compensation for an unexciting vocational and home life. He had written poems as a youth, love poems to the Anna he never married, and it was these that were first published. He made friends with poets like Coleridge, Wordsworth, Southey, and Charles Lloyd, and journalists like Hazlitt and Leigh Hunt, and wrote imitatively, entering into the swim with them and thinking very much of the potential fame and immortality writing might bring. His poems appeared in periodicals or in volumes with the work of his friends; some, for instance, appeared in the second edition of Coleridge's *Poems* in 1797 and some in *Blank Verse* (1798), which he and Lloyd edited together. He even tried a novel, *Rosamund Gray*, in 1798. The trouble was that his poems were less sublime than those of his friends, lighter and more sentimental, and less successful. He alternated between high aspiring hopes and a ready acceptance of his own inferiority. He would refer to his writings as 'sketches' or 'fragments', and in 1796, after his mother's death at the hands of Mary, he had actually burned all his manuscripts as 'vanities'. He had an early sense of the heights which the professional writer must scale, and too great a sense of his own incompetence and unworthiness. His most serious attempts were made in drama. Loving Shakespeare and the Elizabethans, he tried to write a play which could stand comparison with theirs, and published *John Woodvil* in 1802 at his own expense: he lost £25 and the play received a bad press and was never produced. Later, coming to more practical terms with the theatre, he wrote a farce, *Mr. H*, which was taken off after one performance at Drury Lane, but was relatively successful later in the United States. There was also a tragicomedy, *The Wife's Trial*, which was never produced. For a long time his other writings were very minor: articles and verses for periodicals, dramatic criticism, which he never liked, because he saw himself as a man 'never judging system-wise of things, but fastening on particulars', jests for the *Morning Post* at sixpence a joke, political epigrams for the *Examiner* and the *Champion*, and editing for a while with John Fenwick the anti-ministerial paper *The Albion*. With Mary he found a true if minor outlet in writing for children: *Tales from Shakespeare* (1807), which earned him sixty guineas, and other books, especially *Poetry for Children* (1809). He liked an audience of children, and he was at home with the Elizabethans.

Reconciling himself to minor achievement, Lamb published a final and definitive edition of his writings in 1818, but the best was yet to come. It was Thomas Manning who first encouraged Lamb to stop imitating others in vain aspirations and to attempt to express himself in print. The main difficulty was Lamb's diffidence about being thus egotistical. Leigh Hunt brought him out with essays for *The Reflector* in 1811–12; but this collaboration came to an abrupt halt when Hunt satirized the Prince of Wales in prose, carrying on some gentle verse satire by Lamb in a previous issue, and was gaoled for two years for seditious libel. Eight more years elapsed before John Scott finally elicited *Elia* for the *London Magazine* in 1820. In two years Lamb earned £170 from periodicals, and a further profit of £30 when the collected *Essays of Elia* appeared in 1823. But Lamb was never a best-seller: the *Last Essays* in 1833 did not make a profit, and no second edition of *Elia* appeared in his lifetime in this country, although there was better success in the United States. 'I am the publisher's ruin,' he said, and, in defiance of the market, 'Damn the age! I will write for antiquity.'[1] There was much that was archaic in his style and appeal. Hood found him 'a literary Modern Antique, a New-Old Author, a living Anachronism'. The Victorian Alfred Ainger believed that with Lamb 'we live again with the thinkers and dreamers of long ago'. But it was some time before public favour caught his idiosyncratic taste, and Lamb died before he knew he would become the subject of near idolatry. What we get, then, from Lamb at his best is an innocent, unexploited egotism, a description of life from a unique perspective, honest by virtue of its very diffidence. At the last and best, Lamb is 'at his ease in the old arms of humanity', to quote Hazlitt, fulfilling himself with the true devotion of the profession of letters, at work with patience, gentle compassion and generosity, and lively imagination, upon human nature, who and what we are and what we do here.

Lamb never liked Byron or Shelley, because he could never understand or sympathize with their misanthropy. For similar differences, Carlyle, a man who believed that the population of Britain was 'thirty millions, mostly fools', did not like him. Lamb was saved from any retreat into an ivory tower of pride by his diffidence and devotion to humanity. The poets were much more apt to rub against a public hostility so fundamental that there was no alternative but retreat. Shelley's case was archetypal. As the heir to a baronetcy, a large property and a substantial fortune, he led a life of irresponsible leisure. As the writer of long romances, he had his public in print: it was never comparable with Byron's, partly because Shelley's romances

[1] Letter to Procter, 22 January 1829.

were never purely escapist, but held within them his doctrine of political anarchy. When Byron was moved by a political cause, he made his sympathies active, by going to Greece to fight in the war of independence against the Turks. When Shelley was moved, by Peterloo or other symptoms of the industrial distress of the day, he wrote about it. Both men were in a sense the darlings of their society, up to a point, and both, finding society in the end fundamentally hostile rather than approving, took refuge in voluntary exile abroad. The sexual freedom they both advocated, as part of a larger philosophy of anarchy, was tolerated for a while, on the basis that sensitive artists might be forgiven their emotional excesses, but homosexuality, incest and sodomy were a different proposition from a succession of mistresses. Shelley could never reconcile himself to the real public and the real social context in which he found himself; and the result was, in Tennyson's words, that he seems to 'go up in the air and burst', or in Arnold's phrase, he becomes an 'ineffectual angel beating his wings in a void of his own creation'.

Shelley's reaction to his environment was to cut himself off from it as completely as possible. A poet becomes in his eyes a different and unique species of man. Since a poem 'is at once the centre and circumference of knowledge', poets are the 'hierophants of an unapprehended inspiration . . . the unacknowledged legislators of the world'.[1] Since poetry is 'the record of the best and happiest moments of the happiest and best minds', the poet is 'the author to others of the highest wisdom, pleasure, virtue and glory' and ought to be 'personally . . . the happiest, the best, the wisest, and the most illustrious of men'. As T. S. Eliot dryly remarked, 'with Shelley, we are struck from the beginning by the number of things poetry is expected to do'.[2] As for himself, he reveals that his feelings were often 'awakened to such a state of unnatural and keen excitement that, only to instance the organ of sight, I find the very blades of grass and the boughs of distant trees present themselves to me with microscopic distinctness'.[3] His wife Mary said that 'No man has such keen sensations as Shelley. His nervous temperament was wound up by the delicacy of his health to an intense degree of

[1] *A Defence of Poetry*, E. Rhys, ed., *Essays and Letters* (1886), p. 7.
[2] *The Use of Poetry and the Use of Criticism* (1933), p. 88.
[3] Quoted by Mary Shelley, note on *Prometheus Unbound* (1819).

sensibility, and while his active mind pondered for ever upon, and drew conclusions from his sensations, his reveries increased their vivacity, till they mingled with, and were one with thought, and both became absorbing and tumultuous even to physical pain.'[1] Such an attitude towards himself expresses itself in part in his behaviour: attempting suicide, believing that he was dying from tuberculosis, stalking naked after bathing through his wife's tea parties, and, as one weary host put it, 'seeing visions and alarming the whole house'. It also finds expression in the way he treated his poetic audience.

Shelley believed that a poet writes for himself and has no need of an audience; he is 'a nightingale, who sits in darkness and sings to cheer its own solitude with sweet sounds; his auditors are as men entranced by the melody of an unseen musician, who feel that they are moved and softened, yet know not whence or why'.[2] His wife describes his ivory tower in these words: 'He sheltered himself from . . . disgusting and painful thoughts in the calm retreat of poetry, and built up a world of his own—with the more pleasure, since he hoped to induce some one or two to believe that the earth might become such, did mankind themselves consent.'[3] He did not care whether his work were successful in print or not; print was only useful in enabling him to reach a few kindred spirits. Walter Scott, bewildered by Shelley's vast claims, offered the poet some practical advice which by its very nature reveals the kind of ethos Shelley had taken arms against: 'I would . . . caution you against an enthusiasm which while it argues an excellent disposition and a feeling heart, requires to be watched and restrained, tho' not repressed. It is apt, if too much indulged, to engender a fastidious contempt for the ordinary business of the world, and gradually unfit us for the exercise of the useful and domestic virtues, which depend greatly on our not exalting our feelings above the temper of well-ordered and well-educated society.'[4] Poor Scott, who may have been talking about another planet altogether, for all the relevance Shelley found in his remark! The publishers, and the printed-book readers, accepted the poet as a phenomenon not to be explained in human terms. As the publisher of the posthumous edition of *Epipsychidion*

[1] *Essays, Letters from Abroad etc.*, I. 251.
[2] *A Defence of Poetry*, *op. cit.*, p. 10.
[3] Note on *Prometheus Unbound* (1819).
[4] Letter, 1 May 1811.

explained, about the poet's flight to the Mediterranean, 'the author hoped in the Sporades to realise a scheme of life suited perhaps to the happier and better world of which he is now an inhabitant, but hardly practicable in this'. For all Shelley's love and devotion for poetry, and his deep social conscience—'To defecate life of its misery and its evil,' said his wife, 'was the ruling passion of his soul'[1]—it is likely that the profession of letters would have come to an abrupt halt if his attitude towards writing had become general. In the last analysis, Shelley despairs of ever making any professional connexion between the writer and his public, of ever making real and immediate the service he thought he could render society. Behind his explosive hope and revolutionary energy lies a pessimism and a negativeness (perhaps the reason why his ideals are so often expressed in orgiastic floods of negative words). Many shared his despair: 'It requires a mind as subtle and as penetrating as his own to understand the mystic meanings scattered throughout the poem.'[2] It is Blake's madness, in another form.

Later poets followed Shelley's path of retreat, but the best seem to have been saved by a patience and perseverance, and perhaps a balanced sense of humour, which Shelley lacked. Tennyson's story might have been one of despair too. His grandfather was a wealthy solicitor and landed gentleman, but his father had trouble with his inheritance and had to take orders to earn a living, becoming a frustrated man, moody, and beating his wife, so that his family left him. His brothers and sisters were unbalanced: Frederick was sent down from Cambridge, Charles took opium, Edward was insane, Arthur had twitchings, Emily was driven into melancholia when she lost Arthur Hallam, and Septimus used to go around saying, according to Rossetti,' I am the most morbid of the Tennysons.' 'They are all strangely brought up,' commented the grandfather. When Alfred was 4 or 5 he used to go out on stormy days with his arms outspread, chanting: 'I hear a voice that's speaking in the wind', and at the age of 11 he had a manuscript book inscribed:

Vol. I The Poetry of Tennyson.
Vol. II The Lyrical Poetry of Tennyson.
Vol. III The Prose Writings of Tennyson.

[1] Mary Shelley, ed., *Poetical Works* (1839), preface.
[2] Note on *Prometheus Unbound* (1819).

As an adult he startled the American Hawthorne with his 'picturesque figure' and 'morbid painfulness', and captivated Elizabeth Browning with his 'frankess, confidingness and unnexampled *naïveté*', when he was moved by his own poems, so moved, Rossetti said, that the tears ran down his cheeks.

But he had also a patient nature: Carlyle found him 'dusty, smoky, free and easy . . . swims outwardly and inwardly, with great composure in an inarticulate element as of tranquil chaos and tobacco smoke . . . a most restful, brotherly, solid-hearted man'.[1] It was his balance which made him probably the best critic among the later Romantic poets (it was his taste which set the standard of Palgrave's *Golden Treasury*), and enabled him, when an adversary growled 'If an author pipe of adultery, fornication, murder and suicide, set him down as the practiser of these crimes', to reply mildly, 'Adulterer I may be, fornicater I may be, murderer I may be, suicide I am not yet'. He needed his strength. He reached print in 1826, in a volume by three of the Tennyson brothers, and again in 1830 and 1832, but the verse was ridiculed in the *Quarterly Review*, and by 1834 only 300 copies had been sold of the 450 impression of the 1830 volume. He relied on a small income from family sources and struggled on, putting aside thoughts of marriage. His perseverance won through. His 1842 poems found at last a favourable press, from Dickens and Samuel Rogers, although there were still vitriolic critics who refused to accept him, like the man who said that one or other of the vowels in the title *Maud* ought to be cut out—it didn't matter which. Slowly he won acceptance, becoming a Crown pensioner in 1847, Poet Laureate in 1850, and receiving the degree of Doctor of Civil Laws at Oxford in 1854. By 1859 he had published his first *Idylls of the King*, in 40,000 copies at 7*s*. each, and sold 10,000 in the first week. He was then offered 5,000 guineas for his next volume. *Enoch Arden* in 1864 ran to 60,000 copies in the first edition. Magazines like the *Contemporary Review* paid him £500 for a single poem, and the Americans offered him £1,000 for any three-stanza poem and £20,000 for a lecture tour.

It is not the best of Tennyson which achieved the highest sales, but he did much to educate the public to accept not only

[1] Letter to John Carlyle, 5 September 1840, D. A. Wilson, *Carlyle on Cromwell and others* (1925), p. 122.

his own best, but also the best of Shelley, Keats, and Byron. He revived public interest in Dryden. He inveighed against the magazine habit: 'Reading magazines breaks one's mind to bits —one ought to give up the newspapers.'[1] He brought stability to the literary profession at a time when, certainly as far as poetry was concerned, security was hard to find, and he was a sound influence among the new mass public audiences achieved in the later decades of the century. For all the pessimism of his philosophy in post-Darwinian society, he was practical in his actions. For all his conventionality he was a supporter of every reformist movement of his lifetime and was opposed to the growing unscrupulousness of high-pressure capitalism. For all his years of isolation and failure he never retreated into a personal mystique. He never posed. As Jowett reported, he was 'Absolute truthfulness, absolutely himself, never played tricks. Never got himself puffed in the newspapers. . . . He would have wished that, like Shakespeare, his life might be unknown to posterity.'[2] He saw poetry as a healing agency in a wounded society, and professionally devoted himself, within his lights, to the job of healing, in a real contemporary context rather than in the clouds of Shelley's dreams.

The equivalent among the prose writers was Thomas Carlyle, although Carlyle had more than a dash of the misanthropy and despairing self-regard which waylaid Byron and Shelley. Even at the time when he was beginning to taste success, Carlyle complained, in 1838, 'O that literature had never been devised. I am scourged to it by the whip of necessity.' This son of a stonemason started life with less than Tennyson. His first ambition was the Church, and then teaching. Indeed, he started off as a teacher of mathematics at schools in Annan and Kirkcaldy, and was still hoping for a university chair, in St Andrew's or London or Glasgow, as late as 1836, when he was in his forties. It gave him Johnsonian pleasure to reject the chairs offered him, when he no longer needed them, by Edinburgh and St Andrew's in 1841. What turned him away from mathematics and astronomy was an alternative ambition of 'literary fame', 'the wish of being known'. It was this ambition which induced him to move to

[1] Quoted in C. Tennyson, *Alfred Tennyson* (1949), p. 452.

[2] 'Notes on characteristics of Tennyson', in Hallam Tennyson, ed., *Tennyson and his Friends* (1911), p. 186.

Edinburgh with his savings of £90. He refused to work as a journalist, despising the trade, and began with contributions in prose and verse for magazines and the *Edinburgh Encyclopaedia*. He translated Legendre's *Geometry* in 1824 for £50, and then wrote a *Life of Schiller*, which was accepted for serial publication in the *London Magazine* for £100. He went on to take up translations from German, but returns were small, and he had to augment his income with interludes of private tutoring, positions worth up to £200 a year. Tutoring, however, was 'selling the very quintessence of his spirit', and even after his marriage to Jane he preferred to live in retirement, on a farm which others might work for him, leaving him free to persevere with his translations and his reviews for the *Edinburgh Review*, the *Foreign Review*, the *Foreign Quarterly Review*, and later, *Fraser's* and the *Westminster*. He recognized that he was no poet, and the one novel he attempted was a failure, yet he resisted all attempts to interest him in journalism (Jeffrey wanted him as his successor as editor of the *Edinburgh Review*). He went on ploughing a lonely furrow, sure of his own genius and of the value some day of his literary devotion, yet not being able to present himself, or his patient wife, with any positive proof that he was a genius at all.

The first completed work which gave expression to his range of talents for historical-critical-philosophical writing, in a prose all his own, was *Sartor Resartus*. No publisher would accept it in book form, but it was serialized in 1830 in *Fraser's* (indeed, it did not appear as a book until 1838, and then only on the guarantee of friends; and yet a few months before his death a cheap reprint sold 30,000 copies in a few weeks). The public impact was virtually nil, although in the United States greater interest was shown. When he moved to Chelsea in 1834 his wife and he had savings of only £200–£300, and the future was not encouraging. Indeed, in 1833 he reported that he had not earned a penny from his writings in twenty-three months. But he refused a post on *The Times* and persevered. 'My friends,' he commented dryly, 'think I have found the art of living upon nothing.' The turning-point came with *The French Revolution* (1837). Inauspiciously, John Stuart Mill lost the manuscript and insisted on recompensing Carlyle with £200. When the book was finally published it found little success in this country, but

Carlyle earned £400 from American sales. Then Harriet Martineau organized courses of lectures for him, four in all, which raised between them £835. On the death of Jane's mother in 1842 his wife inherited between £200 and £300 a year. From this time the Carlyles became both prosperous and famous: they were caught up in the circle of Lady Harriet Ashburton (Lord Ashburton left them £2,000 in his will in 1864), and returns from print became substantial, a new edition of *The French Revolution* and *Miscellanies* earning £600.

By 1854 the family income was about £400 a year, not large, but comfortable in a house where the rent was only £30 a year and the housekeeping totalled £230. They travelled first-class, and were soon able to keep two servants and run a brougham. When the *History of Frederick the Great* appeared in 1858 it ran into three editions a year, two of 2,000 and one of 1,000. After long struggles Carlyle had at last approached the class of Macaulay, who about the same time was earning £20,000 for the third and fourth volumes of his history. He became the great man who was elected Rector of Edinburgh University, who was called to the Queen, who was presented with the Prussian *Ordre pour le mérite*, who received the attention of artists like Millais and Watts, and who characteristically refused the offer of a pension and a G.C.B. from Disraeli. Yet, most of the triumph was reserved for the period after the death of his wife, and he was bitter about it: 'If they would give me £10,000 a year, and bray unanimously their *hosannahs* heaven-high for the rest of my life—who *now* would there be to get the smallest joy or profit from it?'[1] Carlyle believed in himself, and had overridden many obstacles to achieve his goal, at the personal cost of a life of cantankerousness, domestic and public conflict, and a bitterness which became more and more ingrained as time went on.

This kind of single-minded dedication to literature had its price for the wives, too. Jane Carlyle was a capable talented woman whose letters reveal that she might have had a literary career as well as her husband; but, as she said, marrying 'a man of genius' carried special responsibilities and involved personal sacrifice. In a state of relative poverty, she had no choice but to turn all her energies to domestic chores, for which she had little

[1] Letter to Jean Aitken, 23 June 1866, D. A. Wilson and D. W. MacArthur, *Carlyle in Old Age* (1934), p. 85.

natural aptitude. Her inheritance came too late to affect the pattern of her married life: her claims for personal fulfilment took second place to Thomas, even if the only way she knew she was making him happy was by observing when he stopped grumbling. On Carlyle's side it must be pointed out that her martyrdom was brought to his attention as frequently as was useful. And they remained united in a real sense: other wives of men of genius committed suicide, went mad, or lost all touch with their husbands.

In contrast, but rather exceptionally, Robert Browning was ideally matched in Elizabeth. Quite apart from any felicities of temperamental sympathy, her private fortune, inherited from her father, was sufficient to free her husband from all domestic anxieties, and leave herself free to write her own poetry (Victorian critics acclaimed her 'the greatest poetess whom the world has yet seen'). Browning needed her help: like Carlyle, he single-mindedly devoted himself to literature. His first poems were published in 1833 when he was only 21, and he went on to publish another thirty-five volumes, the last coming in the year of his death fifty-six years later. For long periods he had to publish at his own expense, in pamphlet form; the market was so small that Edward Moxon, a literary publisher who had been helpful to Wordsworth, Southey, and Lamb, refused to take the risk of a collected edition. In the end, like Tennyson, Browning won his public over. After *The Ring and the Book* in 1868, as the Victorian critic George Saintsbury reported, 'though still anathematized by a very few, he was grudgingly tolerated by more, admitted by the general, and wildly and foolishly adored by a certain sect'. There is a caricature by Beerbohm of the poet having tea with the Browning Society at Girton College, Cambridge, in which Browning appears ruddy, masculine, hearty, and sublimely uneccentric, surrounded by fans who are clearly worried and confused by the real man in their midst: 'Poets', they seem to be saying, 'ought not to be quite like this.' Browning was by nature cheerful and optimistic: Mary Gladstone in 1877 said that 'he talks everybody down with his dreadful voice, and always places his person in such disagreeable proximity with yours, and puffs and blows and spits in your face'. But one wonders how much of the natural Browning would have survived if his environment had been Carlyle's, if he had not had the good fortune of the security given him by his wife.

Charles Dickens had no such fortune. This son of a dockyard clerk, who fell into debt and into the Marshalsea Prison, had to earn his living the hard way. He started life as a newspaper reporter at the age of 17, and like Johnson, worked his way through to literary eminence from the bottom. His first attempt at fiction came in his early twenties, when he sold the sketch, *A Dinner at Poplar Walk*, later incorporated in *Sketches by Boz*. He then tried essays in the *Old Monthly* and *Chronicle*, and published a collected *Sketches by Boz* in 1836 for £350. The idea of a picture illustrated by a short story or essay was a popular one at the time, and Chapman and Hall commissioned him to write the prose commentary for a series of Cockney sporting pictures in shilling numbers, the artist being first Seymour and then Phiz. In April 1836 he began earning £14 for each monthly instalment: thus began the *Pickwick Papers*. His aptitude for fiction attracted the editor of *Bentley's Miscellany*, a new monthly, who commissioned the two novels to be called *Oliver Twist* and *Barnaby Rudge*. Simultaneously, Chapman and Hall commissioned a successor to *Pickwick Papers* in *Nicholas Nickleby*. Since Dickens was engaged in other work also, as a journalist, the load had to be reduced, and he succeeded in freeing himself from Bentley by borrowing £2,500 to buy the copyright of *Oliver Twist* and to cancel other contracts. He also bought out the rights to *Sketches by Boz*, which had been published by a third firm, Macrone, and put all his eggs in the basket of Chapman and Hall. He stayed with this firm until 1844, when he switched to Bradbury and Evans, receiving £2,800 for a fourth share in whatever he might write in the next eight years. Thus began an increasingly prosperous career, in which eighteen novels appeared in thirty-four years, published in part form or as serials in periodicals. His journalism continued: he was for a short while editor of the *Daily News*, and editor also of two of the periodicals in which his own stories appeared, *Household Words* and *All the Year Round*. There was other literary work, like an edition of the *Memoirs of Grimaldi*.

Dickens lived in closer contact with his audience than many novelists and artists of his time: people could, and did, write to him about his stories, begging him, for instance, between one instalment and the next, to reprieve Little Nell. He was a writer subject to the attentions and pressures exercised, for example, by modern radio writers over scripts about the Dales and the Archers. He worked from hand to mouth, an instalment at a time, and never wrote his novels as an organic whole. He was influenced not only by his fan mail, but by other extraneous considerations such as competition from rival periodicals. As Edwin Muir suggests, he was 'congenitally melodramatic' by nature, but many of the exaggerations of his view of life, the extraordinary coincidences, the gratuitous horror and nightmare, the grotesqueness and disorderly profusion of his situations, may be directly attributable to the professional context in which he worked. As with Scott, the highly successful salesman all too often obscures the genuine artist at work in a unique field of literary imagination.

In contrast, the other great novelist of his day, seven years his junior, George Eliot, preserved her professional integrity while achieving a similar measure of commercial success. Technically, she was supported through life, first by her father, and then by George Henry Lewes, the man with whom she lived, as in marriage, for most of her adult life. But Mary Ann Evans lived at a time when women were beginning to take up professions in their own right, and, though no careerist, she devoted herself to the profession of letters and was capable at all times of supporting herself. Lewes adored her as a genius, and she thought of him as the leading thinker of his time, and altogether their real relationship was one of mutual comfort and support, with none of the problems that beset the Carlyles and other literary couples. She first became a writer by translating theology by Strauss, Spinoza and Feuerbach; she tried a few poems for her own amusement, and then theological articles for periodicals and reviews. From 1851 to 1853, in her early thirties, she was literary editor of the *Westminster Review*, coming into contact with contributors like Mill, Froude, Newman, and Harriet Martineau. Once she had joined her life with Lewes, she abandoned journalism as such, and was encouraged by her 'husband' to attempt fiction. There was still much masculine prejudice to overcome (all but one of her previous writings had been published anonymously), and hence the adoption of a masculine *nom de plume*. *Scenes of Clerical Life* appeared in 1858, in part-form in *Blackwood's Magazine*, at fifty guineas a part. She immediately caught the eye of critics like Carlyle, Thackeray, and especially Dickens, and found an immediate market for her novels. *Adam Bede* appeared in the same year and was an immediate success, running through seven editions and 16,000 copies. Excluding the copyright, she earned £1,600, and the publisher, Blackwood, promised for the future £2,000 on every 4,000 copies of her novels published.

George Eliot only tried one book as a serial: *Romola* (1862–3), which was bought by *Cornhill* for £7,000. She hated the experiment and never repeated it. On the other hand, her two biggest successes were published in eight monthly parts, *Middlemarch* (1871–2), which sold over 25,000 copies in four years, earning over £7,000, and *Daniel Deronda* (1876). The novels were, however, written as a whole before the first part appeared. She desired no kind of intimacy with her audience, preferring to remain quite aloof. Indeed, she never read the critics, in case she should be discouraged by ill-considered praise or blame: 'Far worse than any verdict as to the proportion of good and evil in our work is the painful impression that we exist for a public which has no discernment of good and evil.'[1] In extenuation, it might be said that she needed to erect arrogant barriers against the world: her 'marriage' was ostracized by society at large, and her agnosticism and scepticism were the subject also of painful criticism. She believed that 'there is no private life which has not been determined by a wider public life', and was making sure that her barriers sensibly kept her ideas and way of life as insulated as possible from the interference and knowledge of the public. The insulation was sensible for her literary career, too; she remained free to develop as an artist, and her last work is by general agreement her best. Secure, she was able to enlarge upon her distinctive view of life, its tolerance and moral sternness, its idealism and pessimism, side by side.

By the 1870's the literary profession presented a crowded scene which the historian recognizes with scant justice. There was Matthew Arnold, the first Professor of Poetry to turn English Literature into a subject of specialized university study, the law-giver, of Olympian manners—'the sound of his voice and the wave of his arm was Jove-like'—who insisted that poetry was 'a complete *magister vitae*', a religion at a time when 'there

[1] Quoted in L. Stephen, *George Eliot* (1907), p. 146.

is not a creed which is not shaken'. But the author of *Essays in Criticism* and *Culture and Anarchy* was a salesman, too: he had two publishers, Macmillan and Smith, Elder, and played them off against each other, scrutinizing sales prices with acute vigilance. 'I make literature put my boys to school,' he said, 'and literature failing, I want £200.' Then there was William Makepeace Thackeray, who perhaps would rather have been an amateur dilettante than a professional, and a painter or a barrister rather than a writer. His first connexion with literature was as a newspaper owner, but when the *National Standard* and the *Constitutional* failed, he was caught up more and more in writing, for *The Times*, for *Fraser's*, and many other periodicals. He hung on to some pretence of amateur status by adopting various pseudonyms. But finally he was involved wholly with a professional life, tempting the market with Christmas books, becoming a popular contributor to *Punch*, and serializing his novels in *Cornhill*, of which he became the editor at a salary in the end of £2,000 a year.

Another great figure was John Ruskin. With wealthy parents he led a life of leisure, developing his interests in painting and architecture and writing about them. But, like De Quincey, his large inheritance, in the region of £200,000, was dissipated, chiefly in generous gifts to needful friends and causes, and he was compelled to take up literature seriously for a livelihood. In his early fifties he started his own publishing business in Orpington, and made a success especially with *Fors Clavigera*, which appeared first at 7*d.* a number, then 10*d.* For the last fifteen years of life he was the successful salesman who made an income of £4,000 a year, chiefly from books. Like other writers of his time, Ruskin found a serious audience in the new working men's colleges, where he lectured and gained new readers. Working at the same time were William Morris and his friends, whose socialist sympathies were bringing them into contact with readers in the lower social strata, who had never previously before exercised any significant influence in the printed-book market. A revolution was at hand.

All through the nineteenth century the reading public had been widening, outwards and downwards through all levels of society. Educational reform, cheaper methods of mass production, and the social sympathies of writers had all helped gradually to bring about, for the first time, the possibility of a mass market, and it is time some of the implications and results of this revolution were examined. It is all too easy to associate with a wider reading public an inevitable lowering of standards, too easy to forget that the profession of letters could not be finally secure except on the basis of a very wide general public. This chapter describes the difficulties writers had experienced in preserving their integrity in times before the mass market was a significant reality at all. From this viewpoint writers have always had, and always will have, a struggle to assert and maintain standards, whenever a new public is gathered into their audience. But, after all, this is what a profession is *for*: if the professional service is useful, or necessary, for some, it must be extended to all who will find it useful, or necessary. The doctor and the lawyer are not mere social luxuries. If the writer is to claim a professional value and competence on a par with theirs, he must be prepared to extend his service, asserting that value and competence until a new public is prepared to accept his standards. The conflict between the artist and the salesman intensified in the last decades of the century; but it was a necessary conflict seeking a necessary resolution, and the profession of letters was by now strong enough to take up the challenge.

# X

## The Mass Market

*The English are, so far as I know, the hardest worked people on whom the sun shines. Be content if in their wretched intervals of leisure they read for amusement and do no worse. They are born at the oar, and they live and die at it. Good God, what would you have of them?*

DICKENS[1]

IN 1801 the population of Britain was 10,500,000. By 1901 the figure had trebled, and more, to 37,000,000. There is sufficient explanation here for the steady increase in book production throughout the century, allowing for a reasonably proportional increase in the number of people who were by class and tradition educated and literate. Doubtless, the encouragement given to private, charity and factory schools, following the first State grants to education from 1833, increased steadily the number of 'working-class' readers, as did the work of the Mechanics' Institutes and early University Extension Movement. But a mass market, in any proper sense of the term, did not arise until the decades at the end of the century, after State education had been established in 1870 and free elementary education in 1890. When in mid-century Archibald Constable talked of 'literature for the millions', he was referring to volumes priced at 6*s*. each!

When Lane of the Minerva Press established his circulating library in Leadenhall Street in 1770, a library which by 1802

[1] Quoted in Charles Knight, *Passages of a Working Life* (1864), iii, 17.

held 17,000 volumes and had an agent in every principal town, the borrowing charge per volume sometimes amounted to 2*d.* a day. The greatest of the nineteenth-century libraries, Mudie's, which regularly bought for its clients 600 copies of the *Quarterly* and the *Edinburgh Review*, or as many as 3,000 copies of a book like Disraeli's *Lothair*, charged an annual subscription of a guinea. These prices represented an economy to middle-class readers, who might have paid otherwise £1. 11*s.* 6*d.* for a three-volume novel, but were entirely out of the reach of the majority of the population. Charlotte Yonge, Ouida and Marie Corelli, and Mudie's other best-sellers, were not therefore the product of a mass market.

Similarly, the great periodicals of the century were intended for a minority public. The *Edinburgh Review* and *Quarterly*, selling about 14,000 copies each in 1818, reached saturation point at this level. The *Westminster Review* did not better a circulation of about 3,000. Leigh Hunt's *Examiner* at best sold 7,000. The best-selling number of the *Cornhill* was probably its first in 1860, when 110,000 copies were sold; by 1871 its circulation had dropped to 20,000 and by 1882 to 12,000. The *Fortnightly Review* in 1872 saturated its market with 25,000 and the *Saturday Review* about 1880 with 10,000. Even the *Athenaeum*, which appeared as a fourpenny in 1831 with high hopes of attracting working-class readers, stopped at 18,000. This is a great age of periodicals: in 1859, 115 were started in London alone—but the vast majority of all these magazines were bought and read by a middle-class minority. There were a few genuine ventures for a mass public. The Society for the Diffusion of Useful Knowledge, founded in 1827, ran a *Penny Magazine*, which reached a circulation of 200,000, but failed financially in 1846. Chambers's *Edinburgh Journal* had a circulation of 90,000 in the 1850's. And Charles Knight's *Penny Cyclopaedia* had a sale of 75,000 in 1833; but significantly the readership dropped to 55,000 when the price was increased to 2*d.* in 1834, and to 20,000 when the price became 4*d.* in 1843.

It was the same with newspapers. Before new legislation abolished advertising duties in 1853, the stamp duty in 1855, and excise taxes on paper in 1861, English newspapers had tiny circulations and were few in number, a particularly unfavourable state compared with, say, the United States at this time. The mass newspapers, like William Cobbett's *Political Register* and Henry Hetherington's *Poor Man's Guardian*, which during the 1830's had a circulation of 20,000, were essentially irregular, even illicit, journals. A special Coronation number of the *Observer* in 1821 sold 61,500 copies, and the issue of the *Sun* which commemorated the Coronation of Queen Victoria went into twenty reprints. But in 1829 only 630,000 papers were sold each week, a proportion of one copy to every thirty-six inhabitants: as Bulwer Lytton pointed out in the House of Commons, the comparative proportion in the state of Pennsylvania was one to every four. The best of the dailies, *The Times*, did not reach a circulation of 5,000 until 1815; and in 1853 it was still selling only 60,000, although this figure was three times that of all the other morning papers put together. The situation altered drastically after 1855. Penny dailies appeared, the *Sheffield Daily Telegraph*, the *Liverpool Daily Post*, the *London Evening News*, and then the *Daily Telegraph and Courier*, which claimed by 1875 'the largest circulation in the world', 200,000, compared with the 150,000 of its nearest rival, the *Daily News*. Halfpenny papers put in an appearance in the 1850's, particularly with evening editions, and in the 1870's there were a few examples of papers selling at a farthing. In 1851 there were 563 newspapers and periodicals in the country; by 1862 there were 1,165 newspapers and 213 magazines; by 1870, 1,390 newspapers and 626 magazines; by 1880, 1,986 newspapers and 1,097 magazines; by 1890, 2,234 newspapers and 1,778 magazines; and by 1900, 2,488 newspapers and 2,446 magazines. By 1863 a Sunday paper, *Lloyd's Weekly News*, was selling over 300,000 copies, and over a million by 1896. By 1870 there were ninety-nine dailies compared with only fourteen in 1846. By 1900 Alfred Harmsworth's *Daily Mail* had a circulation of 700,000 daily, and similar figures were attained by weeklies like his *Answers* and its predecessor, George Newnes's *Titbits*. This is truly the mass market.

A number of factors combined to produce these revolutionary developments. Increased literacy and an end to repressive legislation were two of them. Others were technical. In 1800 hand presses could produce only 5,000 copies of a newspaper in a day. By 1850 steam power produced 40,000 in four hours. By 1900 web press printing from continuous rolls, and other innovations allowed the rolling off of 200,000 in an hour. Linotype and Monotype machines increased the speed of typesetting. New chemical pulp processes increased the production of paper from 11,000 tons, all hand-made, in 1800 to 652,000 tons, all machine-made, in 1900. Paper prices dropped from 1*s.* 6*d.* a pound in 1800 to 3*d.* a pound in 1900. There were other technical advances in the reproduction of illustrations and in the means of distribution. In the last decades of the nineteenth century all these factors come together to set the mass market on its inexorable progress towards the mass circulations of today, when weekly magazines exceed 2,000,000, daily papers 4,000,000, and Sunday papers reach above 8,000,000. Sales were advanced by all kinds of stunts: competitions, insurance policies, treasure hunts, £10,000 prizes for first flights, and the like. But the popular paper had come to stay.

It is sometimes argued that in these decades we ceased to be a nation of book-readers and became a nation devoted to the newspaper and periodicals. But it seems to be true that an increased readership in one direction encourages, rather than discourages, increased readerships in others, and the book trade seems to keep pace with the papers. Between 1816 and 1851 the number of new books published each year averaged about 1,250. By 1913 the figure had risen, steadily and persistently, to 9,541. Despite setbacks in the world wars the annual figures have continued to increase into our own times, reaching 17,137 in 1937, 19,962 in 1955, and 23,783 in 1960. There are several qualifications, which must be made in due course, about interpreting this growth as a story of literary progress, but by and large the literary profession has gained in strength from the mass market.

At the height of Dickens's fame there were novels of the *Gentleman Jack* variety which sold, in penny weekly parts, ten, twenty and thirty times more than his. In hard covers, there has always in modern times been an *East Lynne*, a *Gone with the Wind*, or a *Cruel Sea*, to sell upwards of half a million copies, to the despair perhaps of more literary novelists whose books will conceivably attain a more lasting reputation in the history of letters. But the technical advances which were precipitated by the immediate and ephemeral needs of a mass public also helped publishers achieve mass sales for books of lasting quality. Cheaper paper brought a reduction in the percentage cost of paper in book production from 20·5 in 1740 to 7·1 in 1910, and in the nineteenth century machines reduced printing costs by 25 per cent. There were more skilled compositors available: in London, 11,355 in 1900 compared with 1,751 in 1845. It became possible by 1900 to produce cheap hard-cover editions at prices between 1*s.* and 3*s.* 6*d.* Developments following the Copyright Act of 1842 released, about the turn of the century, all kinds of great works for mass publication in pocket editions, and in rapid succession Nelson's *Classics*, Oxford's *World Classics*, Collins's *Pocket Classics*, and Dent's *Everyman's Library* were established in the first decade of the twentieth century, to perpetuate as best-sellers the works of Jane Austen and Dickens, Mill and Boswell, Gibbon and Charlotte Brontë. New means were established for communicating worth while literature to a mass public: book clubs (*World Books* has a membership of 150,000), the book token system originating in 1932 to secure for books a proper proportion of the gift trade, and paper-backs, following the inauguration of *Penguin Books* in 1935 (through which agency E. V. Rieu's translation of the *Odyssey* sold over 1,000,000 copies between 1946 and 1955).

In the long term the real best-sellers are not novels which sell vast numbers in the first years of circulation, but works like translations of the *Bible*, editions of Shakespeare (Dent's *Temple* series sold over 5,000,000), Bunyan's *Pilgrim's Progress* (now translated into 147 languages), the *Golden Treasury*, and so on. One often hears complaints about changes brought about by the mass market. It is true that in modern industrial communities the proportion of paper devoted to books is very small, in the United States less than 1 per cent. Bookselling, always a difficult proposition, has increasing difficulties in this century, and it is important not to minimize these. In 1957 only 32,000,000 hard-cover adult books were sold in the United States, although there were 233,000,000 paper-backs sold, and nearly 26,000,000 encyclopaedias and other subscription books. The pattern of bookselling and bookbuying has certainly changed a good deal. But all the new activity is in truth the broad base of a pyramid, on the apex of which the sale of good literature continues on a broader scale than ever before. The kind of audience provided by *Penguins* in print, and the B.B.C. Third Programme in broadcasting, would not have existed if the mass market had not been achieved for other purposes. This is the inference to be drawn from the careers of the leading professionals of letters in the period from 1880 to the present day. In brief, they all seem to have depended upon one assumption: ultimately, they agree, 'giving the public what it wants' breeds its own ennui; people tire of entertainment which merely feeds stock responses and which fails to satisfy, properly, deeply, imaginatively, their curiosity about the workings of human nature; ultimately, then, provided increased leisure is made available, people will turn from the weaker literature which merely skims the shallows of life to the writers who have new perspectives and deep experiences to offer.

Wordsworth was one of the first writers to attribute the rise of cheap fiction to the social consequences of the Industrial Revolution, and to express dismay about the way bad reading blunted 'the discriminating powers of the mind, and, unfitting it for all voluntary exertion,' reduced it 'to a state of almost savage torpor'.[1] There have been many voices since, crying with Carlyle 'Universal Shoddy', or with Lawrence 'Ugliness, ugliness, ugliness'. George Gissing summed up the case against the popular Press when he suggested in 1904 that its readers seemed to want only 'the lightest and frothiest of chit-chatty information—bits of stories, bits of foolery, bits of statistics, bits of jokes. . . . Everything must be very short, two inches at the utmost. . . . Even chat is too solid for them; they want chit-chat.'[2] But there have been other writers, not necessarily more sympathetic, but perhaps more tolerant, who have riposted, with Dickens, 'Good God, what would you have of them!' Ruskin started from the assumption that 'the man who has been heaving clay out of a ditch all day, or driving an express train against the north wind all night, or holding a collier's helm in a gale on a lee shore, or whirling white-hot iron at a furnace mouth, is not the same man at the end of his day, or night, as one who has been sitting in a quiet room, with everything comfortable about him'.[3] And, in defence of the *Daily Mail* and similar papers, Lord Northcliffe once suggested that, before the rise of the popular newspaper, 'journalism dealt with only a few aspects of life. What we did

[1] *Lyrical Ballads* (1800), preface.
[2] *New Grub Street* (1904), p. 419.
[3] *The Crown of Wild Olive* (1865, 1919 ed.), p. 27.

was to extend its purview to the whole. . . . The old type was convinced that anything which would be a subject of conversation ought to be kept out of the press.'[1] This is an important debate still inconclusive in times of greater leisure and commercial television. It is a fact that the popular Press and popular fiction alike have tended to draw attention away from what might be termed responsible interests, seeking news and novelty in crime and sensation, in the bizarre and the abnormal; but they have also aroused, satisfied and maintained a certain curiosity about human nature which is near to the central purposes of literature, and one would quarrel with them not because of what they do, but because of how they do it: the argument would be concerned with quality.

The career of George Bernard Shaw indicates the kind of conflict, and the kind of victory, available to the dedicated man of letters in our own century. Before he was 30 it was apparent that the theatre, already long established as an entertainment industry, had entered a new period of favour with audiences obtained from all sections of the community. After Queen Victoria's patronage in mid-century, the theatre was once more respectable and even genteel. The West End of London had become a social rendezvous for spectators travelling in from a vast urban area: here seven new theatres were built between 1860 and 1870, and ten between 1880 and 1890. Acting was once more an honourable profession, with knighthoods bestowed upon leading practitioners. Some 20,000 plays were produced between 1850 and 1900, a number vastly in excess of any other half-century of English history. New financial arrangements, whereby authors received a percentage of the takings, killed the hack system, and made it profitable, in times of the 'long run', for managers to cultivate authors who could establish a reputation for quality rather than quantity. Dion Boucicault, for instance, earned £10,000 for *Colleen Bawn*, whereas previously as a company hack he had never earned more than £400 for a single play and had been usually paid £50 an act. Conditions were propitious for a returning interest in the theatre by the men of letters, and quite apart from hacks like Douglas Jerrold, C. H. Hazlewood, George Pitt, and Sydney Grundy, careers in playwriting were achieved in Victorian times by Tom Taylor, who

[1] Quoted in Harold Herd, *The March of Journalism* (1952), p. 241.

at different times was a professor of English Language and Literature, a barrister, Secretary to the Board of Health, and Editor of *Punch*; by Charles Reade, who had been Vice-President of Magdalen College, Oxford, and a successful novelist; by amateurs like Leopold Lewis, professionally a solicitor, and new professional writers, earning respect for their plays as literature, of whom a leading example was Sir Arthur Wing Pinero.

In short, the theatre was ripe for the efforts of a writer who would restore its lost seriousness, who believed as Shaw did that 'the best dramatic art is the operation of a divinatory instinct for truth'. Shaw set out early to educate himself as a writer. In his early twenties he gave up commercial posts, lived with and upon his mother, and set out to write, methodically, five pages a day. Between 1879 and 1883 he wrote five novels, which publishers refused, Macmillan on four separate occasions. In his first nine years in London he earned only £6 by his writing. William Archer helped him to reviewing work, and his first year of book reviews for the *Pall Mall Gazette* earned him £117. He went on to become, successively, art critic for *The World*, music critic for T. P. O'Connor's *Star*, music critic for *The World*, and finally in 1895 drama critic for Frank Harris's *Saturday Review* at a salary of £6 a week. Reasonably secure now, and even more so after his marriage in 1898 to a wealthy Irishwoman, he turned his attention increasingly to play-writing. Under the influence of the first London productions of Ibsen in 1889 and 1891, and after he had written his book *The Quintessence of Ibsenism*, he wrote plays about social problems of the day, about landlords, feminists and prostitutes. *Widowers Houses* was produced by the Independent Theatre Society and *Mrs. Warren's Profession*, after being banned by the Lord Chamberlain, was privately produced by the Stage Society in 1902. He created critical tumult in the Press and lived through a period of violent public reaction: when *Mrs. Warren's Profession* was played in New York in 1906 the entire cast was arrested, but subsequently acquitted, on a charge of disorderly conduct, and even his friends disowned him, Archer, for instance, suggesting that Shaw 'cannot touch pitch without wallowing in it'. His aim, he said, was to civilize England through drama, 'to force the spectator to face unpleasant facts', to break up the English tradition of spending the evening sitting 'in separate families in separate houses, each person silently occupied with a book, a paper, or a game of halma, cut off equally from the blessings of society and solitude'.[1]

Having failed to win substantial public sympathy by colliding head-on with popular prejudice, Shaw next attempted pleasanter plays, dealing with romantic follies rather than crimes. In *Arms and the Man* he used the conventional form of romantic comedy to satirize romance; in *Candida* he used the form of domestic comedy to satirize conventional domestic bliss; in *You Never Can Tell* he used the form of Society comedy to debunk Society. He was helped by his association with Granville-Barker at the Royal Court, where *Arms and the Man* ran with mediocre success for eleven weeks. *Candida* in the end was produced in the provinces, and *You Never Can Tell* was withdrawn from the Haymarket after a fortnight's rehearsals. These were serious plays, discussing the consequences 'sometimes terrible, sometimes ludicrous, of our persistent attempts to found our institutions on the ideals suggested to our imaginations by our half-satisfied passions, instead of on a genuinely scientific natural history'.[2] Shaw wanted the theatre to survive by 'a constant supply of interesting plays', plays which did not deal in the 'obvious conflicts of unmistakable good with unmistakable evil', plays which concerned themselves with 'ourselves in our own situations' in such a way that audiences would ask questions of themselves and seek values and revaluations. But the impact upon the public remained unsatisfactory for a long time, even after 'plays for Puritans' like *The Devil's Disciple* and *Caesar and Cleopatra.* Shaw had to wait until 1914 before he achieved a first big success with *Pygmalion*, which earned Tree, the producer, £13,000 in three months.

He proceeded meanwhile to print the plays and his dramatic criticism, prefacing his volumes with long dissertations, not always strictly relevant, which explained himself to the public. His political work helped to get himself known: he was on the executive committee of the Fabian Society between 1885 and 1911, and wrote many pamphlets; he was a borough councillor in St. Pancras between 1900 and 1903; and with Sidney and Beatrice Webb he assisted in the launching of *The New Statesman* in 1913. Even more useful to him was the reputation for forthright eccentricity that he gradually achieved for himself, 'one of

[1] Preface to *Plays Unpleasant*, *Prefaces* (1934), p. 690.
[2] Preface to *Plays Pleasant*, *Prefaces*, p. 703.

the most successful of my fictions', he confessed. 'Whoever the author,' concluded Edward VII of one of the plays, 'he is, of course, mad.' It paid Shaw, as it paid Swift in earlier times, to have the public say this kind of thing of him. He established a successful public image of an *enfant terrible*, dedicated, as J. B. Priestley once said, to the purpose of disturbing 'Victorian smugness and Edwardian ease'.[1] The exhibitionism came naturally to him: 'Some people,' he said, 'are born with a terrible desire to be laughed at: this has prevented me from becoming a great author.' Maybe the dazzling wit is frequently a literary superfluity, inorganic in a particular work, but certainly Shaw's stunts, and the irrepressible sense of humour from which they stemmed, were priceless assets in making the public listen to what he had seriously to say. In the end, most people agreed with Margaret Cole: 'You may disagree with what Shaw says, or foam at the mouth while reading it. But you cannot possibly say that you have no idea what he means.'[2] His fiction helped Shaw to an audience, alike for his political books, like the *Intelligent Woman's Guide to Socialism* and *Everybody's Political What's What*, and for his plays.

By the time *Man and Superman* was published in 1903, Shaw could afford to separate himself from any anxiety about pleasing his public. He told *The Times* dramatic critic that this play was intended for a 'pit of philosophers': 'I plank down my view of the existing relations of men to women in the most highly civilized society for what it is worth. It is a view like any other view and no more, neither true nor false, but, I hope, a way of looking at the subject which throws into the familiar order of cause and effect a sufficient body of fact and experience to be interesting to you, if not to the playgoing public of London. I have certainly shewn little consideration for that public in this enterprise; but . . . it will take my books as read and my genius for granted, trusting me to put forth work of such quality as shall bear out its verdict. So we may disport ourselves on our own plane to the top of our bent.'[3] As it happened, the play was never a failure. After a moderately good first season at the Royal Court, it was a complete success on Broadway, making the producer £40,000 in

[1] *News Chronicle*, 3 November 1950.
[2] *Fabian Journal*, February 1951.
[3] Preface to *Man and Superman*, *Prefaces*, p. 161.

seven months. In a sense, Shaw was perhaps too successful. He seems to have built up, particularly in his later years, an arrogance that was impervious to all criticism, cut off from the challenge and support of an active relationship between the author and his public. Living in a world of his own, he came to see men, as has been remarked, as 'ideas walking', a publicist's vision, in the end, rather than a dramatist's. He left himself vulnerable to T. S. Eliot's indictment: 'Mr. Shaw never was really interested in life.'

Little damage was done to the plays immediately preceding the first World War. *Major Barbara*, *The Doctor's Dilemma*, and *Pygmalion* especially, seem to be written from a state of balance and indeed compromise: the hard intellectual content is softened by a warmth of human sympathy, deriving from Shaw's involvement at that time in a healthy context with his public. He took great interest in the productions of his own plays, loved his actors and actresses, and was personally involved in making his plays presentable in the living theatre; his interest was entirely genuine (he refused the Presidency of the Royal Academy of Dramatic Art because he felt that an actor should hold that position, and he always held that he owed far more to actors than they to him), and he was a good producer. The war, however, brought about his isolation: 'Truth telling,' he once said, sadly, 'is not compatible with the defence of the Realm', and his forthright views won him many enemies and general unpopularity. And the world was very changed by 1919: there was no smugness and ease for him to sweep away, and society was awake to a new grim order of life without any assistance from Shaw. In the first few years, when society acted upon the slogan 'Back to normality', conditions were still reasonably favourable to him. From this period date his last good plays, including *Saint Joan*, which was written exceptionally quickly to exploit the interest aroused by Joan's canonization in 1920. But gradually Shaw seems to have been left in isolation, a prophet who had outlived his own prophecies. He was never more esteemed, being awarded the Nobel Prize for Literature in 1925, and having the Malvern Festival established in his honour in the 1930's. He grew wealthy. By 1931 he was earning £16,000 a year in the United States alone; his wife left him £154,000; he became the largest shareholder in the Welwyn Garden City Company; when he died he left a six-figure fortune. But he lived essentially on a solitary pedestal; he was still a hard and methodical worker, turning out his 1,500 words a day from his retirement at Ayot St. Lawrence, completing the 40,000,000 words he penned during his long career of seventy years; but his plays, particularly, suffered from his isolation. Although he lived on until 1950, only *The Apple Cart* (1929) reflected any of the brilliance of the years immediately before and after the war. What Shaw had to say seemed increasingly irrelevant, and when, uniquely, the lights of Moscow and New York were dimmed simultaneously at his death, the honour was bestowed chiefly upon the memory of a great Edwardian.

But the last decades of Shaw's life should not be allowed to conceal the fine achievement of a dedicated man of letters, who virtually single-handed restored to the theatre an intellectual and spiritual content it had lacked for a century and a half. Without Shaw, Eliot and Fry, Osborne and Wesker, Pinter and Whiting would have had to deal with a theatre unaccustomed to challenge and experiment. Shaw produced many reasons why he should have devoted so much time to writing plays. His favourite defence he used for the benefit of the Lord Chamberlain: 'I write plays with the deliberate object of converting the nation to my opinion in these matters. I have no other effectual incentive in writing plays, as I am not dependent on the theatre for my livelihood. If I were prevented from producing immoral and heretical plays, I should cease to write for the theatre, and propagate my views from the platform and through books.'[1] He often insisted that a man interested only in play-writing would write very uninteresting plays. Certainly, he saw the opportunity in a mass market to sell a particular message, and the urgency of his political views is an inseparable part of the man. But it is also true, as Maurice Colbourne suggested, that 'he wrote plays, not because he wanted to, but because he couldn't help it'.[2] As he confessed himself, 'Whether it be that I was born mad or a little too sane, my kingdom was not of this world: I was at home only in the realm of my imagination.'[3] Even as a politician he was essentially a visionary rather than a practical man: he was not in

[1] Preface to *The Shewing-up of Blanco Posnet*, *Prefaces*, p. 409.
[2] *The Real Bernard Shaw* (1949), p. 17.
[3] Preface to *Immaturity*, *Prefaces*, p. 648.

his element in Trafalgar Square. Without the theatre as an outlet for his imagination, Shaw could not have lived. And, after the decline and decadence of the early nineteenth century, so much of his thinking about the theatre was exceptionally apposite. Society needed to be told that 'drama makes the theatre, not the theatre the drama', that 'the man who writes about himself and his own time is the only man who writes about all people and about all time', that the theatre was a kind of church with an apostolic succession back to Aeschylus.[1] These convictions and this earnestness produced no wholesale or overnight conversion, but the theatre became a place again in which serious writers could once more honestly discuss and describe human nature without unreasonably compromising the truth of their imaginations to fit in with popular prejudice and convention.

Other writers followed in Shaw's path, particularly the Irish dramatists from the Abbey Theatre in Dublin, in the years following 1904. W. B. Yeats insisted, like Shaw, on 'the ancient sovereignty of words'. He, too, agreed that 'we have to make the theatre a place of intellectual excitement'.[2] Many of the innovations he introduced in Dublin were sound: he eliminated stagy mannerisms and movements by the drastic procedure of rehearsing his actors in barrels; he simplified the form and colour of scenery and costume, and all exterior representationalism, to get away from the confining restrictions of the 'picture stage'; and, finding prose, especially the prose speech of modern educated folk, bloodless ('it cannot become impassioned, that is to say, vital, without making somebody gushing and sentimental'),[3] he attempted a return to poetry, taking his cue from other experimenters of the time like Stephen Phillips, Lascelles Abercrombie, John Masefield, and John Drinkwater. But Yeats failed in almost everything. He was even more removed from his audiences than Shaw. He was essentially a late Romantic poet, who believed that a long poem was 'a region into which one should wander from the cares of life';[4] he was a member of Madame Blavatsky's Theosophical Society, believed in spiritualism, fairies, astrology and automatic writing, and claimed to be in

[1] Preface to *Our Theatres in the Nineties*, *Prefaces*, p. 743.
[2] *Essays* (1924), p. 421.
[3] *Ibid.*, p. 339.
[4] Quoted in Katherine Tynan, *The Middle Years* (1916), p. 51.

touch with spirits who gave him 'metaphors for poetry'; he was of Protestant birth and rationalist upbringing; he was aristocratic by nature, arrogant in his attitudes, and though one of the founders of the Irish Academy of Letters, recoiled from any suggestion of professionalism, relying chiefly upon a comfortable private income for his livelihood. All these factors tended to put him apart from his colleagues in Dublin. He had no successors at the Abbey. His own plays, lyrical rather than dramatic, were all one-act in duration, and were produced after the main play of the evening, 'to satisfy', as has been tactfully said, 'the few who remain in the theatre for the entire evening'.[1] Finally disgruntled by his failure to create, as he had hoped, a peasant art, and by seeing round him the greater commercial success achieved by prose realists, he became even more aloof. Influenced by the Japanese, he experimented with masks and music, drum-taps and silence, trying to create a ritual which would establish what he called a 'distance' between imaginative art and 'a pushing world'. In the 'unpopular theatre' of his chamber drama, he was at last free to seek 'the theatre's anti-self'.[2] These are sad words which reveal the measure of his failure, as a man of letters, to come to terms with the living theatre.

Though much more of an amateur in the theatre, J. M. Synge was happier there. He had a small private income, which he augmented by music, freelance journalism and literary criticism. His work for the theatre is restricted to six plays (he died when he was only 38). But he was saved from Yeats's despair by several sound beliefs. He insisted that 'all art is a collaboration' between the artist and his audience; this is why he concentrated particularly on creating a rich language which could be shared. He realized, too, that 'on the stage one must have reality, and one must have joy',[3] and sought for ways of avoiding the false joy of musical comedy and the joylessness of realistic intellectual drama. He rejected all historical themes and argued that 'every healthy mind is more interested in *Tit-Bits* than in *Idylls of the King*, or any of the more or less artificial retellings of classical or saga stories'.[4] Above all, he believed that 'the drama is made

[1] F. R. Higgins, in L. Robinson, ed., *The Irish Theatre* (1939).

[2] *Plays and Controversies* (1927), pp. 212 ff.

[3] *Playboy of the Western World* (1907), preface.

[4] *Note Books* (1907). *Plays* (1932), p. iii.

serious—in the French sense of the word—not by the degree in which it is taken up with problems that are serious in themselves, but by the degree in which it gives the nourishment, not very easy to define, on which our imaginations live'.[1] He was thus able to write plays which are honest as literature, and yet also commercial propositions in an entertainment industry. He had to overcome nationalistic prejudices, but his best play, *The Playboy of the Western World*, while it was greeted on its first performance with pumpkins and custard-pies, was generally accepted in Dublin, as George Moore says, as 'the most significant play of the last two hundred years'.

In the theatre it has proved especially difficult to work with the commercial market and to produce within it drama of more than ephemeral character. There is the unfortunate case of Sean O'Casey, a writer devoted to the work for his livelihood and therefore exposed more than Yeats or Synge to the corruptions of the trade. Perhaps for this reason O'Casey was determined to avoid compromise. When he left Ireland in 1926, after the nationalistic riots which greeted *The Plough and the Stars*, he settled in Devon, avowedly an exile from every creed, every party and every literary clique. He concentrated upon his art, for instance upon the development of expressionistic techniques. But while he thus avoided the necessity of pleasing particular audiences, he incurred all the risks of isolation: it is difficult for a dramatist to dedicate himself to professional service without having real roots in a particular, living theatre. Until *The Bishop's Bonfire* in 1955, O'Casey's plays reveal the price paid for isolation: and he had to suffer the indignity of having *The Silver Tassie* rejected by the very theatre which had brought him an international reputation, of seeing *Purple Dust* staged only at the Liverpool Playhouse, *Oak Leaves and Lavender* put away after a first unsuccessful production in Hammersmith, and *Cockadoodle Dandy* attempted only by a little theatre in Texas and an amateur society in Newcastle. This is a problem about which more must be said elsewhere. It is sufficient to note here that Shaw, and those who came immediately after the period of his greatest influence, broke down some of the barriers that had existed between the theatre and the profession of letters. Though new difficulties presented themselves, the theatre

[1] *The Tinker's Wedding* (1909), preface.

had once more become an outlet for professional writers.

For the novelists the growth of the mass market has tended to create pressures similar to those experienced by poets in the early nineteenth century. An industry has been established to supply long prose stories for mass sale, either in the form of paper-back editions and 'pulp magazines' or in the form of hard-back editions at a price within the reach of individual readers of all sections of the community (with considerable sales also to the public libraries, where over 70 per cent of the books borrowed tend to be fictional). The essence of this trade is that certain specific tastes are met: hence the various divisions of subject—crime, detection, romance, western, science fiction, sex, and so on. Schools of journalism and writing have arisen to train writers to meet these tastes in an efficient way. Novels written to formulae in this way sometimes become literature, within the meaning of the term defined in previous chapters: sometimes a genuinely imaginative exploration of human nature is offered in this form. But generally these novels present nothing novel: their whole effort is designed to relax the reader by entertainment which appeals to preconceptions, prejudices and tastes definable in advance. Such books, however, command at their most successful a very wide sale and handsome rewards. The professional novelist as a result runs the hazards of his own particular Scylla and Charybdis: if he writes to a formula, he earns a living but loses his professional values; if he deserts the formula, he satisfies his own values but antagonizes his readers and imperils his income. Hardy, Lawrence, and Joyce lived their careers in this context of conflict, as did all serious novelists of their times.

Thomas Hardy always thought of himself as a story-teller rather than a novelist, a term which he disliked. He had no pretensions in prose, and thought of the novels as 'hand-to-mouth', unimportant by the side of his poetry. He had been apprenticed at the age of 16 to an architect who restored churches, and had decided at an early age that he would earn his living through architectural work and satisfy his soul by writing in his spare time. His poems were rejected by editors, but this did not matter very much: '*Writing* verse gives me great pleasure, but not publishing it. I never did care much about publication.'[1] Later, the urge to make public his literary gifts

[1] Letter to Sir Sydney Cockerell, 28 February 1922.

became stronger; he turned to the novel speculatively, expecting no better reception for the prose than for the verse. And at first he met with failure. His first novel, *The Poor Man and the Lady*, written in 1869, was turned down by Macmillan and other publishers; the second, *Desperate Remedies* (1871), was published at his own expense, at a cost of £75, and had a poor reception from the critics and from the bookshops; the third, *Under the Greenwood Tree* (1872), was published commercially but anonymously, and was another failure, although it had a good press and was sold in a 2*s*. paper-back edition. *A Pair of Blue Eyes* (1873) was a moderate success when published, the first in his own name, by Tinsley Brothers as a serial in twelve monthly parts; then came the first solid success, *Far From the Madding Crowd* (1874), serialized in Leslie Stephen's *Cornhill*. Stephen had taken his young author to task and had succeeded in toning down his natural pessimism and socialism and in securing a happy ending. For some years Hardy compromised with his public. He rejected Stephen's timidity about *The Return of the Native*, which the editor thought might offend the ladies; but in general he did not seek to run too far ahead of public taste. His novels won him international fame, being serialized not only in *Cornhill* and *Good Words* but also in the European edition of *Harper's Magazine* and in the American *Atlantic Monthly*.

At this point Hardy seems to have decided to write about life as he saw it with less tact and greater honesty. He knew now he was able to 'hold his own in fiction—whatever that might be worth', and he determined to give freer expression to the whole of his distinctive view of life. The novels become darker, embodying his belief that 'this planet does not supply the materials for happiness to higher existences', that 'happiness is but the occasional episode in a general drama of pain', that man's nature and man's aspirations were irreconciliable: the more sensitive the nature, the more malign the universe. Gradually the public recoiled from his agnosticism, from his insistence that the 'difference of sex is but a difference of degree', from his pagan stoicism and cosmic darkness. *The Athenaeum* decided that *The Woodlanders* (1886) was 'Distinctly not for the Young Person'. Despite Hardy's reputation, *Tess of the D'Urbervilles* (1891) was rejected by two editors and published in the end only in emasculated form. And the emasculated *Jude the Obscure* (1894) was greeted everywhere as 'garbage', as 'titanically bad': bishops wrote letters to the *Yorkshire Post*, there were public burnings and personal attacks upon the author's morals. Hardy turned in regal disgust from the scene, and never wrote another novel, contenting himself with the writing of short stories and with more poetry, especially *The Dynasts*.

The storm died down in time, and Hardy was rehabilitated in public esteem: he was awarded honorary degrees at five universities and honorary fellowships at Oxford and Cambridge; he was made President of the Royal Society of Authors in 1908, and awarded the Order of Merit in 1910 and the Gold Medal of the Royal Society of Literature in 1911. When he was buried in Poets' Corner at Westminster Abbey in 1928 one of the pall-bearers was the Prime Minister. But to the end of his life this great writer continued to regard himself primarily as a poet, and to think of the novels as the product of an interregnum in his life, a period when, if he pleased the public he did not please himself, and if he pleased himself he did not please his public. The mass market offers no easy road for the true artist: Hardy's career exemplifies what might be achieved by a brave man who was prepared to await the verdict of the years.

D. H. Lawrence similarly had a massive courage. He was forthright about the future of the novel: 'Instead of snivelling about what is and has been, or inventing new sensations in the old line, it's got to break a way through, like a hole in the wall. And the public will scream in agony and say it is sacrilege. . . . But gradually, first one and then another of the sheep filters through the gap, and finds a new world outside.'[1] In complete conviction he abandoned his first career in teaching as soon as he saw the opportunity to devote himself to writing. Yet from the beginning of his literary career, while he was still struggling with poverty, he had to contend with public hostility. When Jessie Chambers sent some of his poems and stories to the *English Review* in 1909, Lawrence was lucky in finding immediately an editor, Ford Madox Ford, who recognized his genius and gave him space. From the beginning, then, he had friends among the writers, artists and *élites* of the day. Popular support came very much more slowly. The first novel, *The White Peacock* (1911), was a fair success, but its successors, *The Trespasser*

[1] *Phoenix* (1936), p. 520.

(1912) and *Sons and Lovers* (1913), both lost money on first publication, and the latter aroused the first public storm. *The Rainbow* (1915) earned Lawrence £190, easily his best return to date, but the book did not weather the storm: Robert Lynd, a typical voice, dismissed it as 'a monstrous wilderness of phallicism'; a thousand copies were seized by the police after protests from the National Purity League and the book was suppressed as obscene. These were difficult times for Lawrence: he published poems, a travel book, a play and other writings, but he was dependent a good deal of the time upon the hospitality of his friends and upon gifts which he would return, if there were any other alternative way of survival. He had also fallen in love with Frieda Weekley-Richtofen, a German baroness, married, with three children, to a professor at Nottingham University; after a divorce, he married her in 1914. An unconventional artist married to a German was bound to suffer in jingoistic years when, for instance, the Chief Secretary for Ireland said in a public speech that 'he for one would forbid the use, during the war, of poetry'. He and his wife were extradited from coastal areas. The market for his writings dried up.

Recognition came slowly. One turning-point was his victory in 1920 in the vice case brought in the United States against *Women in Love*. The magistrate's ruling was that there was nothing in the book either obscene, lewd, lascivious, filthy, indecent or disgusting. By 1922 Lawrence's earnings in the United States amounted to over 5,000 dollars in the year. In 1924 he had in the bank £303 and 2,285 dollars. In his own country support for him spread outwards from his circle of colleagues, friends and enthusiasts. *The Lost Girl* (1920) was one of his worst novels, but it won the James Tait Black Prize of £100 from Edinburgh University. *The Plumed Serpent* (1926) is not good Lawrence, but it ran into five editions in five years, followed by cheap reprints. Lawrence's view of life was not one which commended itself easily to the mass market: it was associated too easily in the public mind either with a 'highbrow' image which seemed to have little relevance in common life or with a picture of sexual licence and anarchy against which conventional instincts rebelled. It took Lawrence many years to break down the unfairness of these images: indeed, the job was not complete in his lifetime. Lawrence insisted that 'life is only bearable when the mind and the body are in harmony, and there is a natural balance between them, and each has a natural respect for the other', that 'what man wants most passionately is his living wholeness and his living unison, not his own isolate salvation of his "soul". . . . What we want to destroy is our false, inorganic connexions, especially those related to money, and re-establish the living organic connexions, with the cosmos, the sun and earth, with mankind and nation and family. Start with the sun, and the rest will slowly, slowly happen.'[1] The novel was essential to him in expressing this view of life: 'Somehow you sweep the ground a bit too clear in the poem or the drama, and you let the human world fly a bit too freely. Now in a novel there's always a tom-cat, a black tom-cat that pounces on the white dove of the word, if the dove doesn't watch it; and there is a banana-skin to trip on; and you know there is a water-closet on the premises. All these things help to keep the balance.' 'Only in the novel are *all* things given full play . . . out of the full play of all things emerges the only thing that is anything, the wholeness of a man, the wholeness of a woman, man alive, and live woman.'[2]

Lawrence saw the novel as a medium of social reform, with a fervour akin to that of the great eighteenth-century novelists. 'It is the way our sympathy flows and recoils that really determines our lives. And here lies the vast importance of the novel, properly handled. It can inform and lead into new places the flow of our sympathetic consciousness and it can lead our sympathy away in recoil from things gone dead.' 'Now here we see the beauty and great value of the novel. Philosophy, religion, science, they are all busy nailing things down, to get a stable equilibrium. . . . The novel is the highest example of subtle interrelatedness that man has discovered. Everything is true in its own time, place, circumstance, and untrue outside of its own time, place, circumstance. If you try to nail anything down, in the novel, either it kills the novel, or the novel gets up and walks away with the nail.'[3] 'Now I absolutely flatly deny that I am a soul, or a body, or a mind, or an intelligence, or a brain, or a nervous system, or a bunch of glands, or any of

[1] *Apocalypse* (1931).
[2] 'Why the Novel Matters', *Phoenix*, p. 538.
[3] 'The Novel', *Reflections on the Death of a Porcupine* (1925).

the rest of these bits of me. The whole is greater than the part. And therefore, I, who am man alive, am greater than my soul, or spirit, or body, or mind, or consciousness, or anything else that is merely a part of me. I am a man, and alive. I am man alive, and as long as I can, I intend to go on being man alive. For this reason I am a novelist.'[1] As the son of a miner, brought up in the ugliness of a mining village, he could not rest content with convincing merely the intellectuals. He saw his view of life helping most to revolutionize the quality of life of those in whose life there was least quality. He devoted his life with professional single-mindedness to writing to this end. He turned his hand to everything that might express more widely his perspective and philosophy.

Besides the novels, twelve of them, there were eleven volumes of poems, many volumes of short stories, several plays, travel books, essays, translations (especially of modern Italian works), one history, a great many pieces of criticism, and one book about the paintings to which he turned late in life. This is the record of a professional career as earnest as Pope's or Carlyle's. He worked in almost continuous uproar. Stifled by industrial England, he worked from exile, having no home but moving between Italy, Ceylon, Australia, the United States, Mexico, France, and Germany. He had time for few friendships. From 1924 he struggled against the increasing hold of tuberculosis. But in time he won the public recognition he required. This is reflected in his vastly increased earnings. When *Lady Chatterley's Lover* was at last published in 1928, privately in Florence, Lawrence made a profit of £1,024 in the first year. The 1929 volume of poems entitled *Pansies*, against all the trends of the market, made a profit of £500. For some short stories he was paid £300 each. By December 1929 his essay, *Pornography and Obscenity*, was selling 12,000 copies a week. By 1928 he was writing articles for the newspapers at two thousand words, the work of one and a half hours, for £25 each. At his death in 1930 he left £4,000, exclusive of the value of his books, paintings and manuscripts.

Final recognition did not come until Lawrence posthumously conquered the mass market by publication in Penguins, of which event the most notable, though not necessarily the best, index

[1] *Phoenix*, p. 535.

is the sale of 3,500,000 copies of *Lady Chatterley's Lover*, following the obscenity trial of 1960. In this series *Sons and Lovers* has been reprinted in nine editions in twelve years. There is a sense in which the notoriety of the trial has drawn the attention of the mass public to elements in Lawrence which, taken out of context, mislead readers about his essential view of life. But the success of the whole series of novels is not explained so simply: by and large, one may fairly conclude that here is an outstanding example of the victory of a dedicated man of letters within the mass market, and public taste is immeasurably the richer for it.

Even more so than Lawrence, James Joyce struggled through a career in which for long decades there was no hope of reconciling the artist's values and the taste of the printed-book market. In his teens he wrote a play, some poems and various papers, and at 18 had his first article published, on Ibsen, in the *Fortnightly Review*. He was determined from the beginning to be a writer, and with this ambition went off to Paris at the age of 20, living on less then a pound a week, going without meals for two days at a stretch, trying to master his craft and resolved not to give in. He returned to Ireland when his mother was dying and spent another year there, finding no kind of security until he took a temporary post as a schoolteacher. At 22 he eloped to Switzerland with Nora Barnacle, the woman whom twenty-seven years later he was to marry, and taught at the Berlitz Institute in Zurich for £80 a year. Teaching proved congenial and brought him a livelihood for many years, apart from a brief period as a bank clerk in Rome. He established himself as a private tutor of English in Trieste, charging rates which increased, as he became more popular, from 10*d.* to 5*s.* an hour. This kind of teaching gave him the security and the time he needed to write his books. He had set himself a particularly difficult ambition: nothing less than the evolution of an entirely new kind of prose style, expressing a stream of consciousness from which nothing was omitted. For a long time nobody knew what to make of it: even his family were bewildered. 'Isn't it extraordinary,' he once asked, 'that none of my family read anything I write?' To which question Nora's amiable reply was: 'Don't you think Jim is making things very difficult for himself by writing the way he does?' Joyce's single-minded dedication was almost inhuman: he was utterly sure of himself, refused to swerve or compromise in any way, and roughly overrode all the suggestions made by his few friends.

The publishers were dismayed not only by the new style but by the risk that Joyce's free language would involve them in obscenity actions. The omens were entirely inauspicious. Even Lawrence condemned him: 'My God, what a clumsy *olla potrida* James Joyce is! Nothing but old fags and cabbage stumps of quotations . . . what old and hard-worked staleness, masquerading as the all-new'.[1] The two writers were indeed hostile to each other: Lawrence found *Ulysses* dirty, and Joyce found *Lady Chatterley's Lover* lush. It is little wonder the publishers demurred: two contracts were signed, but each time the publishers recanted and nothing happened. Joyce's first published book was, in fact, his poems, *Chamber Music* (1907), although he always insisted: 'I am not a poet'. Five hundred and nine copies were printed at 1*s*. 6*d*., but the volume sold badly and Joyce did not earn a penny. To augment his income he had a hand in different business enterprises: he acted as an agent for the Italian firm which opened the first cinema in Dublin; and he entered for the Guinness slogan competition and could never understand why his entry, 'My brand old Dublin lindub, the free, the froh, the frothy freshener' was turned down in favour of 'Guinness is good for you'.

But in manuscript his work gradually made an impression on fellow writers. These writers and their wealthy friends were establishing new periodicals and publishing firms, means whereby *avant-garde* authors could reach a public in print without having to compromise with the mass market. They were also prepared to help men of genius with monetary gifts. When Joyce was caught in Switzerland by the war, an American woman called McCormick gave him 1,000 Swiss francs a month; later Harriet Weaver gave him 500 a month. Other patrons helped him settle in Paris after the war and release himself from a burden of teaching which, with sickly eyes, he found an increasing strain. In the years from 1914 onwards the tide turned for Joyce. Harriet Weaver and Dora Marsden secured the serialization of *A Portrait of the Artist as a Young Man* in *The Egoist*. Grant Richards published *Dubliners*, his collection of short

[1] Letter to the Huxleys, *Letters* (1932), p. 742.

stories. In 1918 the play *Exiles* was printed in Britain and the United States and in a French translation. An American edition of the poems appeared. And then the great novel, *Ulysses*, began appearing in parts in *The Egoist* and, after an obscenity trial, in the American *Little Review*. There followed the long battle for book publication. Another patron, Sylvia Beach, first published *Ulysses* in Paris under the imprint of Shakespeare and Company: 1,000 numbered copies were sold in a month; a second impression of 2,000 followed, of which 500 were confiscated in the United States. In 1924 a third impression of 500, intended for Britain, was confiscated at Folkestone. By 1925 there were seven impressions, and by 1930 eleven. The rewards were high, the American sales alone by 1924 totalling 21,144 dollars, of which Joyce earned 10 per cent in royalties. But there was no copyright: the book was vulnerable to pirate printers, including the American periodical *Two Worlds Monthly*. In the end free publication was permitted in America in 1932 and in Britain in 1936: wide sales followed (the American sales in 1934 alone ran to 35,000 copies), and translations into French, German, Polish, Czech, Spanish, Russian, and Japanese. And the way was clear for Joyce's later work, *Pomes Penyeach* (1927) and *Finnegan's Wake*, which appeared first in limited editions and pamphlets and then in book form in 1939. It is doubtful if Joyce ever achieved, or ever could achieve, the conquest of the mass market that was Lawrence's final victory: his style is in no sense a thing to be shared with a mass public. Like Shaw, Joyce seems to live on into an age in which he had no part to play; like Lawrence, he was always a man apart from his fellows. The mass market accentuates, in so many cases, the isolation of the artist, the dilemma first experienced by the Romantic poets. But just as the theatre developed within itself professional and amateur groups who were concerned with defending high standards of writing against the encroachment of commercial corruption, so for the novelists there were little magazines and writers' groups who also saw themselves as the leading defenders of values. In time these small groups win over adherents and converts from the mass public, so that by one means or another values are preservable. To say this is not to underestimate the intensity of the conflict; neither does it overestimate the power of the corruptive forces.

And while these more flamboyant careers embody the conflict of the first decades of the mass market, other quieter men were carving out their own place in the profession of letters with less distress. One thinks of H. G. Wells, or Hilaire Belloc, or G. K. Chesterton, or Arnold Bennett, or Joseph Conrad, or, perhaps most typically, E. M. Forster. Forster's career has nothing dramatic about it. The son of an architect, he had private means of a modest kind, sufficient to enable him first to travel and then to set about a career as a professional writer. After some political work for the Liberals and articles for the *Independent Review*, he published four novels and began the fifth, which was not completed until 1924. There followed volumes of short stories, biographies, historical works and criticism, together with literary work for Labour politics, including a year as literary editor of the *Daily Herald*. The success of *A Passage to India* brought him the prestige which led to the invitation to undertake the Clark Lectures at Cambridge and then to a fellowship at his old college, King's. Thereafter he led a quiet life as a don and occasional writer. Forster insisted that the novel should tell a story: 'the novel that would express values only becomes unintelligible and therefore valueless'.[1] And he had other principles which made his path easier towards the mass market of Penguins: a love of suspense and surprise and perhaps melodrama. But his view of life was unique: no other writer quite captures with the same skill the power of the 'chance collisions of human beings', the mysterious tenderness of the call of sex to sex, the inconstancy and instability of all true human relationships. Forster's view offers none of the comfortableness demanded of life in the formula novel; yet he was convinced that the novelist's social purpose was to enable his readers to understand what in real life they could not understand, and he quietly dedicated himself to professional service in this way.

There are many others who served the true purposes of professional literature within the mass market in which there were increasing numbers of 'professionals'—so-called because they were full-time writers, earning their living wholly from print—who served no such purpose. The result of the interaction of the 'true' professionals, many of them by commercial standards part-timers and amateurs, and the 'false' professionals, many of

[1] *Aspects of the Novel* (1927), p. 61.

them the heirs of Pope's Grub Street, is a complex pattern, which perhaps now ought to be described more comprehensively, since it forms the basis of the profession of English letters today. The lesson to be learned from these first decades of the mass market, the age of Shaw and Hardy, Lawrence and Forster, was not the simple pessimistic one that the *Daily Mail* and the *News of the World*, *Tit-Bits* and *Woman*—and, if you like, *Reveille* and commercial television—would ultimately swamp literature's true function of exploring through the imagination the complexities of human nature. The great writers recognized the necessity for standing firm in a context in which dangerous corruption was an omnipresent temptation; but they also proved their contention that readers will ultimately turn to what they really need. This conclusion may ring a little hollow to those dismayed by the modern homes in which, according to American advertisements, a row of *Reader's Digests*, neatly stacked in a place of honour, is proof of culture. But it is a conclusion upon which our modern generation of writers acts. There is always the proviso that good reading depends upon adequate leisure, and it is still unfortunately true, in modern industrial communities, that leisure surprisingly is far from adequate. Getting and spending, as Wordsworth said, we still lay waste our powers. But Lord Northcliffe and Lawrence were allies, at least in this: in seeking to persuade the public at large to devote more, and still more, time to reading. This perhaps is still the main problem, and the mass market in print is no enemy of literature in this respect.

# XI

# The Profession Today

*What stuns us into a realization of our supersensible destiny is not, as Kant imagined, the formlessness of nature, but rather its unutterable particularity: and most particular and individual of all natural things is the mind of man.*

IRIS MURDOCH

We have been aware throughout this story of the gathering force of the profession of English letters: piece by piece the profession has put itself together, establishing its fundamentals, consolidating its fabric, cementing its structure with true principle. By our own day it ought to be a sizeable feature of the social landscape. The most extraordinary thing, however, about the modern scene is that, with the naked eye at least, the profession is not visible at all; and society certainly accords it no separate existence. The industry of literature is plain for all to see, powerful, ubiquitous, inobviable. But, as we have seen, the industry is not the profession: the men of letters who are dedicated to the specific quest of the imagination which identifies them are concealed within the total mass.

We know our doctors and solicitors and other professionals by the brass plates on their doors, their plain and unarguable social status and service. Even our other artists, the painters, musicians and so on, have certain means of social identification and places where they enjoy professional status, like the colleges, the art galleries, the concert halls and the like. But the literary professionals are lost in the crowd. There is no academy capable of housing the entire profession; there is no union as inclusive as actors have in Equity; organizations like the Royal Society of Literature and the Society of Authors are voluntary in character and therefore non-inclusive. The literary profession can never have the means of controlling its own members, the powers of admission and expulsion enjoyed, for instance, by the doctors. No one will ever have the authority to keep a nominal roll. And yet society has never had more need of its imaginative writers. Since 1945 the physical cosmos surrounding humanity has simultaneously become vaster and smaller; suddenly man has discovered that he has his finger-tips on the ultimate controls, only to realize simultaneously that everything is hideously out of control. We have big thoughts of nuclear energy, of space travel, of united nations and world government, of mass production and mass movements; and yet we are extraordinarily insecure and indeed immature in our personal relationships, and concentrate with curious single-mindedness, especially in our novels and plays and films, upon sex, upon the relations of man and man, and man and woman, uncertain about our very fundamentals. Our legs in their big boots take giant strides, but our heads and hearts do not seem large enough. As always, we turn to the artists to help us, to inform us, with the kind of information science, with its precise answers and generalizations, cannot give us. We assume that the artists, perhaps alone among all other public servants, will remain concerned with the infuriating and unutterable particularity of nature, and of human nature in its inexpressible individuality: unutterable and inexpressible, that is, except in art. Iris Murdoch, who prizes so highly in the epigraph to this chapter this 'unutterable particularity', does so because she believes that the discovery of it is an act of love. 'Love', she says, 'is the perception of individuals. Love is the extremely difficult realization that something other than oneself is real. Love, and so art and morals, is the discovery of reality.' People have never more needed to know this reality, this love. Literature, with its primary concern for the things that make men human, stands at the heart of our desperate survival.

And yet since 1945 it has become clear that the literary profession has been disappointed in its hope of inheriting from the mass markets and mass media a haven or heaven of security and financial independence. Instead of steady progress to higher social status and richer rewards, there is evidence of retrogression comparing the situation today with the situation before the war. Indeed, the Society of Authors predicted in 1953 'the end of professional authorship as we have known it in the past'. The contemporary scene is discussed by Richard Findlater in a recent pamphlet.[1] He estimates that of the 45,000 or 50,000 living British authors, excluding 5,000 technical or educational authors, only about 6,500 or 7,000 are properly professional, in the sense of writing full-length books, or film scripts, or plays (for television as well as the theatre) 'with some degree of continuity and productivity'. Various investigations, conducted by the Society of Authors and literary agents, reveal that, of these professional authors, some 60 per cent (one investigation puts the figure as high as 77 per cent) earn £500 a year or less from their writing, a poor yield in comparison with the national average wage of over £15 a week. Only a small proportion, perhaps 13 per cent, earn from writing more than £1,500 a year. Pre-war comparisons are difficult, since writers and publishers are notoriously shy about revealing their incomes, and inflation is an added problem, but the situation has clearly worsened. Findlater suggests that a novice in 1938 could get by with £4 a week, providing himself with a furnished bed-sitter, visits to the cinema and theatre, and a weekly meal in Soho, and could easily earn this money with articles. Today a novice would need £12 a week and would find the greatest difficulty in earning so much. The inscrutable Civil Servants in charge of the Census have recognized this decline: in 1951 writers were accorded the social status of Class I, along with lawyers and doctors, while teachers were included in Class II, and actors and musicians in Class III; but in 1961, writers, actors and musicians are all graded together in Class II.

Changed economic conditions are to blame. While national expenditure on books, newspapers and magazines increases all the time, from £176,000,000 in 1954 to over £190,000,000 in 1961, and while the total turnover of publishers also increases, from £41,500,000 in 1951 to nearly £79,000,000 in 1961, many factors have combined to ensure that the rewards of authors have been diminished rather than increased. Book-

[1] *What are writers worth?* (1963).

production costs have increased by something like 100 per cent since 1939: more books are sold each year, but there is a smaller profit per book sold, a shorter sale-life for books in the shops, and a greater dependence upon overseas sales from which receipts are diminished by high discounts. Bookselling remains a difficult business: seventeen representative booksellers in 1952 averaged a net profit of only 1.22 per cent. Publishing is increasingly concentrated in a few expanding groups, some controlled by outside commercial and industrial interests: Ian Parsons, of Chatto and Windus, estimates that while before the war a turnover of £100,000 was sufficient to make a net profit of £20,000, now at least double this turnover is needed to make the same nominal profit. The commercial libraries are tending to disappear: there are now only 4,000 left, and their memberships fall each year. Not only are the small *2d.* lending libraries now virtually extinct, but the chain libraries, too, diminish, the latest defection being the W. H. Smith chain in 1961 with its 286 branches and 60,000 subscribers. Despite the continuing annual increase in borrowings from public libraries, public authority spending remains almost static at about 10 per cent of the book trade's output: some authorities still spend less than *2s.* per year per head. And quite apart from the book trade, other openings for writers close up year by year: between 1949 and 1962 seventeen daily and Sunday newspapers closed down, leaving three major groups in control of 67 per cent, in 1961, of the total circulation of daily papers, compared with only 45 per cent in 1948. In the past forty years nearly 250 weekly papers have closed down, and twenty-five of the twenty-seven fiction magazines. As we shall see, some compensation comes from the growth of paperback publications, and from new openings in television, but not as yet on a scale to relieve what is undoubtedly a recession for those seeking to earn a living from writing.

In short, the contemporary scene would appear rather bleak, if it were necessary to equate the profession of letters with those who seek to earn a full-time living from writing. Fortunately, there is no such need. The history of the profession reveals that in every age some of the most dedicated professionals have lacked the facility, and indeed the ambition, to earn all their living from literature. Indeed, many full-time writers have failed to be truly professional, in the sense of the word used in this history. It is still true that a large proportion of the 'authors', for whom Richard Findlater shows such concern, are public entertainers; their function is an honest and a necessary one, providing the public with familiar food, with romance and excitement and adventure of a kind that caters for the 'rehearsed response'. More than ever, people need relaxation and escape in certain specific types of literature: the public demands this food and many writers live to satisfy the demand. But such a service, however valuable and necessary, cannot be graced with the title of a profession: such subservience to giving the public what it wants, what it *knows* it wants, places writers who have nothing else to offer in the category of craftsmen rather than artists. If the craftsmen are having a harder time, because of changes in public taste and economic values, there is no reason to assume that the times augur badly for the future of the profession of letters, provided that congenial alternative methods of earning a living exist. It is the survival of the artists which matters above all else. This is not to deny that the artists may have grounds for disquiet in the contemporary situation; nor that many true professionals (there are many instances in our own time) do not ultimately seek to free themselves from other occupations and devote all their time to writing. My point is merely that it is not enough to take into account only the cash rewards of the book and periodical trade.

From another point of view, writers have never been so happily at home in society as in the twentieth century. There is now no longer an iron choice between doing what one wants to do and starving, and doing what one is forced to do and dying as an artist. Indeed, it is now only an exceedingly old-fashioned writer, and perhaps a very young one, too, who adheres to the Victorian 'Bohemian' ideal that starvation is better than any kind of 'prostitution'. There now exist several allied professions which have been particularly developed in this century and in which the writer can earn a living without necessarily prostituting his art. In them a writer can find a refuge which actually encourages and nurtures his art, because they share at least in part his interest in the employment of words. There is no longer any stigma against earning a living outside art, just as there is no longer any need for the artist to adopt the anti-social defences of the last century. The Victorian notion that a man of artistic sensibility is *essentially* half-mad and wholly rebel was itself the product of peculiar social circumstances of limited provenance, which are not repeated elsewhere in literary history and have disappeared in our own times. The modern 'beatnik', it will be argued, is the product of a special kind of artistic self-indulgence rather than of artistic necessity.

The 'professions of words' in which the writer finds congenial company may be listed briefly. Primarily, there is teaching, particularly the teaching of English, in universities, colleges and schools. This is an occupation which has assumed importance only in our century: Oxford did not establish a Chair in English Literature until 1904, and Cambridge not until 1910. Other homes for the writer are provided by certain sections of journalism, publishing and public relations concerned with literary editing, criticism and advice: there is now a circle of editors and critics who have become, perhaps *faute de mieux*, powerful patrons of literature of a new kind. We must also add certain sections of show business, films, broadcasting and television, even to some extent the theatre, which employ literary skills and advice.

A large proportion of the literary profession today is employed in these 'professions of words', most of them entirely happily and usefully. Samuel Johnson might well envy them, across the years, their felicitous combination of independence and support. A few examples will illustrate the pattern. In another age, T. S. Eliot might have been a businessman; he was the son of the President of the U.S. Hydraulic Press Brick Company, and he spent a few years in Lloyds Bank during and after the 1914–18 war. But in the twentieth century he is mainly a don: he holds degrees in at least eleven universities and has held teaching posts in Highgate School and in the Universities of Harvard and Cambridge. He is a learned man, member of academies in four countries, a student of philosophy, metaphysics, logic, psychology, Indic philology, Sanskrit and literature. He has been assistant editor of the *Egoist*, editor for seventeen years of the *Criterion*, and he has also served, with special distinction, as a director of Faber and Faber. In his career there is a happy correlation between all these occupations and the poems, plays and criticism: the whole forms a unity expressive of his total dedication to imaginative literature. C. Day Lewis is another example: he has been a schoolmaster for nine years, an editor of books and pamphlets for the Ministry of Information during five years of the war, a writer of detective fiction, a literary adviser to a firm of publishers, a lecturer at Cambridge and a professor at Oxford, altogether a handsome cross-section of the professions of words. And like the writer who began in the 'twenties, and the writer who began in the 'thirties, Kingsley Amis, who began in the 'forties, has spent all his life, apart from military service, as a don, first as a lecturer in Swansea and then as a fellow of Peterhouse, Cambridge: it is only recently that he has resigned teaching to take up full-time writing.

One of the most dedicated of contemporary professionals is Iris Murdoch. She set herself an exacting apprenticeship to the novel, with the result that the first of her long string of novels did not appear until she was 34. In the meantime she became a wartime Civil Servant, then a relief worker in refugee camps, and finally fellow and tutor in philosophy at St. Anne's College, Oxford, where she married a fellow don, John Bayley, who is a tutor in English and also a writer. Other novelists have found temporary homes in the Civil Service: Angus Wilson, for instance, whose work in the Foreign Office included replacing the losses occasioned in the British Museum Library by enemy bombing; he later became Deputy Superintendent of the Reading Room. Joyce Cary was employed in the Nigerian political service, and Lawrence Durrell was in the Embassy at Cairo and press representative in Rhodes. Christopher Fry has augmented his income from writing in a variety of ways: teacher, repertory actor, secretary, editor, director of repertory in Tunbridge Wells and Oxford, and resident dramatist of the Arts Theatre Club. These careers are typical and representative, true of modern writers of all generations, from the time of Gerard Manley Hopkins through to the writers of the 'sixties. It is rare to find a writer who has had no connexion with the professions of words, and even rarer to find writers emulating the example of Samuel Beckett, who abandoned his work as a university lecturer to exile himself in Paris, living on the slenderest of means while he taught himself how to write. Nowadays writers are glad to seek out congenial secondary occupations, and they normally stay in them well after they can afford to leave them.

The cause of this happy change in attitudes is clearly the fact that writers tend to be better educated these days. I suppose some three-quarters of contemporary writers have been to a university, a proportion comparable with the Renaissance. There is nothing extraordinary about the fact: there are more opportunities for formal education nowadays, and it is less and less likely, as the years go by, that anyone with a talent for language will miss them completely. Writers are thus better fitted to take up other work. And those writers initially without a university education inevitably are drawn into a university context, for lecturing in particular, as happened to Walter de la Mare, Rudyard Kipling, John Masefield, Edith Sitwell, Dylan Thomas, Jon Silkin and many others. Writers are still to be found working as doctors, lawyers, architects, engineers and so on, but most start or finish or involve themselves for substantial periods in the professions of words.

Nevertheless, despite this relative insulation against the hard economics of the book trade, writers of all kinds have experienced, and had to adapt themselves, to some major changes in the pattern of communication with their audience. Briefly, there have always been three different kinds of audience, reached through the three different media: oral recitation together with manuscript circulation; periodicals and journals; and printed books. There is nothing rigid about the relative degree of importance of these channels. The printed-book audience assumed primacy only in the nineteenth century: in the Renaissance, as we have seen, the manuscript-oral audience was far more important. The particular change in pattern visible during this century, and intensifying since 1945, has been a relative decline in the printed-book audience, and increasing importance for the other two. The periodicals have assumed a dominant role as patrons and critics, and a new oral audience has been presented to authors by radio and television.

The effect upon authors depends very much on the kind of literature they write. The poets have experienced change most sharply. They are no longer the national figures of Victorian times, bards of the drawing-room, reaching remote audiences through best-selling books. Nowadays, Geoffrey Cumberlege, of the Oxford University Press, estimates that 'a slim volume of poetry by a living author who is not well known but whose poetry is undoubtedly good, will achieve a sale of some 300 copies'.[1] John Pudney calculates that such a volume would be published at a loss of between £70 and £150.[2] Three hundred years ago, when the country had a population less than a tenth of its present size and a literate public twenty times smaller, a new poet who was reasonably good could expect an audience as large as this. Nor is this relative decline in book sales confined to England or to Europe; in the United States, John Ciardi has asked 'Why is it . . . that in a nation of 146 million presumably literate people, the average sale for a book of poems is about 500 copies?'[3]

The situation has varied considerably within the twentieth century. Books of poetry sold well between 1912 and 1922, eleven years when 'more than 1,000 poets published more than 2,000 volumes between them';[4] in the middle 'thirties, when Stephen Spender earned over £500 on his first three books and Day Lewis over £100 on his first three; and in the years of the last war, when John Pudney, for instance, could sell 100,000 copies of one book, sales of 10,000 were not unusual, and even a completely unknown poet could achieve sales of 3,000 or more. It is notable that each of these periods marked a time of national crisis, which induced a *camaraderie* among poets, a hunger for poetic consolation in the reading public, and, more importantly, a sense of community. In such times minority tastes are apt to be extended more generally through the public at large. In quieter decades it is now quite clear that the book-buying public is not prepared to support the slim volumes, the poet's work 'in progress'. They have reverted to the custom of only buying poetry when it is established as good. Most of the best-selling books of poetry in our age have been either collected editions or anthologies. T. S. Eliot, Gerard Manley Hopkins, John Masefield, A. E. Housman, W. H. Auden, W. H. Davies, Dylan Thomas, and, more recently, John Betjeman have achieved reasonable success in collected editions. Maybe the measure of the success has diminished since the nineteenth century: the first impression of Eliot's *Collected Poems, 1909–1935*, which achieved eleven impressions between 1936 and 1947, was of 6,000 copies, compared

[1] In a personal letter to the present author.
[2] *The Bookseller* (26 January 1952), p. 120.
[3] *Mid-century American Poets* (New York, 1950), p. xvi.
[4] J. Isaacs, *The Background of Modern Poetry* (1951), p. 31.

with the 30,000 copies of the first impression of his play, *The Cocktail Party*, published simultaneously here and in the United States. The second edition of Hopkins's *Poems* achieved ten impressions between 1930 and 1944, a disappointing figure for the publisher, Geoffrey Cumberlege, who suggested that 'the sales appear rather small in relation to the amount of discussion and writing that is in constant process'. But there is clearly a market for this kind of book, and for anthologies. The Oxford University Press has reported that, of the 530 titles in the World's Classics series, Palgrave's *Golden Treasury* has had the biggest sales, both in the whole history of the series and annually. Similarly, probably the outstanding best-seller of modern poetry is the *Faber Book of Modern Verse*, which ran into fifteen impressions between 1936 and 1948.

In compensation, the poets have used the periodicals and journals to communicate their work in progress. In the boom years periodicals sold as well as books. In 1912–22, the era of the *Poetry Bookshop* here and *Poetry* (Chicago) in the United States, a whole host of little magazines thrived, such as *Blast*, *Art and Letters*, *The Egoist*, *Coterie*, *The Tyro* and others. In the political 'thirties the left-wing reviews were popular *media* for poetry, and Geoffrey Grigson established *New Verse*. In the last war there were *Penguin New Writing*, with a public of 50,000 or more, *Horizon*, *Voices*, *Our Time* and similar periodicals. But even in years which have been lean for the printed-book poets, there has always been a crop of little reviews, many of them local, all of them short-lived, but soon followed by successors: *Poetry and Poverty*, *Poetry and Audience*, *Oasis*, *We Offer . . .* , *Poems in Pamphlet*, *Fantasy Poets*—these are a few of the post-war examples of periodical and pamphlet print, selling at prices ranging from 1*s*. 6*d*. to 1*d*. Most poems published in books have first seen print in periodicals. When James Kirkup, for instance, published *The Submerged Village*, he acknowledged permission to republish from these journals: *The New Statesman and Nation*, *The Spectator*, *Time and Tide*, *The Listener*, *Tribune*, *Poetry Quarterly*, *The Wind and the Rain*, *Outposts*, *The Evening Standard*, *The Northern Review*, *Glass Hill*, *The Canadian Poetry Magazine*, *The Poetry Review*, *Writers of the Midlands*, *An Anthology of Northern Poetry*, *The Occult Observer*, *Poetry*, *Mandrake*, *The Times Literary Supplement*, *The Leeds University Verse*

*Anthology*. In this list Kirkup reveals that his poems have had all kinds of home: the periodical which does not specialize in poetry, and the quarterly which does, the review which specializes in something else but manages a corner for poetry, the local anthology, the daily paper and the weekly.

The periodicals provide a convenient channel for the poets. Nowadays, poets are not centralized in London, but are to be found all over the country. But it is not necessary for Mr. A in Oxford to transcribe a manuscript from Mr. B in Glasgow for his friend Mr. C in Swansea. He simply tells Mr. C to look for Mr. B's latest in the week's *Listener*. In this sense the periodicals augment manuscript circulation and compensate the poet for the lack of centres in which he can meet his colleagues. More importantly, the periodicals provide the poet with a public which appraises him, discusses and influences his activities, and passes him to the book publishers as a writer of established reputation. The book publishers wait for the verdict of the Sunday papers and weeklies, and these depend upon the verdicts of the little reviews. The power of patronage thus rests upon a few editors and their professional advisers, as it does in the printed-book trade. The system has many faults, since individual editors are themselves vulnerable to all kinds of critical failing, from sentimentality to undue susceptibility to fashion. But it is a viable system which looks like holding together for many years to come.

At the same time, particularly in the years since the war, oral recitation of poetry has again become popular. The radio and television companies have developed programmes, the Arts Council has subsidized touring shows like those developed with the Apollo Society, and individual poets in whom the bardic tradition appears to linger have taken poetry to clubs and pubs. Some, like Christopher Logue, Michael Horowitz, and Adrian Mitchell, with 'Live New Departures', have followed the example of the American negro, Langston Hughes, and found a place for poetry in jazz concerts. Much of these experiments are a form of protest against coterie writing, or an attempt to get away from the influence of the universities and make a connexion with the mass public.

Perhaps some experimenters are unduly optimistic. A writer in *The Times Literary Supplement* has suggested that the reign of the printed image is over 'and we would seem to be entering an era of a predominantly oral poetic culture'. It is difficult to believe that audiences have changed much since 1944, a good year for poetry, when a Broadcasting Committee under Lord Beveridge reported on a survey which asked a representative selection of listeners to place in order of preference seventeen kinds of programme: variety, plays, light music, musical comedy, military bands, cinema organs, brass bands, religious services, dance bands, discussions, talks, short-story readings, features, grand opera, symphony concerts, chamber music and poetry readings. It was discovered that listeners with a university education placed poetry fourteenth, with only dance bands, brass bands and cinema organs lower, while listeners with an elementary or secondary education placed poetry sixteenth. Over all sections of the audience poetry reading was the only item always in the last five, whereas, an interesting comparison, plays were always in the first five. Louis Macneice, after much experience, concluded that the broadcasting poet 'scales down his words': 'because it requires performance, such poetry is bound to be to some extent impure'.[1] But oral poetry, whatever its faults, has returned in a variety of *media*, from the concert to the gramophone record, and even unsuccessful experiments at least achieve two objects: the audience is extended outwards from the minority who read books and periodicals; and new rewards compensate poets for the decline in the printed-book market. The important thing is that poets with proper professional standards should attempt, continually, one way and another, to extend their audience, so that the field is not left open to what Auden called 'grotesquely bad verses written by maiden ladies in local newspapers'.

Many imaginative writers who in other times would have specialized in poetry have turned to the theatre. Most of Eliot's work since 1935 has been dramatic, and the writers who came to light in the 'thirties, like Auden, Isherwood, Macneice and Dylan Thomas, have felt the attractions of the post-Shavian theatre. Essentially, modern poetry, attempting a quintessence of a highly complex way of life, is bound by laws of its own nature to be complex, of a kind difficult to convert into an oral medium, and apt therefore to limit itself, at its best, to a small

[1] *Times Literary Supplement* (21 November 1952), p. 761.

audience. As Eliot suggests, in non-dramatic poetry, 'the question of communication, of what the reader will get from it, is not paramount: if your poem is right to you, you can only hope that the readers will ultimately come to accept it'. But in the theatre, 'you are aiming to write lines which will have an immediate effect upon an unknown and unprepared audience, to be interpreted to that audience by unknown actors rehearsed by an unknown producer. And the unknown audience cannot be expected to show any indulgence.'[1] In a mood of enthusiasm, Eliot has allowed himself such extravagant remarks as: 'I myself should like an audience that could neither read nor write.' But it must be reported that the experiments to take poetry into the theatre have failed: neither Eliot's philosophy nor Fry's wit nor the Marxist enthusiasm of Auden and his friends, writing political revues and plays for the little theatres, has created an era notable for poetic drama. Despite the support given to poetry by the little theatres, the theatrical societies (one year recently even the National Federation of Women's Institutes limited its annual dramatic festival to poetic drama), and above all by the great festivals at Edinburgh, York and elsewhere, the theatre remains stubbornly addicted to prose.

But within the prose theatre other kinds of imaginative experiment have been successful. The theatre has not been so alive since Jacobean times. The combined effect of so many explorers of the imagination working simultaneously—John Osborne, Harold Pinter, Samuel Beckett, Arnold Wesker, Robert Bolt, Shelagh Delaney, John Arden, N. F. Simpson, Henry Livings, Hall and Waterhouse, and many others—has made an impression even on the metropolitan theatre of London's West End, an entertainment industry traditionally providing idly amusing after-dinner plays for a polite public seeking relaxation rather than new experience. The influence of the Royal Court, the Theatre Workshop, and the Royal Shakespeare Company at the Aldwych has encouraged a new spirit of independence in managements and some capacity to lead rather than to follow public taste. A writer's theatre was helped forward by the establishment of the English Stage Company in 1956. Arts Council grants influence the trend towards the worth while, and those for drama have increased from £76,193 in 1952–3 to £252,144

[1] *Poetry and Drama* (1951), pp. 21–22.

in 1961–2. Above all, competition between the television companies has resulted in something akin to a renaissance of drama through this medium. There is a wealth of new experiment available on the television screen: it has become a matter of prestige for the companies to seek out and to reward good new material, and as a result a general freshness of writing has met with a large and ready audience not experienced in this country since the Elizabethan Globe.

For dramatists these are not only exciting times but rewarding times. True, the numbers of theatres shrink; there are fewer productions on tour; long runs clog up the theatres that exist and plays not immediately successful tend to have a shorter life. But the successful playwright adds to his income from repertory, amateur and foreign rights. Film rights can be exceptionally rewarding: *Seagulls over Sorrento* earned £10,000 in this way, and this figure is relatively unexciting compared with figures over £100,000 offered for plays like *Separate Tables*. True, cinemas decline in numbers, too, from 4,568 in 1952 to as few as 2,711 in 1961, but from the writer's point of view this is no disaster if one of the results has been, as is undoubtedly the case, a demand for scripts of better quality: the popularity of 'new-wave films' is one indication of the opportunities now available to writers, both with new film-plays and with adaptations of novels. In terms of regular rewards radio and television alone provide a good living. According to the Radiowriters Association, 55 per cent of radio scriptwriters were earning between 30*s*. and 40*s*. per minute of production time, while 20 per cent were earning over 40*s*. a minute. The TV and Screen Writers Guild now includes among its members more than 500 full-time writers, 40 per cent earning more than £20 a week, 11 per cent over £80 a week, from writing of all kinds. The market is larger each year. In 1955 the B.B.C. bought only twenty new television plays; by 1960 the B.B.C. and I.T.V. were screening 500 hours of drama each year.

It would seem that the good modern playwright has little reason to be grieved by the scale of his rewards, nor by fears of the corruption of his art by commercial interests. He tends to be more anxious about the actual composition of the audience which gives him his livelihood. The motive behind Joan Littlewood's work in Theatre Workshops, behind Shelagh Delaney's plan for a provincial Arts Theatre, behind the campaign of Arnold Wesker, Clive Barker and others for a 'Centre 42', a theatre for working men and women, has been essentially a desire to speak, in the flesh, to an audience of the whole people rather than a fraction of the whole. Wesker estimates that the theatre today, including the provincial houses, repertory halls and festivals, attracts only some 3 per cent of the total population.[1] This small minority is an educated group which has developed a taste for the theatre and which is able and willing to pay the price of the seats. Whereas the cost of renting a television set, including the price of an aerial and licence, amounts to little more than £2 a month, a man might well spend the same money taking his wife to the theatre for just one evening's entertainment. In any case, it is argued, the average working man never thinks of going to the theatre: the whole ritual, the art itself, he assumes, is not for him. It is galling for writers with a working-class background themselves to find a major channel of communication so blocked. And the mass audiences of films and television cannot give writers the same sense of direct communication with their public, the same satisfying sense of social service.

There is no immediate consolation available for artists with this kind of anxiety. It is no solution if diligent trade unions, urged on by their education committees, subsidize Centre 42 festivals, and the general reaction of the audience is that of the man in the Golden Lion at Wellingborough who complained in the Press that 'these artists get in the way and stop us playing skittles'! It is one thing to establish the means of a livelihood, the time to write in peace what one wants to write. It is quite another to convince the public of the value of the service rendered, to get away from the role of mere entertainer. The poets who are now developing oral poetry, and the dramatists seeking new audiences, agree in believing that the solution is the creation of a genuine collaboration between the artist and his public. T. S. Eliot recognized that 'the working man who went to the music-hall and saw Marie Lloyd and joined in the chorus was himself performing part of the act'. The problem, then, is to get more people into the act, and this is essentially a question of education. Paul Claudel, writing in 1893–4 in *L'Echange*, held that

[1] In lectures devoted to enlisting support for his Centre 42.

> Man grows bored and the ignorance he was born with sticks to him,
> And not knowing a thing about how it begins or ends, that's what makes him go to the theatre.
> And he is looking at himself, with his hands resting on his knees.

The problem is to persuade more people to be content with looking at themselves, to be interested in becoming more secure, more human, more alive, and to break the hold of mass entertainment which satisfies the more strident demand of human nature to escape from itself and thus to go to sleep. The major problem in the literary profession now is not so much the scale of rewards nor even questions of social status, but the bridging of the gap which exists, and has always existed, between the minority who respond to their imaginative needs, and the majority who still fail to recognize that the profession has any service it can render them. As this history demonstrates, education is a long, slow process. Much has been done; much is being done, particularly by the artists who are not reluctant to go out to meet their public and explain themselves; much remains to be done, and for a long time to come.

The novelists are more fortunate than the poets and dramatists in making use of what has been, for two hundred years, the most popular of literary forms. In the first place, quite apart from eccentric instances like Joyce's *Ulysses*, there is not the same gap as exists in other forms between the physical presentations of good writing and bad writing. The reader used to Patience Strong is apt to feel an abrupt jolt on opening *Four Quartets*; the viewer accustomed to *Cheyenne* is likely to demur when the next programme turns out to be a Pinter play; *L'Année Dernière à Marienbad* is apt to bewilder the cinemagoer brought up on English film comedy; but the reader habitually looking along the library shelves, where all fiction is housed in a superbly classless society, is just as likely to take home an Iris Murdoch, and enjoy it, as a Denise Robins. The differences are differences of quality in language and enlightenment rather than total disparities of style and presentation. One might go further and add that all novels, however unexacting and unoriginal, require a minimum of co-operation from the reader: before the necessary suspension of disbelief occurs and he is caught up with the author on an imaginative journey, the reader must work himself, whatever the novel. A degree of concentration is required, more effort than from, for instance, the passive spectator of television: the pictures go on regardless, but the words stop flowing when the reader stops reading. This is why it is not true, as John Wain suggests, that the novel is a 'packaged product', belonging to the 'world of consumer goods', in the sense that it does not require the active participation of the audience in the way of oral poetry or arena theatre. And because the novel-reader is accustomed to doing work, because the best novels are readily accessible to, and digestible by, relatively uneducated readers, the department of novels is the most democratic part of the republic of letters.

In terms of rewards there is not the same gap as heretofore between the 'popular' and the 'serious' novelist. Among the best-selling romantic novels, stories of a kind eligible for serialization in women's magazines, an outstanding example is Victoria Holt's *Mistress of Mellyn*, which sold 22,000 copies in this country, and 45,000 in the United States. Netta Muskett does very well to keep up regular sales of about 12,500 copies. More usual is a sale of between 2,000 and 6,000, of which 60 per cent represents home sales and 40 per cent sales abroad. The average reward for the good romantic novelist is somewhere in the region of £150 per novel. This scale of rewards is open just as much to the serious artist as it is to the commercial craftsman. True, romantic novels are often reprinted, sometimes printed first as women's serials: of Alex Stuart's forty-five novels in the last twelve years, all but three earned British serial rights; the standard rate of fee, to all but the top names, is between twenty-five and forty guineas an instalment. And commercial novelists are able to produce more, four a year quite usually, and up to sixteen in exceptional instances, obviating restrictions imposed by publishers by writing under pseudonyms (Alex Stuart has five). And there are strip-cartoon rights also available. But, by and large, the large rewards in novel-writing come from reprint in paperbacks, film rights and reprints abroad. The paperback business increases phenomenally: in 1953 less than a thousand titles were produced in this medium; by May 1960, 5,866; by June 1962, 9,578, a 65 per cent increase in two years. Between 1951 and 1960 the sale of Penguins, the leading paperback, leaped upwards from nearly 10,000,000 copies a year to over

17,000,000. From the point of view of the author, royalties of $7\frac{1}{2}$ per cent on a run of 30,000 or 50,000 paperbacks, even if he has to share some proportion with his hardback publisher, is worth more than royalties of 10 per cent on 3,000 hardback copies. And, by and large, the serious novelist has a better chance of reprint in paperbacks than the writer of conventional westerns or romances, just as he has more chance of attracting the attention of the film-makers and publishers in Europe, the United States, the Soviet Union, Japan and so on.

History indicates that art thrives, that the best art becomes available, when there are the fewest stratifications of public taste, when, in fact, the *élite* of society and society in general share, broadly enough, the same tastes. Because of the gulf between mass entertainment and the culture of the *élites*, at one time most commentators despaired of the future of the literary art in the twentieth century. Forecasts tended to be Jeremiads. It is still common to read, in one history or another, of the end of western European culture, of the decline into mediocrity of English Literature. While such pessimism may have its justifications, the facts of the situation since 1945 hardly warrant such sweeping conclusions. In poetry today homogeneity does not exist, and poetry is clearly experiencing a period of eclipse: but poetry has known eclipse before, and one remembers Samuel Johnson's despair after the consummate artistry of Pope. In drama there is the encouragement of the struggle towards homogeneity, and the evidence of a renaissance which has produced better plays than the theatre has known since Shakespeare. With the novel homogeneity has never been broken, and the gloomy forecasts of thirty years ago have not come to pass. Eliot was wrong: the novel did not end with Flaubert and James, nor did it end with Lawrence, nor with the despairing innovations of Joyce and Virginia Woolf. One critic, K. W. Gransden, recently complained: 'When did we last have a novel which transformed our world?' and suggested that 'The plain fact about many novels is that their authors offer what they think we want to read, not what they themselves are compelled to discover about life.'[1] But it is plainly true that only a handful of great artists ever transform the world, and one cannot expect a Lawrence

[1] 'Thoughts on contemporary fiction', *A Review of English Literature* (1960), p. ii.

very often. Throughout history the enlightenment of art has usually taken more modest forms: it has helped society to understand itself, to value itself, to live with its particular problems. It is true that many novelists overtly set out to give the public what it wants, but there are plenty of writers, especially since 1945, who have understood and served the national need for imaginative enlightenment about fundamental problems. Like the Elizabethans, we recoil from a cosmos which we cannot control and fall back upon the eternal questions of human relationships. And after Lawrence, it is inevitable that we should be interested in problems of sex and marriage, should be most moved by the tenderness of the call, as Forster suggested, between man and woman. Surprisingly perhaps, if it is not heretical to say so, there were a great many things Lawrence did not and could not know. This is perhaps our major interest; the novel exists as a medium of exploration available widely throughout the whole community, without as well as within the *élites*; and a whole series of good novelists have helped us explore. The roll includes Iris Murdoch, Lawrence Durrell, Angus Wilson, William Golding, Kingsley Amis, John Wain, John Braine, Alan Sillitoe, Stan Barstow, David Storey, Lynne Reid Banks, and many others. Perhaps if we stopped looking for the great novel, we might better appreciate the health and vigour, and indeed the astonishing fertility, of the last decade or so of novel-writing.

One last remark about our own times. In an age of enforced specialization it is encouraging to observe so many writers with more than one string to their bow. Some writers as yet have only a limited range: Iris Murdoch, for instance, has only her novels, a book on Sartre and other philosophical papers, although other people are adapting her work for television and the theatre. But Eliot set an example which many follow: not only a poet and a playwright, he was also the leading critic of his generation. The 'thirties offered several examples of authors of wide range, notably W. H. Auden, who turned from poetry to drama, travel books, criticism, and opera librettos. Among the writers who have come to the front since the war, Lawrence Durrell has written in four different genres: first as a poet publishing slim volumes and then a selected and a collected edition; he next turned to travel books, three in succession; then to novels, five altogether; and latterly to plays, to *Sappho*, *Acte* and *Faustus*. Among a generation younger again, David Holbrook's example of industry is one which Defoe and Carlyle would entirely approve. Beginning only a few short years ago, in 1957, he has already published or is about to publish, two books of poems, two novels, two books of short stories, five works of criticism, five anthologies of various kinds including the *Cambridge Hymnal*, several educational textbooks, a book about children's games, a libretto for a ballad opera and a sequence for voices. And this range is typical of many of the younger writers. Faced with this contemporary evidence of professional dedication, the historian of the profession of letters must conclude that his is not an epitaph but merely an interim report on the profession to date. We leave off the story in midstream, as it were, with the flood still rolling strongly towards new areas of achievement in the future.

From our present vantage-point, it is possible now to see the evolution of the profession as a whole, what has been done and what remains to be done. We have seen how in fourteenth- and fifteenth-century England, at the beginning of English as a language, certain necessary elements were gathered together to make possible a profession. The medieval Church found a practical need for vernacular literature and gave to such writings a status of dignity, concerned as they were with the profounder truths of human nature. The need for recreation in the feudal communities connected literature with the open questions of human nature which dogma naturally tends to seal and close, with imaginative adventures widely available through oral recitation and manuscripts. At the same time, individuals were seeking the means whereby they might devote much of their working time towards the avocation, if not vocation, of writing books.

During the Renaissance literature came to enjoy a national esteem and importance it had not so far been vouchsafed. Wider literacy, the development of the printing press and of the printed book market, the greater opportunities for leisure, the revived interest in *belles-lettres*, all these factors contributed. But the Court which led the way in the establishment of a literary art hindered the establishment of a literary profession. Talent was concentrated at Court through an elaborate system of patronage, which encouraged generations of brilliant amateurs, to whom writing was an accomplishment but not a vocation. The courtly amateurs connected literature with personal experience, with the things that make men human, but they condemned print and many kinds of public writing: their art was essentially a private one. The stigma attached to print, and the suspicion of a Puritan-minded reading public that fiction was shameful and foolish, prevented for a long time any development of imaginative literature in the printed-book market. Only in the theatre, for special reasons, was a profession possible in which writers could simultaneously earn a living and devote their lives to literary art. Shakespeare and his colleagues in the public playhouses were the first true professionals, and even here their best opportunities were restricted to two or three decades at the turn of the seventeenth century.

But inspired by classical examples of what literature could do, and what sort of place it could occupy in the community, first Spenser and then Milton pioneered a new trail in professional print. As a result of the Civil Wars, print became the normal and entirely respectable medium of communication with any audience and new impetus was given through a whole range of prose arts, from the biography and the essay to the novel. New *media* arrived: newspapers, periodicals, miscellanies, anthologies, encyclopaedias, and so on. The new forms and *media* provided writers with the means to a living, and opportunities of serious and increasingly imaginative expression. With the arrival of criticism, literary editions and scholars concerned with English Literature as a subject worthy of study comparable with the classics, literature addressed a national forum. In Augustan England the profession was finally established and the writers from Defoe to Johnson were the first complete professionals, while the audience was organized through coffee-houses, clubs, literary societies, subscription patronage, and a steadily growing printed-book market. The dedicated writers were still outnumbered by the drudges and hacks, on the one hand, and by the amateurs on the other, but there is a distinct line of progression. The two extremes, the amateur like Waller uninterested in rewards and the journalist like Defoe struggling with his integrity for the sake of rewards, finally come together, until with Pope, Fielding, Johnson and their successors there is an accord and balance: security is achieved without loss of independence, high status without the stigma of commercialism, and dignity without the slackening of full-time industry and devotion.

The main problem then, as literature gradually extended its audience into new areas of society, was to maintain proper standards of discovery and enquiry where the public was all too readily satisfied with 'entertainment' which did not nourish their imaginative curiosity. The growth of an entertainment industry destroyed English drama, at least for two hundred years and more, as long ago as the early eighteenth century; and has provided a constant temptation for writers in other forms. The literary profession has had to guard against the dangers of public demand, in order to maintain the quality of the work done, the service rendered by the profession. It is all too easy to play to the gallery, and console oneself with the thought that at least one is helping the harassed and the weary to 'enjoy themselves', to 'escape from life', to 'relax and be happy'. On the other hand, too little attention to public taste and demand robs an author of his audience altogether. The Romantic dilemma, the problem of the late eighteenth and early nineteenth century, was to reconcile the opposite claims of professional standards and general popularity. The dilemma sharpened with the Industrial Revolution, when the writers claimed, as the latest extension of classical precept, a special inspiration, a peculiar vision of truth which should not be socially corrupted or circumscribed, while the reading public demanded an immediate and practical use for dreams and visions, not as a means of truth and an understanding of life, but as a kind of anodyne to compensate for the poverty and ugliness of the age. Substantial private means helped many writers remain true to themselves; a few weathered the storm in the thick of things; others fell into despair or various kinds of aberration. The literary profession of the nineteenth century embraced, side by side, idealists and frauds, honest professionals and dishonest amateurs, men of unquestionable genius and men of most questionable ingenuity, a complex scene which became even more complicated as the mass market evolved.

The true professionals, Carlyle, Scott and Dickens, and the amateurs of true professional dedication, Jane Austen and Lamb and George Eliot, not only loved their art, but were willing to serve the community and were convinced, too, that their service was good and important and above all necessary. It was this conviction that steadied the profession when the mass market became a reality. We have seen how, despite the difficulties, Shaw restored to the theatre drama of integrity, how Lawrence established his novels against the fiercest possible public opposition, and how in our own day the best writers have worked within the mass market, taking advantage of their readers' opportunities for wider leisure and hunger for reading matter. Nothing stands still. Writers have to be adaptable, and, like modern poets, seek out new oral and periodical audiences; or, like modern dramatists, compensate for a decline in the printed-book market by finding new audiences, on television and elsewhere; all the time seeking to demonstrate that literature is a collaboration relevant to all human beings whatever their occupation or class.

The struggle continues. The primary problem today is one of education, a process which will end the Romantic isolation of the artist from the community, and also bring about a more perfect homogeneity of taste in a wider public. The struggle is important, and not only to the minority who care about literature. This chapter began with the concern of the artist for the 'unutterable particularity' of nature and especially human nature, a concern which is the same as love. If literature has a distinctive 'knowledge' to offer, a knowledge different from that gained through philosophy or psychology or theology or any other intellectual study of human nature, then such knowledge is useful and necessary and the community needs the means of making use of it. F. R. Leavis once told the London School of Economics; 'Without the sensitizing familiarity with the subtleties of language, and the insight into the relations between abstract or generalizing thought and the concrete of human experience, that the trained frequentation of literature alone can bring, the thinking that attends social and political studies will not have the edge and force it should.'[1] These words, intended for economists, have the same meaning when referred to the other specialists of modern society. More boldly, V. de Sola Pinto defines the task of literature (he was thinking primarily of poetry) as that of

[1] *The Common Pursuit* (1952), p. 194.

'humanizing the classless (and at present cultureless) society of the Welfare State by providing it with living images of virtue and truth, which would help to heal 'the schism in the soul' caused by standardization and mechanization, and ultimately to restore the Whole Man'.[1]

Because literature is at its best an activity which co-ordinates, rather than departmentalizes, our knowledge of human nature, it has a general value in the specialized society of today. Yet too many people still think of it as a specialized activity irrelevant to their own specific experience and needs. Too often managerial society discourages its members to look outside their own rut. I once enquired how many members of our modern Parliament (once the Parliament of Donne and Marvell, Waller and Addison, Disraeli and Macaulay, Lytton and Cobbett, Belloc and Churchill) now read and wrote poetry; Alice Bacon, herself a leading educationist, protested that 'it was rather a waste of time to send such a letter to M.Ps. Why not address it to someone less busy?' This, I suppose, was a fair retort by one specialist to another, but it begged the question of the fragmentation of our specialized society and of how far anyone can be too busy to ask and answer questions about his fellow beings and their imaginative use of art and literature.

There is a dangerous anaesthetic at work in modern society: as more leisure has become available, it has been filled up by a multitude of pursuits, many of them passive, docile and unnutritious. All too often the daylight is never let in upon our human nature: it is blocked by habit-making mass entertainment, by time-consuming daily routines of work and leisure, by specializing education and employment. Metaphorically, our heads are all too often down, if not for bingo then for whatever anodyne helps us forget the primary call of our human nature to find out who we are, why we tick, what we do here. The profession of letters is now the most important agency available in society to help us all counteract the pressures of our age and assert our unutterable particularity. And since so much remains to be done, since mass literacy, mass education, mass print, are all still in their infancy, it is just to conclude that far from being at the end of this story of the profession of English letters, we are only at the beginning.

[1] *Crisis in English Poetry* (1951), p. 208.

# Selected References

## CH. II. IN THE BEGINNING


J. W. ADAMSON, 'The Extent of Literacy in England in the Fifteenth and Sixteenth Centuries', *The Library* (September 1929).

J. W. H. ATKINS, *English Literacy Criticism: the Medieval Phase* (Cambridge, 1943).

H. S. BENNETT, 'The Author and his Public in the Fourteenth and Fifteenth Centuries', *Essays and Studies*, XXIII (1938).

— 'Caxton and his Public', *Review of English Studies* (April 1943).

— 'Science and Information in English Writings of the Fifteenth Century', *Modern Language Review* (January 1944).

— 'The Production and Dissemination of Vernacular Manuscripts in the Fifteenth Century', *The Library* (December 1946).

— *Chaucer and the Fifteenth Century* (Oxford History of English Literature, II. I, 1947).

F. W. BATESON, *English Poetry: a Critical Introduction* (1951).

CARLETON BROWN and R. H. ROBBINS, *The Index of Middle English Verse* (New York, 1943).

MILDRED CAMPBELL, *The English Yeoman* (New Haven, 1942).

D. CHADWICK, *Social Life in the Days of Piers Plowman* (Cambridge, 1922).

E. K. CHAMBERS, *The Medieval Stage* (Oxford, 1903).

— *English Literature at the close of the Middle Ages* (Oxford History of English Literature, II. II, 1945).

G. C. COULTON, *Chaucer and his England* (Oxford, 1921).

HARDIN CRAIG, *English Religious Drama of the Middle Ages* (Oxford, 1955).

M. DEANESLY, 'Vernacular Books in England in the Fourteenth and Fifteenth Centuries', *Modern Language Review* (October 1920).

E. P. GOLDSCHMIDT, *Medieval Texts and their First Appearance in Print* (1943).

K. J. HOLZKNECHT, *Literary Patronage in the Middle Ages* (Philadelphia, 1923).

W. P. KER, *English Literature: Medieval* (1912).

C. L. KINGSFORD, *English Historical Literature in the Fifteenth Century* (1913).

— *Prejudice and Promise in Fifteenth Century England* (1925).

H. B. LATHROP, 'The First English Printers and their Patrons', *The Library* (September 1922).

SAMUEL MOORE, 'General Aspects of Literary Patronage in the Middle Ages', *The Library* (October 1913).

G. R. OWST, *Literature and Pulpit in Medieval England* (Cambridge, 1933).

A. L. POOLE, *Medieval England* (Oxford, 1958).

G. H. PUTNAM, *Books and their Makers during the Middle Ages*, II (1897).

W. L. RENWICK and H. ORTON, *The Beginnings of English Literature to Skelton 1509* (1952).

F. M. SALTER, *Medieval Drama in Chester* (Toronto, 1955).

R. SOUTHERN, *The Medieval Theatre in the Round* (1957).

J. SPEIRS, *Medieval English Poetry* (1957).

R. M. WILSON, *The Lost Literature of Medieval England* (1952).

## CH. III. THE RENAISSANCE AMATEURS

A. ALVAREZ, 'John Donne and his Circle', *The Listener* (23 May 1957).

J. M. BERDAN, *Early Tudor Poetry, 1485–1547* (New York, 1920).

C. S. BALDWIN and D. L. CLARK, *Renaissance Literary Theory and Practice* (New York, 1939).

F. S. BOAS, *Sidney, Representative Elizabethan: His Life and Writings* (1955).

DOUGLAS BUSH, *English Literature in the earlier Seventeenth Century* (*Oxford History of English Literature V*) (Oxford, 1945).

JOHN BUXTON, *Sir Philip Sidney and the English Renaissance* (1954).

B. CASTIGLIONE, *The Courtyer of Count Baldessar Castilio*, tr. T. Hoby, ed. J. E. Ashbee (1900).

E. W. DORMER, *Grey of Reading* (1923).

JOHN HOSKYNS, *Directions for Speech and Style*, ed. H. H. Hudson (1935).

R. F. JONES, *The Triumph of the English Language* (1953).

AGNES LATHAM, *The Poems of Sir Walter Raleigh* (1929).

J. B. LEISHMAN, 'You meaner beauties of the night. A study in transmission and transmogrification', *The Library* (September 1945).

C. S. LEWIS, *English Literature in the Sixteenth Century, excluding Drama* (*Oxford History of English Literature III*) (Oxford, 1954).

J. E. NEALE, *Essays in Elizabethan History* (1958).
— 'The Elizabethan Political Scene' (*Proceedings of the British Academy*, XXXIV, 1948).
B. H. NEWDIGATE, *Michael Drayton and his Circle* (1941).
C. PEMBERTON, *Queen Elizabeth's Englishings* (Early English Text Society, 1899).
GEORGE PUTTENHAM, *Arte of English Poesie* (1589).
A. L. ROWSE, *The England of Elizabeth: the Structure of Society* (1950).
V. L. RUBEL, *Poetic Diction in the English Renaissance* (New York, 1941).
I. A. SHAPIRO, 'The "Mermaid Club"' (*Modern Language Review*, XLV, 1950).
SIR P. SIDNEY, *The Defence of Poesie* (1593).
G. GREGORY SMITH, *Elizabethan Critical Essays* (Oxford, 1904).
E. M. W. TILLYARD, *The Elizabethan World Picture* (1943).
C. V. WEDGWOOD, *Poetry and Politics under the Stuarts* (1960).
THOMAS WILSON, *The State of England, 1600*, ed. F. J. Fisher (*Camden Miscellany*, XVI, 1936).

## CH. IV. THE RENAISSANCE PROFESSIONALS

E. GORDON DUFF, *A Century of the English Book-Trade* (1905).
B. B. GAMZUE, 'Elizabeth and Literary Patronage' (*PMLA*, XLIX, 1934).
C. GEBERT, *Elizabethan Dedications and Prefaces* (Philadelphia, 1933).
L. T. GOLDING, *An Elizabethan Puritan* (New York, 1937).
W. W. GREG, *Some Aspects and Problems of London Publishing between 1550 and 1650* (Oxford, 1956).
GABRIEL HARVEY, *Letter-Book of Gabriel Harvey, 1573–80*, ed. E. J. L. Scott (Camden Society Second Series, XXXIII, 1884).
R. B. MCKERROW (ed.), *A Dictionary of Printers and Booksellers in England, Scotland and Ireland, 1557–1640* (1910).
EDWIN H. MILLER, *The Professional Writer in Elizabethan England* (Cambridge, Mass., 1959).
W. R. MUELLER, *The Anatomy of Burton's England* (Berkeley, Calif., 1952).
N. B. PARADISE, *Thomas Lodge* (New Haven, 1931).
V. DE S. PINTO, 'The Street Ballad and English Poetry' (*Politics and Letters*, 1947).
MARJORIE PLANT, *The English Book Trade: an Economic History* (1939).
C. T. PROUTY, *Gascoigne: Elizabethan Courtier, Soldier and Poet* (New York, 1942).
ELEANOR ROSENBERG, *Leicester, Patron of Letters* (New York, 1955).

J. W. SAUNDERS, 'The Stigma of Print' (*Essays in Criticism*, I, 1951).
— 'From Manuscript to Print' (*Proceedings of the Leeds Philosophical Society*, VI, 1951).
— 'The Façade of Morality' (in W. R. Mueller and D. C. Allen, *That Soueraine Light* (Baltimore, 1952)).
PHOEBE SHEAVYN, *The Literary Profession in the Elizabethan Age* (1909).
L. B. WRIGHT, 'Translation for the Elizabethan Middle Class' (*The Library*, XIII, 1932)).
— *Middle Class Culture in Elizabethan England* (Chapel Hill, 1935).

## CH. V. TAKING ROOT

F. S. BOAS, *University Drama in the Tudor Age* (Oxford, 1914).
G. E. BENTLEY, *The Jacobean and Caroline Stage* (Oxford, 1941 ff.).
E. K. CHAMBERS, *The Elizabethan Stage* (Oxford, 1923).
T. W. CRAIK, *The Tudor Interlude* (Leicester, 1958).
J. MILTON FRENCH (ed.), *The Life Records of John Milton* (New Brunswick, 1949 ff.).
W. W. GREG, *Pastoral Poetry and Pastoral Drama* (1906).
J. H. HANFORD, *John Milton, Englishman* (New York, 1949).
L. HOTSON, *The Commonwealth and Restoration Stage* (Cambridge, Mass., 1928).
— *The First Night of Twelfth Night* (1954).
— *Shakespeare's Wooden O* (1959).
L. C. KNIGHTS, *Drama and Society in the Age of Jonson* (1937).
C. S. LEWIS, *The Allegory of Love* (Oxford, 1936).
DAVID MASSON, *The Life of Milton* (1859–94).
W. L. RENWICK, *Edmund Spenser* (1925).
J. W. SAUNDERS, 'Milton, Diomede and Amaryllis', *A Journal of English Literary History* (December 1955).
E. M. W. TILLYARD, *The Miltonic Setting* (1947).
GLYNNE WICKHAM, *Early English Stages, I (1300–1576)* (1959).
BASIL WILLEY, *The Seventeenth Century Background* (1934).

## CH. VI. PROSE, PRINT AND THE PROFESSION

R. S. CRANE and F. B. KAYE, *A Census of British Newspapers and Periodicals* (Chapel Hill, 1927).
BONAMY DOBRÉE, *English Literature in the Early Eighteenth Century, 1700–1740* (Oxford, 1959).
F. HOMES DUDDEN, *Fielding: his Life, Works and Times* (Oxford, 1952).

WALTER GRAHAM, *The Beginnings of English Literary Periodicals 1665–1715* (New York, 1926).
A. R. HUMPHREYS, *The Augustan World* (1954).
ARNOLD KETTLE, *An Introduction to the English Novel I* (1952).
J. J. LYNCH, *Box, Pit and Gallery* (California, 1953).
A. NICOLL, *A History of Restoration Drama, 1660–1700* (Cambridge, 1923).
— *A History of Eighteenth-Century Drama, 1700–1750* (Cambridge, 1925).
— *A History of Eighteenth-Century Drama, 1750–1800* (Cambridge, 1927).
ANTS ORAS, *Milton's Editors and Commentators from Patrick Hume to Henry John Todd (1695–1801)* (1931).
V. DE S. PINTO, *Rochester* (1935).
H. R. PLOMER, *A Dictionary of Printers and Booksellers, 1668–1725* (1922).
— *A Dictionary of Printers and Booksellers, 1726–1775* (1932).
R. QUINTANA, *Swift* (Oxford, 1954).
W. M. SALE, *Samuel Richardson, Master Printer* (Ithaca, New York, 1950).
D. A. STAUFFER, *English Biography before 1700* (1930).
— *The Art of Biography in Eighteenth Century England* (1941).
J. R. SUTHERLAND, 'The Circulation of Newspapers and Periodicals, 1700–1730', *The Library* (1934).
IAN WATT, *The Rise of the Novel* (1957).
RENE WELLEK, *The Rise of English Literary History* (Chapel Hill, 1941).
HAROLD WILLIAMS, *Book Clubs and Printing Societies of Great Britain and Northern Ireland* (1929).

## CH. VII. THE PROFESSION ESTABLISHED

W. J. BATE, *The Achievement of Johnson* (New York, 1955).
A. S. COLLINS, *The Profession of Letters, 1780-1832* (1928).
A. DOBSON, *Eighteenth-Century Vignettes* (three series) (1892–6).
C. K. EVES, *Prior, Poet and Diplomatist* (New York, 1939).
K. EWART, *Copyright* (Cambridge, 1952).
B. FITZGERALD, *Daniel Defoe: a Study in Conflict* (1954).
N. HANS, *New Trends in Education in the Eighteenth Century* (London, 1951).
J. W. KRUTCH, *Johnson* (New York, 1944).
F. A. MUMBY, *Publishing and Bookselling* (1956).
J. NICHOLS, *The Rise and Progress of the Gentleman's Magazine* (1821).
M. PLANT, *The English Book Trade* (1939).

R. K. ROOT, *The Poetical Career of Pope* (Princeton, 1938).
GEORGE SHERBURN (essays presented to), *Pope and his Contemporaries* (New York, 1949).
P. SMITHERS, *The Life of Addison* (Oxford, 1954).
R. STRAUS, *Robert Dodsley: Poet, Publisher and Playwright* (1910).
J. SUTHERLAND, *Defoe* (1950).
LESLIE STEPHEN, *English Literature and Society in the Eighteenth Century* (1904).
A. S. TURBERVILLE (ed.), *Johnson's England* (1933).
MARK VAN DOREN, *Dryden: a Study of his Poetry* (New York, 1946).
K. YOUNG, *John Dryden* (1954).

## CH. VIII. THE ROMANTIC DILEMMA

F. W. BATESON, *Wordsworth: a Reinterpretation* (1954).
H. N. BRAILSFORD, *Shelley, Godwin and their Circle* (1926).
E. K. CHAMBERS, *Coleridge: a Biographical Study* (Oxford, 1950).
WILLARD CONNELY, *Laurence Sterne as Yorick* (1958).
W. L. CROSS, *Life and Times of Sterne* (New Haven, 1929).
H. W. GARROD, *Keats* (Oxford, 1939).
F. KERMODE, *The Romantic Image* (1957).
F. W. KETTON-CREMER, *Gray: a Biography* (Cambridge, 1955).
L. M. KNAPP, *Smollett: Doctor of Men and Manners* (Princeton, 1949).
L. L. MARTZ, *The Later Career of Smollett* (New Haven, 1942).
MARIO PRAZ, *The Romantic Agony* (Oxford, 1951).
JOHN WAIN (ed.), *Contemporary Reviews of Romantic Poetry* (1953).
MONA WILSON, *Life of Blake* (1948).

## CH. IX. ARTISTS AND SALESMEN

J. W. ADAMS, *English Education, 1789–1902* (Cambridge, 1930).
R. D. ALTICK, *The English Common Reader, 1800–1900.* (Chicago, 1957)
W. and R. A. AUSTEN-LEIGH, *Jane Austen: Her Life and Letters* (1913).
EDMUND BLUNDEN, *Hunt: a Biography* (1930).
— *Lamb and his Contemporaries* (Cambridge, 1933).
— *Shelley: a Life Story* (1946).
ASA BRIGGS, *Victorian People* (1954).
G. CARNALL, *Robert Southey and his Age* (Oxford, 1960).
A. S. COLLINS, *The Profession of Letters, 1780–1832* (1928).
AMY CRUSE, *The Englishman and his Books in the Early Nineteenth Century* (1930).
— *The Victorians and their Books* (1935).

JOAN EVANS, *John Ruskin* (1954).
G. H. FORD, *Dickens and his Readers* (Princeton, 1955).
R. A. GETTMAN, *A Victorian Publisher* (Bentley) (Cambridge, 1960).
W. GRAHAM, *English Literary Periodicals* (New York, 1930).
HERBERT GRIERSON, *Scott: a new Life* (1938).
L. and E. HANSON, *The Four Brontës* (Oxford, 1949).
BARBARA HARDY, *The Novels of George Eliot* (1959).
C. HILL, *Jane Austen, Her Homes and her Friends* (1904).
Q. D. LEAVIS, *Fiction and the Reading Public* (1932).
BETTY MILLER, *Browning, a Portrait* (1952).
EMERY NEFF, *Carlyle* (New York, 1932).
PETER QUENNELL, *Byron: The Years of Fame* (1935).
G. N. RAY, *Thackeray* (New York, 1955–8).
E. F. SHANNON, Jr., *Tennyson and his Reviewers* (Harvard, 1953).
LESLIE STEPHEN, *George Eliot* (1913).
R. H. SUPER, *Landor; a Biography* (New York, 1954).
G. B. TAPLIN, *The Life of Elizabeth Barrett Browning* (New Haven, 1937).
C. TENNYSON, *Alfred Tennyson* (1949).
GEOFFREY TILLOTSON, *Criticism and the Nineteenth Century* (1951).
KATHLEEN TILLOTSON, *Novels of the Eighteen-forties* (Oxford, 1954).
L. TRILLING, *Matthew Arnold* (New York, 1949).
R. K. WEBB, 'Working Class Readers in Early Victorian England', *English Historical Review* (1950).
R. WILLIAMS, *Culture and Society, 1780–1950* (1958).
G. M. YOUNG, *Victorian England* (Oxford, 1936).

## CH. X. THE MASS MARKET

ERIC BENTLEY, *Shaw: a Reconsideration* (New York, 1947).
E. L. CASFORD, *The Magazines of the 1890's* (Eugene, Oregon, 1929).
AMY CRUSE, *After the Victorians* (1938).
LOUIS DUDEK, *Literature and the Press* (1961).
ST. JOHN ERVINE, *Shaw: his Life, Works and Friends* (1956).
GERARD FAY, *The Abbey Theatre* (1958).
ISABELLA GREGORY, *Our Irish Theatre* (1914).
EVELYN HARDY, *Thomas Hardy* (1954).
HAROLD HERD, *The March of Journalism* (1952).
RICHARD HOGGART, *The Uses of Literacy* (1956).
HOLBROOK JACKSON, *The Eighteen Nineties* (1913).
NORMAN JEFFARES, *Yeats, Man and Poet* (1949).
F. R. LEAVIS, *D. H. Lawrence, Novelist* (1955).
Q. D. LEAVIS, *Fiction and the Reading Public* (1932).

MARVIN MAGALANER and R. M. KAIN, *Joyce: the Man, the Work, the Reputation* (New York, 1956).

HARRY T. MOORE, *The Intelligent Heart: the Story of Lawrence* (New York, 1954).

S. MORISON, *The English Newspaper* (Cambridge, 1932).

A. NICOLL, *A History of Late Nineteenth Century Drama* (Cambridge, 1946).

A. D. C. PETERSON, *A Hundred Years of Education* (1952).

GEORGE ROWELL, *The Victorian Theatre* (1956).

S. H. STEINBERG, *Five Hundred Years of Printing* (1955).

LIONEL TRILLING, *E. M. Forster* (Norfolk, Conn., 1943).

RAYMOND WILLIAMS, *Culture and Society, 1780–1950* (1958).

— *Drama from Ibsen to Eliot* (1952).

— *The Long Revolution* (1960).

## CH. XI. THE PROFESSION TODAY

W. H. AUDEN, *The Enchafed Flood* (1951).

E. H. CARR, *The New Society* (1951).

J. CIARDI (ed.), *Mid-Century American Poets* (New York, 1950).

D. DAICHES, *The Present Age* (1958).

— *The Novel and the Modern World* (1960).

B. DOBRÉE, *The Broken Cistern* (1954).

L. DUDEK, *Literature and the Press* (1961).

T. S. ELIOT, *Poetry and Drama* (1951).

R. FINDLATER, *What are Writers Worth?* (1963).

D. FLOWER, *The Paper-back: its Past, Present and Future* (1959).

G. S. FRASER, *The Modern Writer and his World* (1953).

J. ISAACS, *An Assessment of 20-century Literature* (1951).

M. L. JACKS, *Total Education* (1949).

B. JACKSON and D. MARSDEN, *Education and the Working Class* (1961).

R. JARRELL, *Poetry and the Age* (1954).

J. LEASOR, *Author by Profession* (1951).

R. LEWIS and A. MAUDE, *Professional People* (1952).

P. E. N., *The Author and his Public* (1957).

V. DE S. PINTO, *Crisis in English Poetry, 1880–1940* (1951).

J. W. SAUNDERS, 'Poetry in the Managerial Age', *Essays in Criticism*, IV (1954).

# Index

For the sake of reasonable brevity, the entries in this index have been limited to the names of writers, the names of the more important patrons and publishers, and the major topics discussed. Bold type indicates the major references.

INDEX